RESERVATIONS

RESERVATIONS

The PLEASURES & PERILS of TRAVEL

STEVE BURGESS

Douglas & McIntyre

DOUGLAS AND MCINTYRE (2013) LTD.
P.O. Box 219, Madeira Park, BC, V0N 2H0
www.douglas-mcintyre.com

Some portions of this book have previously appeared in various forms in *The Tyee* and *Salon*, *Western Living*, *Nuvo*, *Reader's Digest*, *BC Business* and *Swerve* magazines.
Edited by Derek Fairbridge
Cover design by Anna Comfort O'Keeffe
Cover illustration by Adobe Stock / labitase
Text design by Libris Simas Ferraz / Onça Publishing
Printed and bound in Canada
Printed on 100% recycled paper

DOUGLAS AND MCINTYRE acknowledges the support of the Canada Council for the Arts, the Government of Canada, and the Province of British Columbia through the BC Arts Council.

LIBRARY AND ARCHIVES CANADA CATALOGUING IN PUBLICATION
Title: Reservations : the pleasures and perils of travel / Steve Burgess.
Names: Burgess, Steve, 1958- author.
Identifiers: Canadiana (print) 20240301285 | Canadiana (ebook) 20240301358 |
    ISBN 9781771624015 (softcover) | ISBN 9781771624022 (EPUB)
Subjects: LCSH: Tourism—Social aspects. | LCSH: Tourism. | LCSH: Tourism—
    Environmental aspects. | LCSH: Burgess, Steve, 1958-—Travel.
Classification: LCC G156.5.S63 B87 2024 | DDC 306.4/819—dc23

To David Beers,
in lieu of payment

Though you may cross vast spaces of sea … your faults will follow you whithersoever you travel.

— Seneca

Table of Contents

Guilt Trip

I am in Tokyo. I am standing in the apotheosis of human activity that is Shibuya Crossing. Featured in every Tokyo montage ever compiled, it is a hyper-urban realm of permanent video daylight, a confluence of human rivers that is never the same twice. Unfortunately, I am not free to fully appreciate the spectacle. I am temporarily in police custody.

At Shibuya Crossing a web of streets converge beside Shibuya Station, forming a scramble crosswalk surrounded by video billboards and neon so bright that after the sun sets it takes on the ambience of a casino floor. As the signal turns, the crossing floods with pedestrians from every side, a regular, constantly changing display of city life at its most intense. Typically filmed from above by videographers seeking to capture this awe-inspiring hive of activity, it must be experienced—and navigated—at street level for the full effect. Here the human tide runs so strong that the local Starbucks, reportedly the world's busiest, offers only a pared-down menu. No time for your finicky, just-so drink order here—that lineup, endless as an M.C. Escher staircase, must keep moving.

I remember my first visit to Shibuya Crossing. It was years earlier, on my very first overseas trip. I was accompanied that day by Kyoko, a news anchor on Japanese TV with whom I was touring Japan. The scene was old news for her, but on this day she was tasked with playing tour guide (and perhaps babysitter) to an overwhelmed and somewhat jet-lagged Canadian yokel—one who was encountering metropolitan intensity unlike anything he'd seen before. A giant screen and speaker system had been set up to blast the trailer for a Mission Impossible movie, while video billboards all around competed for attention. Then, with a flash of green, a crowd that looked bigger than the population of my hometown was unleashed to surge and wash together in the centre of the intersection before subsiding again as cars, buses and taxis charged through. *So*, I thought, *this is what a real city looks like.*

Now years later I am back, on my own. And I am in trouble. A stern Japanese police officer is marching me across the square to be interrogated by his captain. Despite the language barrier, I understand the charge against me. I stand accused of being a voyeur—a furtive pervert lurking amid the unsuspecting crowd.

The trouble began with a broken camera. Finding oneself without a camera in Tokyo is like running out of Scotch in Edinburgh. Akihabara, the electronics district, offers a nation's worth of gadgetry concentrated in a single high-rise neighbourhood. But I would eventually find my new device, an Olympus E-PL5, at a Bic Camera shop in the Shinjuku district. I marvelled at the staff as they did their best to be helpful with their limited English. It was not their multilingual expertise that amazed me—it was their sanity. The company jingle—a high-pitched five-second ditty that went, "Bee-ka-Bee-ka-Bee-ka-Beek Ca-mer-a"—repeated over the in-store speakers at least once every thirty seconds. How one could work an eight-hour shift without being driven mad like the hunchback of Notre-Dame in his bell tower remains a mystery to me.

I was eager to try out my new toy. Shibuya Crossing was the logical place to go—a photographer's dream. Although the nearby Harajuku district is considered to be Tokyo's trendy fashion centre, Shibuya has its own vibe.

Right beside Shibuya's famous crosswalk is Hachiko Square, named after a faithful Akita dog whose statue is a favourite Tokyo meeting place. In the 1920s Hachiko would wait there every day for his owner, a university professor. After his owner died, Hachiko returned daily to the same spot for nine years until his own death, eventually becoming a beloved national icon.

It is in Hachiko Square that I stand with my new Olympus. Capturing the essence of Tokyo means recording local fashion as well as the commercial riot and controlled chaos of this unique environment. Two young women in trendy Harajuku-style garb—pink bags with stuffed animals attached, pink shoes with bows—stand in front of me, waiting to cross the intersection, and I prepare to photograph them. In my experience local fashionistas are happy to pose for photos if asked, but I prefer candid shots. Composing a picture that will include both the women and the surrounding skyscrapers requires me to hold the camera low and angle it upward. A few metres back I crouch and shoot a number of frames catching the video billboards until the traffic light turns and the young women disappear into the crowd. Turning to review my photos, I find myself nose-to-nose with that policeman. Pointing to my camera, the cop says some words I don't understand and then one word I do: "Upskirt!"

Upskirt photos are a serious issue in Japan. There are even posters warning young women to beware of middle-aged perverts with camera phones attempting to snap upskirt photos on escalators or on subway trains.

I imagine Japanese jails are clean and state of the art; they couldn't possibly be smaller than my Tokyo hotel room with its minimal bedside corridor and single faucet that cleverly swivels for both bath and sink. But I prefer my travel adventures to be voluntary, with an end point of my own choosing. Thus I am now strenuously making my case to the stern-looking cop. "Not upskirt!" I insist. "No! Fashion! Capturing urban environment!"

The cop shakes his head and points toward the police booth located on the other side of Hachiko Square. We march over to meet his superior officer. The precinct captain's English is better. Once again I play attorney for the defence, insisting that my client is no base pervert but in fact an appreciative visitor seeking to record and convey the excitement of Tokyo's beating heart. The captain listens impassively and motions toward my camera. The trial will now proceed to an examination of the photographic evidence.

There is something about a camera that excites suspicion. Even in this era when almost everyone carries a camera in the form of a multi-purpose communications device, there still seems to be something dubious about a camera that actually looks like one. The SLR camera is imprinted on the collective psyche in a way that the phone camera is not.

Ubiquitous though it may be, the practice of photography is still fraught with unease. That mistrust is expressed in the durable myth of various Indigenous peoples from around the world who supposedly believe the act of taking a photo involves stealing the subject's soul. But it is one of those popular beliefs whose origin proves rather hard to pin down (see also: we only use 10 percent of our brains). American anthropologist Carolyn J. Marr documented some early suspicion of photography among Indigenous communities in the US but also suggested that photographic portraits eventually became an indicator of status for many of them. Still, the soul-stealing cliché clearly resonates. Modern paranoia about pervasive surveillance is nothing new. Street photographer Lee Friedlander's famous 1966 picture of a woman with a following man's ominous shadow on her back (Friedlander's) summoned that sense of dread in an era long before CCTV.

There is ongoing resistance to photography among some American Amish communities for reasons that have nothing to do with soul-stealing. One issue is pride—posing for a photo is an act of self-aggrandizement and thus frowned upon in Amish philosophy. In this the Amish were surely ahead of their time. That twenty-first-century trope, the annoying selfie-taker found everywhere from Pisa to Auschwitz, is the very embodiment of what the Amish disdain. In this age of petty social media feuds and the smartphone-driven boom in solipsistic photography, Amish contempt for modern technology looks increasingly rational. Another Amish objection to photography hits even closer to home for me: the Amish simply get tired of being treated like zoo animals. Boorish tourists chasing down plain folk as though they were Disney characters have caused the targets to become understandably hostile to photographers.

Here in Hachiko Square I have encountered a different level of trouble. The police captain and the officer crowd around my little camera screen as I scroll back through recent photos. I had taken a number of shots of the two young women and a few similarly angled shots of another woman. Seeing these causes the would-be arresting officer to gesture vigorously at the camera and mutter. But the photos are all taken from a position several metres behind the subjects. My other photos are ordinary city scenes starring crowds, bikes, motorcycles and billboards.

"I think," the captain says finally, "this is not illegal. But it is bad manners. If these ladies complain"—he holds his wrists together—"you are in handcuffs. You must be careful here in Japan. Tokyo is a safe city, generally. But not Shibuya or Shinjuku. I advise you to use caution."

I promise to do so, thank the captain profusely and scurry away a free man.

No handcuffs this time. But I haven't always been so lucky. Once while visiting my old hometown of Brandon, Manitoba, I was cuffed and placed in the back of an RCMP cruiser after taking pictures of a passing train. My crime: wandering onto private railway property. Another time I was summoned to the Cambie Street headquarters of the Vancouver Police Department for questioning. A suspicious woman filed a complaint after I took a photo of two children building sandcastles on the beach.

I have tried to learn the lessons of my run-ins with the law. Children, however adorable, should not be photographed without parental permission. Don't treat people like zoo animals. When approaching railroad tracks, look both ways for trains and cops.

As generations of street photographers have proved and I sincerely believe, the medium is capable of altering our perspective on the world, and is as deserving of respect (and a degree of artistic licence) as any other art form. Yet I also understand that it is not quite so simple as crying "Art!" Issues involving privacy, consent and the misuse of recorded images cannot be dismissed out of hand. The photographer must navigate objections that rarely arise with other creative media.

In that way, at least, it seems fitting that photography is inextricably linked with travel. Both are deceptively complex. Just as photography often begins with the uncomplicated motive of documenting one's experience, travel is often inspired by a simple desire for novelty and broadened horizons. But complications loom. Pursuing either activity can leave one facing denunciations. One need not be suspected of taking perverted photos to stand accused of unscrupulous and harmful behaviour abroad. In the twenty-first century tourism itself is increasingly being viewed in a censorious light.

The sins of the modern tourist are rarely the sort that land you in handcuffs. These days the indictments tend to be of a more general nature. International air travel impacts the climate, as do cruise ships and vehicle trips; monetization of culture can debase and destroy what is observed; mass tourism devastates the very sites it seeks to exalt. Could it be that every vacation is essentially a guilt trip?

Copenhagen environmental group the World Counts says tourism currently contributes more than 5 percent of global greenhouse gas emissions, with a 25 percent increase in carbon dioxide emissions predicted by 2030. Perhaps the real meaning of the journey, environmentalists argue, is the landscapes we befoul along the way.

Then there is the frequently blundering tread of the blithe globetrotter—the crude misconceptions, boorish behaviour and cultural voyeurism that generate cross-cultural animosity instead of increased global understanding. Tourism may boost economies, but when does economic opportunity cross into exploitation? When does appreciation become desecration? I have visited Myanmar and Beijing, and have an Aeroflot throw pillow on my living room chair. Have my travels played a small role in propping up corrupt and brutal regimes?

Global travel was once a marker of sophistication. As the twenty-first century progresses travel is increasingly being seen as a sort of irresponsible collective behaviour. Once upon a time the traveller was an enlightened seeker. Now the tourist is just as likely to be viewed as one locust in an annihilating swarm.

And that would be me. Joining a payload of ravenous invaders in the belly of a winged beast, I prepare to descend on the landscape. Woe to those locals foraging for a quick bite—we have preceded you. The long, snaking line that filed through customs this morning has reformed at the Tripadvisor-recommended taco truck in the afternoon. We are devouring your lunch break.

I do not like to think of myself as a locust. Unlike Franz Kafka's Gregor Samsa, I have never awoken to find myself transformed into a loathsome insect. But then, I'm not objective. A travel-themed rewrite of Kafka's *Metamorphosis* might feature a cockroach in denial. Everybody else can see what he is, but Gregor Samsa is too busy taking selfies at the Trevi Fountain to notice.

How do I see myself when I travel? I would prefer to pose as an enlightened voyager. But does that matter? Whatever romantic label I choose for myself—traveller, adventurer, explorer—a photograph taken inside a Boeing cabin will show no distinctions. Row upon row we sit, mine one more nodding head in the throng. From Rome to Tokyo to Bangkok, deny it though I may, I am a tourist.

No one has ever worn that label with pride. The stigma is emphasized by the neologism that has emerged among national park rangers and other industry groups: *touron*, combining *tourist* and *moron*. Although often used to describe the idiots who chase down bears and bison for selfies in places like Yellowstone National Park, the more extreme interpretation is that every tourist becomes a touron simply by placing themselves in settings not their own.

But must "tourist" itself be a shameful category? Ask the owner of the taco truck if she is upset about those lineups. Tourism does not just consume—it feeds. Its economic impact is planetary, and its environmental effects are by no means all on one side of the ledger.

Whale-watching has its critics, but compared to the other primary reason humans take to the sea to chase whales, it is the preferred option for marine biologists and whales alike. On the other hand, the penguins of Antarctica gain no benefit from entertaining the increasing numbers of looky-loos brought by cruise ships. The goal there is simply to minimize harmful impacts.

The 2020–2021 travel slowdown caused by the COVID-19 pandemic brought into sharp focus the global effects of tourism and its absence. If today we live in a world more aware of mass tourism's dark side, it is also a world hungrier than ever for the experience of travel. A pent-up desire for movement returned us almost instantaneously to the pre-pandemic state of affairs with barely a pause to reflect and rethink.

Can travel be justified? Can the tourist, and the industry, be vindicated?

I will stand in the dock, as an example. I will tell my stories, face my accusers and find my defenders. But I will not be the only one facing condemnation.

Let the voyage begin.

Flight Risk

I am on a train to Vancouver International Airport, bound for an overseas flight. It's been a while.

Every trip I take to the airport reminds me of my first overseas journey. It was April 2001. I had travelled a lot across North America but that flight to Tokyo would be my first time off the continent. The stakes were high. Not only was it my first transcontinental flight, but I was to be met at the airport by a woman with whom I had shared exactly one dinner date. Our second date was to be a twenty-eight-day tour around the main Japanese island of Honshu. As the Japanese coastline passed beneath my window I studied the mountains, the vegetation, trying to pick out some strangeness that might set this landscape apart from all I had known.

Tokyo's Narita airport baggage claim was decorated with a large illustration of Astro Boy, the popular Japanese cartoon character better known to locals as Mighty Atom. He looked stern, his arm extended forward and bent up at the elbow, his other hand gripping the bicep. Perhaps in Japan, I thought, this gesture is universally understood to mean "Watch your luggage!" rather than the typical Western translation of "Up yours!" Japan was going to be a challenge.

Now I am headed back to Vancouver International for another trip to Narita. This time things are rather different—my bag contains a wide selection of multicoloured masks and I look ahead to a trip with viral complications that did not exist back in that carefree era. Along with all of travel's previous difficulties, in the early 2020s it had become a game of invisible dodgeball.

I am always nervous before a flight. The conception of a journey, the planning—these are pure joy, a favourite project that has the power to beckon you away from your real work for months beforehand. But as departure day approaches, jitters arrive. On the eve of departure I lie in bed and ask: Why? Why are you leaving the TV you love so deeply? Why are you abandoning your refrigerator, so full of carefully curated snacks? And your vermin-free mattress that you know for a fact has not been the site of any disgusting hanky-panky in living memory?

You have decided to uproot yourself. And for what? Death, maybe. Death in traffic after forgetting which side of the road locals drive on. Death from the sky—you've seen air disasters on Discovery Channel plenty of times. Death from a drunken cab driver. Tasty, stir-fried death from tainted shrimp with noodles. Death for chewing gum where prohibited. Some jurisdictions are very strict.

But the plans have been laid. The money has been paid. The envious friends have been told. You cannot forgo the envy of friends—there is Instagram to think of. And so you roll your suitcase into the hall, lock the door and cross the Rubicon. The SkyTrain actually crosses the Fraser on its way to Vancouver airport, but metaphors aren't labelled on Google Maps.

For a lot of people, airports are like peyote—before you get high, there is a period of nausea. I don't really feel that way. For me, arriving at the airport in Vancouver usually cues a positive psychological change. Domestic Man, the worried guy who stared at the ceiling the previous night, becomes dormant when I step off the train. In his place walks bold Odysseus. Nerves give way to anticipation. Even the prospect of hours wedged into a tubular holding cell seems acceptable. It's just part of the journey, like blinding the Cyclops with a sharp stick.

It probably doesn't hurt that my local facility is Vancouver International Airport (YVR). Named number one North American airport at the Skytrax World Airport Awards for twelve consecutive years until 2022, YVR is open, airy and home to art installations that include the late Haida artist Bill Reid's *Spirit of Haida Gwaii: The Jade Canoe*. A massive work once featured on the back of the Canadian twenty-dollar bill, it depicts a vessel packed tight with contentious travellers. The original casting of the sculpture, commissioned for the Canadian embassy in Washington, DC, came in $1.25 million over budget and arrived two years late. No better choice for an airport.

Airports are not just physical spaces. More than any other public facilities—aside from hospitals, perhaps—they are psychological landscapes. Architecturally, functionally, emotionally, an airport changes depending on where you are and where you're bound. Often the domestic terminal will be a little older, a little more cramped, and your state of mind there less expansive. Not that there's anything wrong with going to Winnipeg or Edmonton. But having a ticket to one of those destinations makes the airport feel like a different place than it does when you're holding a boarding pass stamped for Rome or Shanghai. The romance of your destination flows back to your point of departure, bathing it in anticipation and possibility.

You may even be able to cast your mind back to a time when an airport visit was a novel and exciting experience. I recall a teenage visit to Winnipeg, the big smoke two hours east of my hometown of Brandon. My young hosts and I smoked some pot and then made our big stoned expedition: a trip to the Winnipeg airport. Bright lights! Escalators! Wide open spaces! Open late! Surreal when empty! There was nothing like it in Brandon. Nothing else like it in Winnipeg either.

This is not to deny that airports are stressful. Airports are places where people lose their luggage and their minds. I recently watched a video of a woman in the Mexico City airport, apparently having just missed her flight, attacking Emirates airline employees before jumping on the ticket counter and hanging from a monitor. And I recently met a friend whose epic travel misfortunes had given him a unique answer to the question "Who are you wearing?" On the day we spoke Zak was wearing a shirt, pants, socks and (I took his word for it) underwear entirely supplied by airlines. Lufthansa bought his pants and underwear, United his olive green T-shirt, Air Canada contributed socks and a stylish Hugo Boss shirt. This touching generosity was prompted by the fact that those three airlines had lost Zak's bag four times in six days. His luggage had wandered rootless and alone through Munich, Berlin, Paris and Newark while Zak gradually acquired his emergency flight wardrobe. When you hear someone talk about a runway fashion show, this is probably not what they mean.

Travel can always involve unexpected complications. It is worth noting that the TV ad with the bold, affirming slogan, "Because you are a traveller!" is for TWINRIX. It's a hepatitis vaccine.

My suitcase and I have now reached YVR and we're standing in line to check in. There is a man standing in front of me with a suspicious lack of luggage. I strike up a conversation and he tells me he is bound for a wedding in Vietnam—or at least, his family and friends are. His visa hasn't come through and the airline won't board him without one. He has applied for a fast-track version that will be ready in twenty-four hours and now he is back in line, hoping he can convince the airline to accept that state of affairs. Otherwise he faces disastrous fees and delays, and probably no wedding.

I look up and down the line at the impassive faces, most staring into phones. Our Boeing 787 seats approximately 250 passengers. And how many stories?

YVR has its ghosts. One level down from that beautiful Haida canoe there's another notable location, the site of YVR's darkest claim to fame— the spot at International Arrivals where, on October 14, 2007, RCMP officers confronted a distraught immigrant named Robert Dziekański. The forty-year-old Polish man had arrived on a flight from Germany in mid-afternoon. Outside security, his mother, from Kamloops, BC, was waiting to greet him. But Dziekański, who did not speak English, seems to have become lost somewhere in the secure area. Nine and a half hours later he was still there, becoming more and more distraught. He began throwing chairs. RCMP were called and Dziekański was tackled, tasered and restrained. Moments later he stopped breathing. Dziekański had apparently suffered a fatal heart attack.

There is in the Dziekański story the starkest possible manifestation of a traveller's fear—a nightmarish, irrational fear, except that Dziekański is there to make it real. You are jet-lagged, stressed, frustrated, far away in a country not your own. Just how wrong can things go? What's the worst that can happen? Your answer, reported then in shocking headlines and confirmed by subsequent criminal investigations: the worst.

Terrible as it was, that 2007 tragedy does not define the typical anxieties experienced by the average traveller. Yet even the more mundane concerns encountered at airports seem to have a power multiplied by the unforgiving nature of commercial flight. Your plane is not going to idle at the curb for you. Show up late, it's gone. Your support systems may be an ocean away. And even during a relatively uneventful transition from pedestrian to Pegasus you will be treated to a brief taste of daily life at a medium-security federal prison.

The security gantlet can seem petty. But the screening is by no means pointless. Defying warnings, pat-downs, penalties and simple common sense, there are still plenty of folks who are, literally, packing heat. According to *Forbes* magazine, in the first ten months of 2022 the US Transportation Security Administration intercepted over five thousand guns at security checkpoints, close to 90 percent of them loaded. (Gun-happiest airport: Atlanta's Hartsfield-Jackson, with over five hundred weapons seized. Betting favourite Dallas Fort Worth International came in a distant second with a mere 317.) Perhaps it is not surprising. Americans have cherished their guns ever since Moses brought the Second Amendment down from Mount Sinai. And after all, the laws are intended to stop bad people with guns, not honest pistol-packing citizens who will only produce a weapon if someone in front of them fully reclines their seat. No one could have a problem with that. (By contrast, guns—loaded or otherwise—are not really a major issue at Canadian airports, according to Sandra Alvarez of the Canadian Air Transport Security Authority. "It is rare for CATSA to encounter a gun at pre-board screening checkpoints," Alvarez says. "As such, we don't track these items specifically.")

Carry-on baggage can be stressful. So don't be too hard on the couple who abandoned their baby at a check-in counter at Ben Gurion Airport in January 2023. Attempting to catch a flight from Tel Aviv to Brussels, they realized that their baby needed a ticket and didn't have one. Their flight was ready to leave. So they bolted, leaving their dependant behind at the check-in counter. They were brought back to the counter and detained by security, though ultimately no charges were laid.

I get it. It's hard to anticipate what will fit in the overhead bins. And those regulations about how many fluids you can carry onto a flight? Babies violate those guidelines constantly and without warning. Best to be safe. Place your infant in the recycling bin before boarding and let's all have a pleasant flight.

Clearly there's something about airport stress that just tends to set people off. Despite my relatively benign attitude, I confess I've flipped out more often in airports than in any other setting. Never swung from a monitor, but there are incidents I cringe to recall.

Particularly memorable was a morning at Paris's Charles de Gaulle. By the time I got through security it had already been a long, ragged day, but it was still young. I went to the customs booth, seeking a VAT refund for clothing I had purchased. I had receipts. But the customs officer—sitting calmly behind the glass with a well-groomed moustache, crisp blue uniform and peaked cap—asked to see the merchandise as well. That was impossible, I explained. I'd had to pack it. I couldn't bring it through security—it wouldn't fit in a carry-on. "Be reasonable," I said. "Here are the receipts." He looked at me placidly through the glass. "The merchandise, monsieur," he said.

My hands were full of forms. My head was full of fog, my nerves jangled. I lost it. I threw everything straight into the air. "Fuck you!" I screamed. "Fuck you! Fuck you!"

He regarded me from behind the glass, his uniform unruffled, his expression unchanged. In a quiet, even voice, he replied, "Fuck YOU, monsieur."

And that was the end of that.

Shameful behaviour, I confess. But there is another sort of shame that currently attaches to air travellers. These days there is *flygskam*.

In October 2019 at London City Airport, a blind man ended up on the roof of a British Airways Embraer jet. Maybe you think you've had worse airport experiences, but this one at least was no accident. The man was James Brown, a Paralympian taking part in an Extinction Rebellion protest against aviation. Swedish climate activist Greta Thunberg calls it *flygskam*— flight shaming, the growing movement to stigmatize air travel.

Dr. Seth Wynes, post-doctoral fellow studying climate change mitigation at Montreal's Concordia University, believes there is at least some reason for collective shame around air travel. "If everyone got together globally in a consensus-driven process," Wynes says, "and said, 'We want to cut emissions, starting with the most frivolous, where should we begin?' You might say, let's start with aviation. We saw how airline emissions plummeted during COVID because a lot of those flights weren't necessary. You have people taking weekend vacation flights to visit the next country over, people taking business flights that could be replaced with Zoom calls—all of these unnecessary emissions. Pro sports leagues cut their emissions by 20 percent pretty easily just by doing things like playing back-to-back games in the same arena."

Estimates of the contribution aviation makes to global carbon dioxide emissions and consequent warming range from 2.5 to 3.5 percent, depending on what is being measured—emissions or the actual effect on warming, which with aircraft is more complex. "Aircraft do create CO_2 but they also make other greenhouse gases," Wynes says. "They emit high in the atmosphere, which can create cirrus clouds that can lead to extra global warming. We don't know how much extra, but it's worse than if you are just looking at carbon alone."

What can be done to ameliorate emissions from the airline industry? As in other sectors, the debate comes down to supply solutions versus demand solutions. Do you reduce harmful emissions through the creation of clean fuels, efficiency and hybrid or battery power? Or do you achieve reductions by cutting back the number of planes in the air? Technological miracles or *flygskam*?

Like many devoted wanderers, I would like to think technology will ride to our rescue. But it is not as simple as Captain Picard asking the starship *Enterprise* replicator for a mug of "Earl Grey, hot." The consensus among those who study the industry seems to be that we are simply too far away from guilt-free air travel, especially when it comes to long-distance flight.

Giulio Mattioli is a sustainable transport researcher at TU Dortmund University in Germany. "If you were trying to prove the thesis that technology is not enough," Mattioli says, "you would pick the aviation sector, for many reasons. It's just so hard to decarbonize. The plane needs to stay in the air, and fossil fuels have such a high energy density that they are very suited to making things fly. And if you are trying to generate the same energy with, say, solar panels or batteries, the physics of it doesn't work. I don't think there is any credible voice out there saying we can realistically meet the targets with technology only."

There are some technological solutions coming. Vancouver's Harbour Air test-flew an all-electric de Havilland Beaver aircraft in the summer of 2022. European budget airline EasyJet claims a battery-powered aircraft could be operational within a decade, but only for flights of under two hours. The CEO of Airbus has made similar predictions for hybrid technology, with a battery–jet fuel hybrid aircraft predicted to be ready for short-haul flights in fifty- to hundred-passenger aircraft by 2030.

These are not clean New York to Paris flights—no one has a blueprint for those yet. A more promising avenue might be what the industry calls SAF, or Sustainable Aviation Fuels. These alternatives would ideally be capable of replacing jet fuel without the need to reconfigure engines (although one of the more enticing emissions-free options, hydrogen, would apparently require a complete revamp of existing air technology).

New York's Air Company has received a lot of press for its proprietary system that removes carbon dioxide from the air and combines it with hydrogen to produce a sustainable jet fuel. A subsequent flight would release only as much carbon as had been removed from the air to make the fuel, thus breaking even on emissions. Sounds perfect. But although the US Air Force has done a successful test flight using Air Company's fuel, and at least two major airlines have signed up for future deliveries, it's worth noting that thus far the only retail products produced by the process have been vodka and perfume. As CEO Gregory Constantine told CNN, "To get to those large industrial markets like aviation fuel, which is traditionally known as the hardest industry to decarbonize, is going to take time, a lot of money, and a lot of effort."

Mattioli is skeptical of the exciting breakthrough announcements made by airlines and aircraft manufacturers. "Often when they make these announcements they'll say 'We'll have the first plane entering the fleet by then,'" Mattioli says, "but meanwhile they're buying lots of regular fossil fuel planes now to enter the fleet within a couple of years. By the time these things are scaled up it's much longer."

The International Air Transport Association has set a deadline of net-zero carbon emissions air travel by 2050. But a May 2022 report by two UK organizations, Possible and Green Gumption, reveals that the industry has been missing its announced emissions targets for twenty years. "All but one of over fifty separate climate targets has either been missed, abandoned or simply forgotten about," the report said. "Overall, the industry's attempts to regulate its emissions and set its own targets suffered from a combination of unclear definitions, shifting goalposts, inconsistent reporting, a complete lack of public accountability and, in some cases, being quietly dropped altogether."

No less an industry figure than Qatar Airways CEO Akbar Al Baker told CNN in June 2023, "Let us not fool ourselves. We will not even reach the targets we have for 2030. There is not enough raw material to get the volumes of SAF ... What we are trying to do is a PR exercise, saying it will happen, it will be done, it will be achieved—but it won't be able to be achieved."

Adds Mattioli: "I think there's a bit of greenwashing going on."

So if technology won't save us, at least in the medium term, what can *flygskam* offer? Several solutions for discouraging excess air travel are being discussed. Wynes offers up a possible frequent-flyer tax. "Let's say your first flight every year is tax-free," he suggests, "your second flight is hit with a pretty hefty tax, your third flight exponentially larger. You could make it so big that no one goes on six flights. That would cut emissions, and would do so in a pretty fair way."

Mattioli also likes the idea of an escalating frequent-flyer levy, saying it circumvents a couple of common criticisms: "One is that a flat tax on air travel would be unfair to those on low incomes who fly irregularly," he says. "The other criticism is that if you just tax carbon it will make a difference for those on low incomes but those with high incomes will just keep flying regardless."

Mattioli does worry about the implementation. "The main issues would be the practicalities around how you track it," he says. "Do you keep a record of whether it's this person's first flight or ninth flight? It might work in some countries but it would have to work in many countries at the same time. Here in Germany they are incredibly concerned about privacy, so I'm not sure anything like that would ever fly, so to speak."

Paul Chiambaretto doesn't like the idea of a universally applied tax. A professor of strategic management at the Montpelier Business School, Chiambaretto believes any flight taxes should be used strategically. "There are some airlines that do a terrific job at improving their environmental footprint," he says, "and others that do not make an effort. So the challenge is to highlight the good students in the classroom instead of punishing them."

Chiambaretto also thinks nations that institute frequent-flyer taxes will suffer for it. "Air transport is a source of connectivity," he says. "If you are a country that bans more than five flights a year or taxes them heavily, you will be a country that will be unattractive. It will be difficult to attract capital and investment."

One policy already taking hold in Europe is to ban flights of under five hundred kilometres. In April 2022 France banned short-haul flights if a train or bus alternative exists. Austria is adopting a similar policy, while Germany is among the other countries heavily taxing short hauls. It appears to make sense, as in many cases these distances could easily be travelled by train.

But Mattioli was involved in a study that found short flights are not the real issue. They comprise 20 percent of European flights but only 6 percent of fuel consumption. The real carbon-belching beasts are the long-haul flights, the kind I am currently waiting at the airport to take.

If there's a lot of pessimism in the field of climate research, few are as gloomy as University of British Columbia Professor Emeritus William Rees. Now living in my current hometown of Vancouver (and coincidentally, originally from my old hometown of Brandon), Rees is the man who, along with his research partner Dr. Mathis Wackernagel, first used the term *carbon footprint*. He doesn't see himself as a Cassandra. "There's optimism, there's pessimism—those are states of mind," he says. "They have nothing to do with reality. I'm a scientist. I try to look at the data. What are the trends? That's realism."

Rees believes that as fossil fuels run out, international air travel could be the first thing to go. "The coming energy shortage could shut down airlines," Rees says. "If governments get sensible about climate change yet recognize that there are as yet no quantitative substitutes for fossil fuels, then we should see the remaining fossil fuel budget allocated to essential uses only."

Will technological solutions replace fossil fuels? Rees is—perhaps you have guessed—skeptical. "We hear so much about the green economy and moving into a green energy transition, solar photovoltaics, wind power," Rees says. "It ain't gonna happen."

Thus, Rees believes we must significantly reduce our energy output. But he also considers that prospect unlikely. "What happens when we have to reduce fossil fuel use by 80 percent to avoid catastrophic climate change, and there's no energy alternative? Given that everything we do is energy dependent people just forget the extent to which we are propped up by energy."

A frequent-flyer tax would not be the best plan, in Rees's view. He wants to bring down the hammer. "An absolute ban on air travel, except for emergencies, would no doubt still see cheaters and leaks, but would generally be fairer," he argues.

Neither does Rees put much stock in the idea of train travel replacing flights, at least not in North America. "You want to leave Vancouver and go visit your friends in Brandon, that's the equivalent of travelling from Paris to Kyiv," he says. "And you're not even halfway across Canada. We have much bigger distances to travel. A lot of our footprint is in highways and public infrastructure, spread out across this enormous continent."

Rees admits his view of our climatic future is darker than that of his friend and colleague, Dr. Wackernagel. "We differ somewhat," Rees says. "I think we are headed for collapse. He thinks there are policy solutions. I think there are policy solutions, but nobody's going to do them."

While Mattioli does not exactly play the part of Winnie the Pooh to Rees's Eeyore, he is not as pessimistic. He thinks there is public support for some sort of aviation tax, with the proceeds perhaps funding sustainable aviation fuel research and development. "One thing I am hopeful about is airport expansions," he says. "Many are campaigning for a moratorium. Let's try not to make things worse. The risk is that we do the same thing we did for cars, where in order to anticipate demand we expand supply, and by expanding supply we are encouraging more demand, and fuelling this self-reinforcing cycle. If we were to say, 'Let's keep airport capacity at the same level,' I think that would be much more acceptable to the public."

Certainly if air travellers are climate criminals, I stand before you in the prisoner's dock. When it comes to *flygskam*, I could qualify for frequent-shame points. The flight I am waiting for at YVR is the first of ten I have scheduled for 2023, some long, some short. According to the emissions calculator at Less.com, my scheduled flights will push out 1,045,560 tonnes of exhaust. Exhibit A in the case for the prosecution, and it's heavy.

Mattioli, though, does not wish to play the role of my accuser. "I don't consider my activity in research or on Twitter as an attempt to 'prosecute' individuals and their behaviour," he tells me. "It's more about pointing out problems that we collectively may have to make hard choices about. Those hard choices may or may not require that some individuals change their behaviour. But whatever we decide, there are trade-offs there."

Mattioli is diplomatic about my personal behaviour. But he is certainly capable of marshalling a damning case. And even if it is merely a voice in my head that reads out the list of charges, the evidence is real.

My journeys have raised issues that are not solely about climate change. Almost any veteran traveller's steps are also dogged by personal questions— questions of behaviour, of motivation, even questions of identity. Is it just about relaxation and recreation? Is it about exploration? Or is there more? Your bag is packed. You're leaving home. What are you looking for?

As we board I look around for the wedding guest bound for Vietnam. I don't see him. But it's a big plane. The rest of us, at least, are on our way.

Motivation

Why did I choose Japan for my first overseas trip?

The plan started out simply. In 2001 I was hosting a talk show on CBC TV, and sketching out a big trip for when our season ended in April. My friends Martin and Laura had both lived in Japan for extended periods. Laura had married Ren, one of her English language students, and now they lived in Vancouver. Inspired by their stories, I began thinking about what would likely have turned out to be a fairly routine tour of Japan. Then I met Kyoko.

On a Friday evening in January I was walking across the plaza of the CBC building in downtown Vancouver, returning from a pre-show meal. A little group stood peering through the studio windows as I passed by. They looked to me like three cabbages and a bird of paradise. Kyoko was a TV news anchor in Kanazawa, Japan, visiting Vancouver with a homestay family. She had convinced her hosts to take her to see a local TV station. Kyoko stood quietly, her face expressionless while they explained their mission. She was strikingly beautiful. I invited them all to come back in a few hours and watch us do the show, which was broadcast live every Friday evening.

I was impatient as showtime approached, standing at the studio door and looking out at the plaza. "Look," said one of Kyoko's hosts as the four of them rounded the corner from the parking lot, "he's waiting for us!"

Kyoko would later describe to me her private reaction. *No*, she thought, *he's waiting for me.*

She was due to return to Japan on Monday, so I had to move fast. I told the group that I was planning a trip to Japan in the spring—true—and that I was interested in Japanese TV, which was also somewhat true, if beside the point. I was more interested in Kyoko. She agreed to a Sunday dinner date.

Over Malaysian food she professed herself surprised and pleased with my ability to understand what she was trying to say and to communicate in turn. Although her English was rudimentary at best, I could usually intuit and then confirm what she meant to say. A long career in broadcasting had also honed my powers of clear and comprehensible speech. I had become a human Speak & Spell. Happily for me, her romantic checklist seemed to include clear enunciation.

Kyoko had a grand plan—she was hoping to enter New York's Columbia University as an international student. Mastering English was key to her hopes, and this had prompted her trip. A planned visit to New York fell through—Vancouver was only a last-moment backup. Her visit had been a disappointment, trapped in the suburbs with her cordial hosts, until Friday. After the show, she told me, they had sat her down to cram for the date as if it were a college exam.

The dinner date went swimmingly. I drove her back to her homestay and as soon as we were in the company of her hosts her demeanour changed, her face reverting to the implacable expression I first saw on the plaza. As we parted she shook my hand. It took a couple of tries before I realized she was slipping me a small strip of cardboard. On one side was a cherry blossom design, on the other her email and phone numbers in Japan.

Tuesday I sent a friendly email from my office computer. "Hi, lovely to meet you, how was your trip?"

Next day in my office I received Kyoko's reply. "I did not mind the long flight," she wrote. "The hours went by quickly because I thought of you and your sweet kiss."

Reflexively I glanced around to make sure no one was there to catch the sudden flush of my cheeks.

Emails began to flow steadily back and forth. Inexorably, the romantic rhetoric escalated. Perhaps the schedule was no different than it would've been had we been dating. But in the absence of any actual contact, the pace seemed faster somehow.

Along the way, the motives behind my spring trip shifted dramatically. What had begun as simple tourism was turning into something more—a shared excursion with Kyoko. It was going to amount to a twenty-eight-day second date.

Why do we travel? What drives us from home and hearth (or thermostat)? Socrates certainly saw no point in it. "Why do you wonder that globe-trotting does not help you, seeing that you always take yourself with you?" said the annoying philosopher. "The reason which set you wandering is ever at your heels." What are we seeking when we roam? If your answer is a mai tai and a stretch of beach, congratulations. Socrates himself would consider those to be achievable goals. Can there be higher ideals driving travel? Mark Twain (who unlike bigmouth Socrates was never sentenced to death by his own neighbours) once wrote, "Travel is fatal to prejudice, bigotry, and narrow-mindedness, and many of our people need it sorely on these accounts."

That's a nice thought. Not everyone buys it.

"The tourist remains mystified as to his true motives," ethnographer Dean MacCannell wrote in his 1976 book *The Tourist: A New Theory of the Leisure Class*. Whatever fuels that mysterious drive, it would seem to be powerful. The flood tide of tourism, temporarily checked by COVID-19, returned as an apparently irresistible wave. Why so persistent?

Dr. Hazel Andrews, professor of culture, tourism and society at Liverpool John Moores University, thinks perhaps there is a search for Eden going on. "If you get to Paradise in the Judeo-Christian religions, life will be better," Andrews says. "Life will be better somewhere else, always somewhere else. This is deeply ingrained, in stories from other cultures."

"One thing I've been looking at recently is the land of Cockaigne, which goes back to the medieval period," Andrews says. "There were fantasies about a paradise on Earth where people were free of hunger, debt, work. It's the idea that there's something better somewhere else."

Journeys to magical places were not always considered purely the stuff of fantasy. The search for the legendary city of gold, El Dorado, drove many Spanish expeditions to the Americas. Francisco de Orellana, the first European to stumble upon the Amazon River, was on a quest to find a golden city. "The early explorers were in part inspired by a search for Utopia, for this place," Andrews says.

If myth and delusion were indeed a spur that once drove exploration, that part of travel hasn't changed very much. Delusion is an inescapable part of the industry. Ads and brochures depict unspoiled paradisical worlds where you will wander like Adam and Eve before the fall, when the reality is overcrowded resort destinations where tourists are treated the way Orange Julius treats an orange.

When dreams smash into reality, the effects can be serious. Paris syndrome has even made it into medical texts. It describes a near-paralysis that can overtake visitors to the City of Light who discover that it is not in fact a shining theme park of fine cuisine and culture but a city with grit, traffic, rude retail staff and sometimes worse. In the spring of 2023 strikes and protests against changes in French pension plans led to heaps of garbage piled on Paris streets. Writing in the *Washington Post*, Lee Hockstader described "ziggurats of filth" and said, "At night, the wide boulevards and winding side streets, already well trod by vermin, have become a Woodstock for rats that must be overjoyed." Not to mention the joy of tourists whose Paris visit was inspired by Pixar's *Ratatouille*.

Like millions of others, Paris was my first European destination (a year after the Japan trip). Why Paris? Everyone has their reasons. Mine did not really come into focus until years later, and the revelation came as something of a shock.

One afternoon in 1973, my friend Al and I went to a movie. New in theatres that summer, it was *The Day of the Jackal*, starring Edward Fox. It's the tale of a professional assassin hired to kill French president Charles de

Gaulle, set against the backdrop of Paris, Genoa and the Italian and French Rivieras. Al promptly fell asleep but I was transfixed.

Decades passed before I saw *Day of the Jackal* again, this time playing on the old TV in my Vancouver apartment. My second viewing of the Fred Zinnemann flick hit me like a slap. This, I recognized, was *my* Europe. There was almost no location that I had not subsequently visited—Paris, Genoa, Provence, the Italian and French Rivieras. The movie had clearly influenced me on a deep level. It had not been a conscious itinerary but it was unlikely to have been a coincidence. My initial sense of excitement and romance at seeing Paris and other locales in person was, to some degree, a flowering of those seeds planted decades earlier in that movie theatre, watching a police motorcycle speed through the streets to the Élysée Palace, or seeing the Jackal in his Alfa Romeo convertible crossing the Italy–France border at Ventimiglia. The romance of Europe had taken root in my teenage mind then. I may never have been inspired to take a shot at a French president, but my continental travels had, to some extent, been programmed by the movies. "You can never underestimate the power of pop culture," says Vancouverite Claire Newell, travel consultant and president of her company Travel Best Bets. "Some want to go to New Zealand to see where the hobbits live. That movie with George Clooney and Julia Roberts [*Ticket to Paradise*] has made Bali go through the roof. It will never go away."

You could make an entire itinerary based only on James Bond locations. You'd have plenty of company. After serving as a backdrop for two Bond adventures over the years, Thailand's hyper-crowded Khao Phing Kan is known—and relentlessly marketed—as James Bond Island. Locals in Glen Etive in the Scottish Highlands complained that the picturesque site had become a party spot and informal garbage dump after being showcased in 2012's *Skyfall*. I once visited Udaipur in India's Rajasthan province and noticed a local bar advertising nightly showings of the 1983 Bond flick *Octopussy*, which included scenes filmed nearby. The sign wasn't a marquee with changeable letters—it was painted. *Octopussy* every night, night after night. Please tip your server.

"That's really where we get our definitions of places, from these cultural representations," says Karen Stein, author of *Getting Away from It All: Vacations and Identity*. "That structures how we perceive, what we're looking for, what we choose to see."

Travel allows people to define themselves. If popular culture drives some to emulate the stars, others have the wherewithal to aim higher—to the stars themselves. In a world where everybody's been everywhere, how can one separate oneself from the hoi polloi? How can one rise above the travelling herd to signal a status that is truly elevated?

Space tourism is still in its infancy but the field already has several contenders. Boeing has the CST-100 Starliner capsule, being developed in collaboration with NASA. Jeff Bezos, Richard Branson and Elon Musk have slip-the-surly-bonds-of-Earth plans available, all of them conveniently priced well outside your budget. In 2021 Captain Kirk himself, William Shatner, went to space for real on one of Bezos's Blue Origin craft. Shatner later said the experience did not fill him with awe at the vast cosmos but rather with an overwhelming sadness for the abused and endangered Earth he saw outside the window.

In an era when the search for new horizons often takes place via Tripadvisor, the exploration motive survives, though it is now sold with amenities. Billionaires and mere multi-millionaires indulge in high-end adventure tourism to the lowest and highest points on the planet. If early explorers went out in search of wealth, these days the gold tends to travel in the opposite direction.

As of this writing, there have been no space tourism disasters. Terrestrial adventuring, however, has been more troubled.

Since Tenzing Norgay and Edmund Hillary first climbed Mount Everest in 1953, the feat has changed somewhat. There are now espresso machines at base camp, and farther up, an ever-changing landscape of frozen corpses. The June 6, 2019 *Colorado Sun* reported on Dr. Peter Lowry, a resident of Golden, Colorado, who, when summiting in May, was forced to squeeze past two fresh bodies. "I did not mentally prepare to see people who had died less than twenty-four hours ago," he told the paper.

That same month, a photo taken near the summit and seen around the world showed a queue of Everest climbers longer than the lunch rush at Katz's Delicatessen. In the 2023 climbing season, seventeen Everest hopefuls were either confirmed or presumed dead. In July the crash of an Everest sightseeing helicopter killed five Mexican tourists and a Nepali pilot.

By that time deaths on Everest seemed hardly more newsworthy than a similar number of fatal traffic accidents. But in June 2023 the world was riveted to another tale of travel misadventure, happening over thirty thousand feet below the Everest death zone. One hundred and five minutes into a Sunday morning dive to the wreck of the *Titanic*, the *Titan* submersible had gone silent.

The miniature sub was operated by a company called OceanGate. Five passengers were aboard for the June 18 dive, three of them passengers who had reportedly paid $250,000 for their seats: British billionaire Hamish Harding, Pakistani businessman Shahzada Dawood, and his nineteen-year-old son, Suleman. The others were renowned seventy-seven-year-old *Titanic* expert Paul-Henri Nargeolet and OceanGate CEO Stockton Rush. A desperate air and undersea search was accompanied by frenzied media reporting on dwindling oxygen supplies and a cinematic countdown to zero hour. It is indelicate but accurate to describe the tone of the coverage as breathless. On Thursday, June 22, came the announcement that the wreckage of the submersible had been found. The evidence was consistent with a catastrophic implosion. There had been no countdown, except on CNN—the end had likely come the moment contact was lost.

"Stockton Rush," said *Popular Science* magazine in 2017, "is kind of like the Jeff Bezos of the ocean." Like Blue Origin and SpaceX, OceanGate sold its excursions as something more than tourism. What they offered was a chance to step into the shoes of pioneers. "Explore the 95% of the seafloor human eyes have rarely seen," OceanGate's publicity said. In 2017 Rush told *Popular Science* his wealthy clients are not mere bums in seats: "We call them 'mission specialists.'"

"Submarines are the safest vehicles in the world," said the OceanGate website. "Since 1974, there has not been a serious injury or fatality on an ABS [American Bureau of Shipping] certified passenger submersible. Over 11 million passengers have been carried in these certified vessels. This impressive safety record is a testimony to the professionalism of the industry members in adhering to safe design and operating procedures monitored by government and industry organizations."

But the *Titan*'s hull was partly made of carbon fibre rather than the usual solid titanium, and the vessel operated in international waters outside of any particular jurisdiction. Even as the search for *Titan* went on, reports emerged that Rush had disparaged government safety mandates as pointless bureaucracy. "We have heard the baseless cries of 'you are going to kill someone' way too often," Rush told one oceanographer. "I take this as a serious personal insult."

PR aside, the *Titan* was not engaged in exploration in the historical sense—the *Titanic* wreck had long since been found. If the doomed submersible discovered anything, it was perhaps that libertarianism does not perform well under thirteen hundred feet of ocean pressure; and that somewhere amid the levels of human wealth there is an invisible line, and if you're above it people will greet news of your sudden and terrible demise with jokes and SpongeBob memes. (From the always-reliable parody paper, *The Onion*: "Critics say submersible should have been tested with poorer passengers first.")

That tendency to snicker at the misfortunes of the hubristic rich is not only a function of modern social media. A Twitter account called Yesterday's Print collected contemporary 1912 newspaper wisecracks about the *Titanic* sinking itself. (From the April 19, 1912 *Tampa Tribune*: "At last accounts, the iceberg was uninjured.") And the snark probably reflects the judgment, justified or otherwise, that dangerous excursions like the *Titan*'s serve no good purpose other than profit. "To me, adventure is a concept that applies only to those men and women of earlier historical times, like the medieval knights who travelled into the unknown," German filmmaker

Werner Herzog once said. "The concept has degenerated constantly since then. I absolutely loathe adventurers."

A voyage to space or the *Titanic* is a last frontier in exclusivity. Wealthy clients are offered a role in a Jules Verne fantasy. But while the "mission specialist" title may have been a fabrication, the risk, at least, was very real. (Days after the *Titan* tragedy, Chicago billionaire philanthropist Jim Crown crashed and died on a Colorado racetrack, a manner of death not available to the ordinary motorist.)

While excursions like the ill-fated *Titan* journey have been sold as tracing a line back to the Age of Exploration, it might be more apt to draw a line sideways to the rest of the modern travel industry. The price ranges may differ, but often what is being sold is an escape from reality, and perhaps from oneself. Some travel is sold as relaxation. But even when it's just a pitch for a luxury resort there is another theme at play—an invitation to announce who you are. I luxuriate, therefore I am.

Why, then, do we travel? A pilgrimage for self-definition? A search for Utopia? An epic quest for margaritas and hot sex? "I don't have the answer," Dr. Andrews says. "I think it goes back to a sort of human restlessness. We as humans have always travelled, whether through our imaginations or physically. It's an important part of life. It's used in a metaphorical sense—we travel though life, life is a journey."

My own motives for travel may be, as MacCannell suggests, obscure to me. But over the years at least one has become clearer. I have often felt a need, perhaps quixotic, to connect. It is not enough for me to pass through a destination and take snaps—somehow I have wanted to establish ties and feel a sense of belonging to the places I go. I have followed this desire, with varying degrees of success, in Rome, Siena, Bangkok, and particularly in Japan.

My first overseas trip now came with a guaranteed connection, one that was perhaps threatening to become more serious than expected.

Martin and Laura seemed quietly appalled. "You've had one date," said Martin. "Your second date will be a solid month joined at the hip."

"In a strange environment where you'll be stressed out and totally dependent on her," added Laura.

All true. But the momentum seemed unstoppable. Our TV season was ending. Two weeks after our final show I was to board a Japan Airlines flight for Narita Airport, where Kyoko would meet me. Our personal-time meter—with a current reading of approximately six shared hours—would restart and run virtually uninterrupted for almost a month.

Ready or not, my ride was parked on the tarmac.

The Fourth Wave

It is an old tradition that New Year's Day sets the tone for the year. Resolutions are asserted, prayers and offerings made for the coming calendar cycle. But when the future announced itself on January 1, 2020, few heard.

I certainly didn't. The tone I was setting mostly involved watching college football and news reports about the ongoing impeachment of President Donald Trump, while reassuring myself that I hadn't wanted an invitation to a fancy-pants New Year's Eve party anyway. Like many other writers, I had blithely published predictions for the year ahead, even as the unknown hurtled toward us all. Only those whose professional responsibilities required constant vigilance were privy to that first faint alarm.

It came via an internal report from the US Centers for Disease Control, titled "China Pneumonia of Unknown Etiology Situational Report," dated January 1, 2020. The three-page document identified the source of the outbreak as the Huanan Seafood Market in Wuhan, China, and said that twenty-seven cases had been reported to date, seven of them serious. The report was not released to the general public, nor were the updates released in the following days indicating that the market in Huanan also sold bats and other wild animals, and that cases of the mysterious infection were beginning to appear outside Wuhan, a city of eight and a half million in China's central Hubei province. The ailment did not as yet have an official name. At that early stage, Chinese officials still claimed that there was no human-to-human transmission—all of the cases, they insisted, had been animal-to-human. That claim would not survive the first week of 2020. By January 6 the CDC had issued a level-one travel advisory (the lowest level) for Wuhan. In spite of what Chinese officials had been saying, local health authorities were already advising people to wear masks and avoid enclosed and crowded spaces.

For those who stand sentinel over global health, this was no bolt from the blue. Back in 2006, C. Michael Hall of New Zealand's University of Otago had warned of a coming "fourth transition," building upon epidemiologist A.J. McMichael's description of three historical transitions in the history of human disease.

The first transition came with the rise of agriculture, which brought humans and animals into close and regular contact. Diseases from smallpox to measles to leprosy are thought to have jumped from domesticated cattle, pigs and dogs. (Even the common cold is believed to have been a gift from horses. Thanks, Trigger.)

Transition number two began around 500 BCE and lasted two millennia, caused by the mixing of people from Europe and Asia, with all the attendant blood and spit and microbe swapping. The Black Death of the mid-1300s, humanity's closest equivalent to the asteroid that wiped out the dinosaurs, falls into this epic phase.

Transition number three is the one celebrated in the US on Columbus Day—the invasion of the New World, as well as Africa, Australia and the South Pacific, by germ-laden Europeans.

"Are we experiencing a fourth major historical transition today?" Hall asked. If so, he implied, you might call this one the tourist wave.

Infectious diseases once thought to be headed for extinction had rebounded, and Hall pointed to tourism as one reason. "Although in health terms tourism only constitutes a relatively small fraction of total human movement," he wrote, "it is highly significant in terms of its potential to contribute to the spread of pathogens because it is a cross-border phenomena and unlike migration, it implies a return to the location of origin." In other words, not all the souvenirs you bring home are in your luggage.

Fourteen years after Hall published his report, new pathogens were in motion. Air travel would play its role in the pandemic, but COVID-19's big international splash would take place on a cruise ship.

Cruising was set for another banner year in 2020. Cruise ships were the fastest-growing segment of the travel industry, with close to thirty million passengers taking a cruise in 2019. The ships themselves had entered a Jurassic era—floating Disney Worlds (some even operated by Disney), capable of holding up to 5,500 passengers and over two thousand crew members. Even larger ships were in the works.

The Carnival Cruise Line vessel *Diamond Princess* was built on a somewhat more modest scale. Christened in 2004, it is thirteen decks high and 952 feet long, or about thirty feet taller and seventy feet longer than the *Titanic*. The *Diamond Princess* sailed from Yokohama, Japan, on January 20, 2020, promising its 2,666 passengers a Lunar New Year holiday tour.

Among the passengers was an eighty-year-old man from Hong Kong. According to the Hong Kong government, this unnamed senior had been in the city of Shenzhen shortly before boarding. Shenzhen, located just north of Hong Kong, is over one thousand kilometres away from Wuhan. But the day before he boarded the *Diamond Princess* in Yokohama, the elderly man developed a cough. He disembarked in his home city on January 25. On February 1 he tested positive for the still-unnamed virus. By that time the *Diamond Princess* had already sailed on.

On January 31 the ship docked in Keelung, Taiwan, about a half-hour drive northeast of the capital city of Taipei, and passengers disembarked for a tour. Later, a study published by the National Library of Medicine would reveal the awe-inspiring multiplication of this new viral transmission network. Through mobile phone geopositioning, officials were able to trace

627,386 Taiwanese contacts with passengers of the *Diamond Princess*. Not only was it a remarkable public health achievement, that calculation was a harbinger of the grim exponential formula that would soon transform the world.

On February 3 there was a raucous farewell dinner celebration on board. As waiters paraded around waving towels and cheering, the voice of the captain came over the loudspeakers, almost drowned out by the celebratory din. "Please be advised that we have new information from public health officials in Hong Kong," the captain intoned.

He then revealed that a former passenger had tested positive for the virus. "You don't hear it too well through the speaker in a busy dining room," passenger Gay Courter later recalled. Heard or not, the announcement seemed to have little impact. The party went on. If the guests had been conscripted into an impromptu production of Edgar Allan Poe's "The Masque of the Red Death," they were as yet blissfully unaware.

The reality would soon be inescapable. On its return to Yokohama, the *Diamond Princess* was quarantined. An initial set of sixty-one tests found ten positives, the first of hundreds. The vessel was soon a self-contained city-state of COVID-19, with the largest concentration of the disease outside of Wuhan itself. Passengers were confined to their rooms. The *Diamond Princess* would offer the world another preview of coming attractions.

With the many marine outbreaks of norovirus over the years, it has become a common wisecrack that cruise ships are like floating petri dishes. In the case of the *Diamond Princess* it would be more accurate to say it was about to become a makeshift laboratory. Everyone, passengers and staff alike, was struggling to figure out best practices for the frightening new disease.

Attempts to quarantine infected passengers internally were haphazard and ineffective. Not everyone was tested. Inequity was built into the situation—while passengers were isolated in their rooms, crew were required to roam the ship delivering meals, collecting linens and cleaning. The virus was not an equal-opportunity entity either—some were more at risk than others. It was, for better or worse, a learning experience for medical investigators, as the tendency for asymptomatic transmission became clear, as did the increased risk for the elderly and those with so-called comorbidities. The virus's ability to mutate was already evident at this early stage—more than one variant would ultimately be detected on board.

In February 2016 the *Diamond Princess* had been hit by a norovirus outbreak, an event that had become almost commonplace in the industry. Cruise ships were well-versed in norovirus control, which involves rigorous disinfection of surfaces. Now the *Diamond Princess* crew went to work once again, following the procedures they knew, wiping down every chair and railing. Meanwhile the airborne virus drifted through climate-controlled rooms that might have been perfectly designed to extend its malignant lifespan. Some passengers, intuitively grasping the situation, even began taping over the ventilation grates in their cabins. Considering the horse dewormer and hydroxychloroquine crazes that were to come, this may have been a rare example of a paranoid reaction that was ahead of the scientific curve.

For trapped and isolated cruisers, information was hard to come by. In one darkly humorous moment, Vancouverite passenger Spencer Fehrenbacher was interviewed live by CBC News on February 15 about the situation on the ship. "Sixty-seven new people have tested positive for the coronavirus on the *Diamond Princess*," anchor John Northcott said. "Spencer Fehrenbacher is on board ... Tell us about that."

"Did you just say there were sixty-seven new cases on board?" Fehrenbacher replied. "I spent all day today and yesterday thinking there were no new cases."

"In that moment," Fehrenbacher later recalled, "I realized that maybe they don't have it under control."

By the time the *Diamond Princess* was finally empty there would be 705 infections and fourteen deaths among its former passengers, and the virus had become a global headline story. On March 13 the government of Canada issued an official health advisory warning people to avoid cruise ships. Yet more than one hundred cruises were launched in the weeks and months after the *Diamond Princess* returned to port.

Particularly virulent was the *Ruby Princess*, which docked in Sydney on March 19. Over 2,700 passengers disembarked and returned to their homes throughout Australia before their test results even came back. The number of infections among *Ruby Princess* passengers would ultimately exceed even the *Diamond Princess*'s totals, with over eight hundred cases and at least twenty-eight deaths. In April 2020 Australian police launched a criminal investigation into whether Carnival Cruise Line had hidden the extent of illness on board. After a twenty-month investigation it was decided that charges would "not be in the public interest."

Eventually seventy-three cruise ships would suffer COVID-19 outbreaks in 2020, with over three thousand infections and almost one hundred deaths. The final cruise of the year did not dock until June 8, and quarantines continued for weeks after.

The infectious agent was initially being referred to as "coronavirus," which it certainly was. But as there are plenty of different coronaviruses, it was a bit like calling your new puppy "Dog." The first official medical term had been "2019 novel coronavirus," until February 11 when the World Health Organization re-labelled it SARS-COV-2, and the disease it caused COVID-19 (for "coronavirus disease of 2019"). Donald Trump began calling it the "China virus," helping to spur a wave of xenophobia even as he engaged in a campaign of denial and disinformation that would ultimately make him as culpable for the climbing death toll as any politician anywhere.

But the United States would not be the first Western country to feel the full effect of the coming wave. As COVID-19 spread to other countries and territories a new leader soon emerged. Like Death riding a pale Secretariat, Italy broke away from the pack. Its infection rate and then its death toll bloomed. Soon all of Italy was in lockdown.

Why Italy? There was some historical precedent. The Black Death of mid-fourteenth-century Europe, a catastrophic pandemic that is to other outbreaks as Batman is to a bat, had spread out from the thriving trading centre of Venice on deadly merchant ships unwittingly carrying plague rats to wide-ranging ports of call. The word *quarantine*, taken from the Italian word for forty, dates from this period as infected ships were made to sit at anchor for forty days. No matter—eventually an estimated one-quarter to one-third of the entire European population was wiped out. That was an era long before the advent of mass travel, a time when Venice generated outgoing traffic as a premier commercial centre. In the twenty-first century, the flow of traffic has reversed. Now the Italian business is tourism.

There is no conclusive proof that Italy suffered early because of its popularity as a travel destination. Other theories were offered up: the age of the population, the initially ineffective government response, and the simple fact that the Italians were unlucky pioneers forced to navigate a perilous new reality and make mistakes for others to avoid. But the nation's unparalleled status as a dream vacation setting almost had to play a role. The first two cases identified in Rome, Chinese tourists, were diagnosed on January 31, even before the outbreak on the *Diamond Princess*. In any major hub, airports are meeting points for millions who flow through and then separate, tracing paths like shrapnel arcing from so many cluster bombs. Countless little viral containers have dropped from the Italian skies since the establishment of commercial flight, a dubious benefit of being one of the most visited destinations on the planet.

By March 9 the prime minister had placed all of Italy under quarantine, shutting down all businesses except for supermarkets and pharmacies. Roman residents were allowed out to buy food and medicine, to make emergency doctor visits or walk their dogs, as long as they stuck close to home. Once they got too far off the block the hammer came down.

Globe and Mail European bureau chief Eric Reguly went for a walk by the Circo Massimo in early April 2020 and was stopped by the Carabinieri, Italy's military police. "Had my journalist documents but they still gave me a hard time," he reported on Twitter. "Carabinieri fined a distraught jogger 400 euros while I was standing there because she was outside her immediate 'hood. One of the carabinieri told me they fined a guy 3000 euros for driving over to a friend's house to have some beers." Another Roman was fined four hundred euros for walking her turtle. Perhaps there was an ambulance behind her.

The once-frantic streets of Rome were reduced to empty corridors. In the Piazza del Popolo there was not a pocket to pick. A city of practised multilingual retailers became monoglots again. Photos offered spooky scenes of a city as full of ghosts as the Colosseum. It was painful to see. And I knew some Romans for whom the pain was very real.

Roman Ruins

"You are a lonely person," the hotel clerk says.

The remark stops me cold. I am picking up my key at the third-floor reception area of the Hotel Orlanda in Rome. It's a place I know well—something of a home away from home, a modest budget inn run by friendly people. Whenever I come back they always give me the same room. I feel defiantly proprietary about that room. As far as I'm concerned room 505 is my own little Roman apartment.

But I don't know this clerk very well. His name is Simone and we've met only a couple of times before. Where does he get off making personal remarks? Lonely, am I? Why? Should I be bringing a new Sophia Loren up the stairs every night?

Yet Simone is onto something. That's what really stops me. Whether he has been speaking with other staffers, or whether he is simply a keen observer of human nature, he has struck at a profound truth. He's a philosopher, per-haps—passing the days in this hotel, watching the human parade check in and out, peering deeply into the souls of the sad tourists who come to Rome in search of some life-changing revelation. With a piercing glance Simone hands you your key and reveals your inner nature, your character, your fate.

"Excuse me," Simone stammers. "My English is not good. I don't mean, 'lonely person.' I mean to say: You are here alone, yes? So you will make a breakfast reservation for one person tomorrow, OK? What time?"

Ah yes, breakfast for one. Just a lonely egg and a toast couple, please.

I'm not really lonely though. I prefer to travel solo. And I feel very at home here. I discovered Hotel Orlanda in 2005 on my second visit to the city, and it is now an essential element of my Roman experience. When I manoeuvre my suitcase out of the ancient phone booth–sized elevator and into the third-floor office, co-owner Marco will give a cheer from behind the counter: "Steve! *Il mio mito!*" His brother Paolo, more reserved, will just smile, shake my hand and hand me the key (along with the air conditioner control, waiving the surcharge). Next morning in the breakfast room their sister Teresa will kiss me on each cheek and ask why I wasn't here last year. They all seem as happy to see me as I am to be there.

But in the spring of 2020 no one was very happy in the city of Saint Peter. As the crisis escalated, I reached out to Paolo, and he emailed a grim report from Orlanda. "In fifteen days we went from 90 percent reserved for March, April and June, to zero," he wrote. "Last night we closed the hotel with zero guests. It is worse than a tsunami since you know it will last at least three months. For now you only see the zeroing of the economic system. The main problem is to pay wages, when you do not collect anything and the government tells you nobody should lose their job. Strength and courage, we will do it."

I always hated the crowds in Rome. Now as photos of deserted streets and closed shops proliferated online it seemed one would need an almost sociopathic level of detachment not to grieve their absence. Obnoxious visitors, it became clear, had long been the lifeblood of that legendary metropolis.

According to myth—a very specific myth—the city of Rome was founded in 753 BCE. Even more precisely, on April 21, a sacred festival day. It seems a safe bet that by April 23 there were dudes in centurion outfits posing with tourists, but the archaeological record does not support this.

During the succeeding centuries life for Romans has not all been *panem et circenses*. There have been barbarian hordes, looting, civil wars, famines, floods, obnoxious Texans demanding overcooked pasta, sticky rivers of melted gelato. The Eternal City has always made it through. But in the spring of 2020, at the venerable age of 2773, Rome faced more problems.

One was disease. The other was desertion. For the first time in millennia, the streets of Rome were largely empty.

The travel industry buzzed along for a while like a lawnmower on a sidewalk. In the first weeks of the pandemic Travelocity and Trivago ads were sprinkled among TV news stories announcing travel bans and cancelled events. Email offers for hotel and airfare bargains still arrived daily. Lottery commercials offered dream vacation prizes even as the government was warning people not to board cruise ships. Reality and game shows filmed earlier offered winners vacation trips. Ultimately there was no escaping the new reality of a world in lockdown.

The real tragedy of COVID-19 was and continues to be measured in human lives. Yet those who were spared its primary effects still suffered consequences both psychological and economic. Businesses were lost, debts incurred and a sense of societal stasis descended. The world seemed to stop.

No industry felt more pain than tourism. Estimated global tourism revenues for 2019 range widely—it seems not everyone includes the same sectors when making calculations—but they generally fall around six to nine trillion US dollars. *Nine trillion*—a nine followed by twelve zeros. Revenues did not entirely evaporate, but the United Nations World Tourism Organization estimates global GDP losses from direct tourism in 2020–2021 at about four trillion US dollars. The open road abruptly closed. The skies cleared. While the drop in air traffic was not quite as drastic as on September 12, 2001, it was comparable. In 2019 Air Canada had an average daily passenger load just shy of 150,000. On April 23, 2020 its fleet carried a total of 2,175 passengers, a drop of about 98.5 percent.

The travel slowdown was atmospherically measurable. A study at the California Institute of Technology found that carbon dioxide emissions dropped by 5.4 percent in 2020, and nitrogen oxide levels also decreased. But the report also found the atmospheric effects were more complex and unpredictable than researchers expected. Methane levels remained relatively constant, leading the report's authors to conclude that long-term climate solutions may depend less on reducing emissions than on changing systems entirely. "Reducing ... emissions permanently will require ... transition to low-carbon-emitting technology," the report said.

Meanwhile the United Nations World Tourism Organization reported that the plunge in tourism had not in fact been some kind of unqualified boon for the environment. In some places the halt in ecotourism had meant a return to more destructive forms of economic activity, such as poaching and slash-and-burn agriculture.

Early on I was among those holding a naive expectation that the pandemic would behave like a tornado, roaring through town, leaving a track of devastation. Terrible, yes, but well-defined, with distinct start and end points. Head down into the shelters when you hear the sirens, emerge at the sound of the all-clear, examine the wreckage and start to rebuild.

Instead life during the pandemic came to seem more like life during wartime. It found an uneasy place between passing crisis and new reality, perhaps less chronic than climate change but more persistent than an earthquake or flood. The pandemic strained the resources of both hospital wards and the Greek alphabet, reaching deep down the list to introduce many of us to *omicron*.

Along the way that initial "we'll get through this" spirit largely vanished. During the original lockdown the world was charmed by videos of Italians standing on balconies singing with and to their neighbours; two years later quarantined residents of Shanghai high-rises were recorded screaming aimlessly into the night. Fortitude had given way to frustration and despair.

And defiance. Much of that came from the paranoid fringes, which unfortunately included the Trump White House. A bewildering and increasingly bizarre parade of conspiracy theories and quackery depressed both vaccination rates and rational observers, who watched in despair as the credulous discussed the merits of injecting bleach and attributed every celebrity death to the deadly effects of the vaccine.

Yet the predominance of wackos among the COVID-denier community could not hide the fact that fatigue had set in across the board. The early months of the pandemic were reminiscent of science fiction with eerily quiet cities and near-empty streets. A couple of years later, when what public health officials described as the sixth wave was showing transmission rates as high as they had ever been, you would hardly know a street photo from one taken in 2019. Traffic was at pre-pandemic levels, sports stadiums were full, border restrictions lifted.

The situation had changed for the better in significant ways—vaccines had seriously reduced rates of hospitalization and death. But vaccinations were far from universal, and sneaky variants had proved repeatedly that breakthrough infections are always a possibility. Nonetheless, it seemed the public was not willing to go through it all again, and politicians were not inclined to ask.

As for the travel industry, one particular car rental ad seemed to speak for all. "The time is coming," it declared, "for us to get out and go again." But was it really that simple? Or might the pandemic provide an opportunity for a change of course?

New US president Joe Biden was not focused on tourism when he announced his Build Back Better plan in 2020. When Canadian prime minister Justin Trudeau echoed the idea, he too was framing the Build Back Better plan in terms of wider economic issues. But tourism, which had been so hard hit, seemed particularly fit for a post-lockdown reboot.

A report by the United Nations World Tourism Organization said, "The crisis is an opportunity to rethink how tourism interacts with our societies, other economic sectors and our natural resources and ecosystems; to measure and manage it better; to ensure a fair distribution of its benefits and to advance the transition towards a carbon neutral and resilient tourism economy."

Was the pandemic pause a genuine opportunity to rethink and reshape the industry? Professor Edward Koh of Bangkok University, who specializes in hospitality and tourism management, is skeptical. "To be honest, I'm not certain how a global restart could be coordinated, let alone a sustainable global restart," Koh says. "One thing we know is that the environment was at its cleanest during the pandemic, and the economic and job situation at its bleakest. The positive takeaway is that many stakeholders planned for a more sustainable future during the pandemic."

Koh cites increased participation in the Global Destination Sustainability Index, an initiative launched in 2010 in Scandinavia with the stated goal of "accelerat[ing] the transformation from destination marketing at whatever cost, towards destination management and stewardship with shared value."

"The number of destinations participating in the Global Destination Sustainability Index is at an all-time high," Koh says, "reflecting increasing interest and responsibility."

One of the pandemic's victims appears to have been travel-industry diversity. A 2020 report by MBS Group found a higher proportion of women than men had been furloughed, put on reduced hours, or made redundant, with women making up 65 percent of workforce reductions. And although everyone suffered, the percentage of people of colour furloughed, put on reduced hours or made redundant was 5 percent higher than their white colleagues.

"There were more people of colour in executive suites before the pandemic," says American travel writer Alex Temblador. "They got laid off. But companies didn't re-hire them. Some of them just got out of travel altogether. They worked so long they got to the top, and then they're not coming back? Why? Speaking to some of them they say, there's no mentorship to push people up from within. They get to a certain managerial level and they don't go higher."

Travel numbers did bounce back, though *bounce* is perhaps not the most accurate word. What happened was more comparable to a failure of the Hoover Dam. In the summer of 2022 pent-up travel demand was unleashed upon a weakened and desiccated travel infrastructure still hobbled by restrictions, leading to epic airport and border lines.

Post-pandemic tourism played out rather like the experience of going to a restaurant when famished. You feel weak with hunger, your stomach howling. You order and wait. At last, food arrives. You eat. A brief moment of satiety races past. But pleasant satisfaction is just a speed bump on the headlong rush to your final destination—painful engorgement, overstuffed with noodles and regret.

The travel industry likewise went from famine to gluttony in the blink of an eye. In 2022 Canadian passport offices were overwhelmed with applications and renewals, issuing almost as many documents in April and May as they usually certify in a year. Around the world airlines and airports that laid off staff during the slowdown found that they could not simply flip a switch and resume pre-lockdown operation levels. Here too Canada was at the frustrating forefront. That summer CNN ranked Toronto Pearson and Montréal-Trudeau as the top two airports in the world if your intention was to be late for your flight. Pearson even achieved the remarkable feat of offering better-than-even odds of a delayed departure. But things were bad all over—TV news cameras panned along lines of frustrated travellers from New York to Paris and beyond. "We found ourselves more in the news than we would have wished over the summer," Olivier Jankovec, director general of airports association ACI Europe, told an industry conference that fall.

That Rome's desperate period of deserted streets was over could be inferred from numerous 2022 news reports. The city once sacked by the Vandals was entertaining their descendants once more. In late May a Saudi visitor drove his rented Maserati down the iconic Spanish Steps and abandoned it there. (The footloose adventurer was eventually tracked down and arrested in a Milan airport.) A couple of weeks later in the early morning hours, two carefree Americans of more modest means began repeatedly launching electric scooters down the famous travertine staircase, eventually causing twenty-seven thousand dollars' worth of damage. Earlier in the spring an Argentine visitor had crashed a drone into the roof of the fifteenth-century Palazzo Venezia in central Rome. A Canadian was caught carving her initials into the Colosseum wall in July, and in September an American was fined 450 euros for plunking himself down on the edge of a recently restored sixteenth-century fountain to chow down a sandwich. In October an American visitor to the Vatican Museums demanded to see the Pope, which in his defence is essentially like asking to see the manager. When his request was refused he toppled and smashed two ancient Roman statues.

Rejoice, you marble city of Augustus—the tourists are back.

Perhaps the surest indicator of the pandemic's subsidence was the demise of Amazon Explore. Launched in September 2020, Amazon Explore was offered up as a way for housebound web surfers to travel virtually. "You could book a virtual wine tasting experience in Argentina, learn how to make smoked fish tacos in Mexico, take a virtual tour of Kyoto's Nanzenji Temple, tour a 500-year-old mansion in Peru, learn about coffee creation in Costa Rica, learn how to make sushi from a home kitchen in Tokyo and more," the press release enthused.

As it turned out, you had a couple of action-packed, couch-based years to do all that. In October 2022, the feature was shelved. Amazon left you with no option but to do those wonderful things in person.

I longed to do just that. No smoked fish tacos in Mexico perhaps, no Maserati down the Spanish Steps. But like so many I was ready to do things—things I loved.

Returning to Hotel Orlanda would be step one. According to Marco, things were on the rebound, albeit not quite back to normal. "Tourism has resumed with good volumes of traffic," he wrote to me in the fall of 2022. "But the problem is that there is a lot of uncertainty in general, so even if today is going well, we cannot plan for tomorrow. There is a staff problem, no one wants to work in tourism anymore, because it is a sector at risk."

A lot of familiar Hotel Orlanda faces did not survive the crisis—at least, their jobs didn't. "We had to fire all the guys at reception," Marco wrote. "Simone, Walter and Maurizio. At the moment it's just me and Paolo."

When I saw news clips of people in Siena serenading each other through the lockdown my heart ached—I recognized the ancient *contrada* songs I had learned on repeat visits to that Tuscan city to watch the Palio di Siena, the historic horse race. Watching footage of empty Roman streets, I saw favourite haunts and wondered if and when I would see them again. The question of whether it was selfish to even try was one I did not like to consider.

Grand Tourists

There are almost always tour buses lined up outside my favourite attraction in Rome. When I walk down Via Caio Cestio to the Cimitero Acattolico, also known as the Cemetery for Non-Catholic Foreigners or simply the Protestant Cemetery, I often see them parked bumper-to-bumper. But no tourists ever emerge from those buses. That narrow side street running along the north wall of the cemetery simply happens to be a designated parking zone for empty charters. Despite its location next to the impressive two-thousand-year-old Pyramid of Cestius, the Protestant Cemetery is not a major tourist draw. Perhaps it's because death can be a hard sell, but it's more likely the result of a happy promotional fluke—the cemetery falls just off the bottom of the free tourist map handed out by most Roman hotels, like my home base of Hotel Orlanda. Whatever the reason, the cemetery is the better for it. The sublime serenity of this urban oasis might not survive the kind of popularity that afflicts Trevi Fountain or Piazza Navona.

There are two sections to the cemetery. The eastern sector, closer to the pyramid, is relatively wide open, dotted with benches where visitors can admire the steep, marble-clad concrete pyramid built as the tomb of prominent Roman Caius Cestius just a few years before the birth of Christ.

At the time Egypt and its perfidious Queen Cleopatra had recently been vanquished and this triumph set off a mania for all things Egyptian. The Pyramid of Cestius was an imitative product of this Egyptian craze in the first century BCE, a little like the replica Eiffel Tower in Las Vegas. Still, the Vegas Eiffel is unlikely to be quite so durable an attraction—two thousand years later the Roman pyramid remains a dramatic sight. In fact, it once seemed to observers too big a deal for a mere rich Roman official. By the Middle Ages the inscriptions with Caius Cestius's name had been obscured from view and it was widely believed the pyramid was actually the tomb of Romulus and Remus, legendary wolf-suckled founders of Rome.

The western sector of the Protestant Cemetery is more densely packed with row upon row of markers over the graves of a remarkably wide array of foreigners, including at least one Confederate officer and a former Canadian ambassador. The famous *Angel of Grief* memorial created by sculptor William Wetmore Story for his wife Emelyn in 1894 is here. Revolutionary philosopher Antonio Gramsci lies here, his grave often graced with fresh flowers left by admirers. Stray cats, well-fed by volunteers, saunter among the headstones and the flowering trees. The quiet beauty of this enclave, located right beside a busy Roman intersection, seems otherworldly.

By Roman standards the Protestant Cemetery is a relatively modern creation. It dates back a few hundred years, believed to have been created for the benefit of the exiled Stuart court of England. In 1719 James Francis Edward Stuart, son of the deposed King James II, set up housekeeping in Rome while he waited in vain to reclaim the throne of Great Britain from Hanoverian usurpers. Prominent though they were, some of these Stuart loyalists were Protestant and thus could not be buried in consecrated ground alongside good Roman Catholics. A new graveyard was needed. Despite the noble status of the Stuart hangers-on, their ultimate destination was nonetheless intended as a ghetto of the damned.

The Protestant Cemetery began doing a brisk business as the final resting place for non-Catholics of every sort. Among its graves are those of young men who came to Rome on the grand tour, never to depart. Chief among the cemetery's pilgrimage sites are the graves of English poets John

Keats and Percy Bysshe Shelley, two friends interred too young in 1821 and 1822 respectively.

Keats is buried in the more spacious eastern section, facing the pyramid. "It might make one in love with death, to think that one might be buried in so sweet a place," Shelley wrote upon visiting. When Shelley drowned after a shipwreck off La Spezia just a year after Keats's death, his tribute to Keats, *Adonais*, seemed to serve as an epitaph for them both. "Go thou to Rome," Shelley wrote, "at once the Paradise, / The grave, the city, and the wilderness."

Neither Keats nor Shelley were really on a grand tour when they died—they fall into the adjacent category of roving artists and/or invalids. The consumptive Keats was in Italy seeking a climate conducive to his failing health, while Shelley, already well-travelled, died in that shipwreck. But other grand tourists of the eighteenth and nineteenth centuries are interred there.

Georg Werpup, twenty-five-year-old son of a Hanoverian noble, was killed in a carriage accident after leaving Rome for Venice in 1765. James MacDonald, baronet of Sleat, also twenty-five, was a brilliant young Scot (a portrait of him and his brother as children hangs in the Scottish National Portrait Gallery). He died in Rome in 1766 of some unspecified disease. The famous biographer James Boswell dubbed him "the Scottish Marcellus," after Emperor Augustus's nephew, another promising noble who died tragically young in Rome. MacDonald's gravestone was designed by his friend, the artist Giambattista Piranesi. He is said to have been the first Protestant to be granted by the Pope the right to a public funeral in Rome.

When you stand in front of these gravestones you are recalling an era when the grand tour was considered a finishing school for every young upper-class European. Keats and Shelley lived and died in an era when leisure travel was the preserve of the wealthy and privileged.

The grand tour was no spring-break fling. Popularized in the seventeenth century, it was typically a long, circuitous European journey undertaken by young men of good birth in order to broaden their cultural, philosophical and moral horizons. An itinerary could last years and generally included Paris, Florence, Venice and Rome, as well as numerous other European stops (often including some difficult trekking over the Alps), and sometimes incorporating periods of study at institutions of higher learning.

It was not intended that young grandees would fall so in love with strange places that they would be tempted to stay and adopt their customs. Rather, the callow heir who left his homeland was expected to return from the grand tour a well-rounded—but still English, or German, or Scandinavian—young man.

In 1678 Jean Gailhard, an Englishman who had served as a chaperone and guide for various young swains, published *The Compleat Gentleman,* one volume of which was dedicated to instructing would-be grand tourists and offering cautionary advice. "Most mischiefs which in Italy befall Strangers are upon the account of Women," Gailhard advises, "in France, about certain points of honor, and in Germany about drinking."

Gailhard also worried about young travellers gaining the opportunity to read novels (or "romances")—possibly corrupting, but worthwhile if read judiciously. But, he warned, steer clear of anything written by Jesuits. "Books of Jesuites do countenance any sinful practice, and corrupt wholly morality," he writes.

Some of Gailhard's themes will resonate with modern travellers, such as his rejection of fear: "For if dangers ought to be so much minded, no body must drink out of a Gold or Silver Cup, because some were poisoned out of the like; no body go to Sea, because some are drowned … so that take away dangers, there is no reward, no merits, nor virtue."

He also advised the wisdom of learning local languages. "This can rid him of the surprizal others are subject to, who coming into a Foreign Country, and understanding not one word of the Tongue, look as if they were fallen from the Clouds." (I hang my head in shameful recognition.)

Gailhard's seventeenth-century travel guide may now be best known for its closing flourish—a series of capsule descriptions of different European peoples in various categories. "In Behaviour: French courteous; Spaniard lordly; Italian amorous; German clownish. In Conversation: The

French jovial; Spaniard troublesome; Italian complying; German unpleasant. In Affection: The French loveth everywhere; The Spaniard very well; The Italian knows how to love; The German knows not how to love."

That's a rather nasty Yelp review for Germans. But in the developing genre of travel guide literature, they would eventually offer a powerful rebuttal.

Gailhard's guide is aimed exclusively at young men—it was they who had the privilege of travel while their sisters properly remained at home. Over the years, however, some upper-class women did venture to make the tour, sometimes with husbands or family, but not always. One of the most notable was a woman who often visited the Protestant Cemetery to weep at the grave of her husband Percy Bysshe Shelley and their child. That woman's name was Mary Wollstonecraft Shelley.

As both traveller and author, Shelley, née Mary Wollstonecraft Godwin, followed in the footsteps of her famous mother, Mary Wollstonecraft. In 1792 Wollstonecraft had published the proto-feminist treatise *A Vindication of the Rights of Woman*, leaving for France shortly afterward. No respectable travel guide would have recommended the trip. The Eiffel Tower would not be built until a century later, so Paris's real must-see that year would have been the busy guillotine in Revolution Square. Louis XVI was beheaded in what is now Place de la Concorde about a month after Wollstonecraft's arrival. She subsequently found herself witness, chronicler, near-victim and sometime defender of the French Revolution. Wollstonecraft died in 1797, eleven days after giving birth to the future author of *Frankenstein*.

In the dismal summer of 1816, Lord Byron, Percy Bysshe Shelley, Mary Wollstonecraft Godwin (as she then was), her stepsister Claire Clairmont, and Byron's physician John William Polidori gathered at a villa on the shores of Lake Geneva. This gloomy vacation is now enshrined as the romantic and literary high point of grand tourism (whether or not their Swiss vacation really qualifies as a true example of the phenomenon). Wet and miserable weather kept them indoors and, lacking Netflix, they entertained each other with readings from *Fantasmagoriana*, a collection of German ghost stories.

One night Byron suggested they entertain each other by coming up with their own ghost stories.

Byron and Shelley were clearly the leading literary lights of the group, and yet the most lasting entries in the resulting competition would come from Polidori and Godwin. Polidori would eventually write the short story "The Vampyre," the first published example of that durable supernatural genre, with a central figure reportedly based on Byron. After a few days of creative torment Godwin would have a vision that led to the book on which her reputation is based, *Frankenstein; or, The Modern Prometheus.*

This fabled Lake Geneva gathering has been depicted many times in book, play and film, and it's no wonder—aside from the seminal literary output, the romantic turbulence and relentless tragedy its members generated left them just a couple of dragons short of a Game of Thrones franchise. Centuries later it can be difficult to sort through all the collective angst.

Clairmont was pregnant with Byron's child at the time of their Lake Geneva stay—at some later point she quite likely became Shelley's lover as well. As for Shelley and Godwin, when they first eloped to Europe in 1814 Shelley was still married to his first wife Harriet Westbrook, who gave birth to his child shortly after the lovers skipped the country. Shelley and Godwin would later have four children of their own, only one of whom would live past the age of three. Byron and Clairmont's child, Allegra, would die of typhus at age five, a tragedy for which Clairmont blamed Byron. After Shelley and Godwin returned to England from Switzerland they learned Godwin's half-sister Fanny Imlay had committed suicide because, Godwin believed, she was in love with Shelley. No wonder Godwin wrote to a friend in 1819, "We have now lived five years together; and if all the events of the five years were blotted out, I might be happy."

As for the men who told and listened to ghost stories beside Lake Geneva in that cold, rainy summer, all three were marked for early death. Polidori would die, an apparent suicide, in 1821, a year before Shelley's fatal shipwreck. Byron's death in Greece followed two years later. *Fantasmagoriana*, it would seem, was a cursed book.

Several developments eventually hobbled the grand tour. The French Revolution and subsequent Napoleonic Wars of the early nineteenth century certainly interfered with tourism (unless one was carrying a musket), and railroads began to change the dynamics of travel. In fact, when steam locomotives began to gain power in the mid-nineteenth century, it was the first time in history that humans could move faster than a galloping horse (unless the human in question had just fallen off a cliff).

But many historians mark the true end of the grand tour era around 1841, with the death knell sounded by one Thomas Cook. Few who read about the catastrophic 2019 collapse of Thomas Cook Group likely realized that this was no mere travel agency made obsolete by the internet, but in fact one of those rare businesses that was itself a transformative force. Cook launched his little company by organizing a rail trip for a group of temperance advocates from his hometown of Leicester. Eventually he progressed to conducting his own "Cook's Tours," versions of the grand tour for customers of more humble birth than the original grand tourists. Cook brochures in the 1930s still advertised the "Grand Tour of Europe," but the happy tourists pictured are not the sons and daughters of nobility. Thomas Cook helped democratize international travel. (Not that Thomas Cook and Son didn't cater to the wealthy too—their innovations included luxury liner cruises that would cost tens of thousands of today's dollars.)

Cook's would not be the only name emblematic of the nascent mass tourism industry; so would that of Karl Baedeker. By the time Cook came along, the German publisher had already launched his leather-bound guidebooks, forerunners of Lonely Planet and Frommer's.

Baedeker was born in 1801 in Essen, then part of the Kingdom of Prussia. His family had long been in the publishing business, and in 1827 Karl started his own firm in the city of Koblenz. Baedeker guides were partly inspired by an earlier English series published by John Murray (who would later accuse Baedeker of plagiarism, and who was, coincidentally, also

Lord Byron's publisher). Baedeker guides first appeared in the 1830s. With Europe largely at peace, and carriage journeys to faraway places gaining popularity, Baedeker guides were full of details on European destinations, maps, lists of must-see attractions, explanations of local customs and mores. The author's goal was to make official chaperones like the late Jean Gailhard unnecessary. In the foreword to his Germany and Austria guide, Baedeker explained his intention "to keep the traveler at as great a distance as possible from the unpleasant, and often wholly invisible, tutelage of hired servants and guides."

Even in the early era of mass tourism, Baedeker was already complaining that overcrowding had led to greed and petty annoyances. In Switzerland's Bernese Oberland region, he writes, "Attempts are made on his purse under every pretence and in every form ... urchins stand on their head and wave their feet; cretins and cripples implore his aid; nearly every hut dispatches a troop of mendicant infants or squabbling urchins; at every turn a virtuoso on the Alphorn is heard, or a quartet of underage Alpine songstresses on parade ... All this is an inevitable consequence of a massive invasion of foreigners, which has exercised a pernicious influence on the morals of the valley."

Baedeker himself died in 1859 but the family business continued to flourish under his sons. In comparison to modern guidebooks old Baedekers are downright awe-inspiring, offering hundreds of pages of small type largely uninterrupted by illustrations. The immensely popular red leather volumes were full of practical information including local fees, typical taxi fares and warnings of local scams. Even Moriarty, arch-enemy of Sherlock Holmes, is seen to consult Baedeker's *London and Its Environs*. Eventually *Baedeker* would enter the English language as a byword for a travel guide.

Understandably, Baedeker guides did not make disparaging remarks about Germans, à la Gailhard—Karl's original guides are fairly bursting with Teutonic pride. But they did traffic in ethnic stereotypes. Baedeker guides were full of disdainful remarks about the wretched, thieving, disreputable inhabitants of lesser nations.

One Baedeker guide included advice on "Intercourse with Orientals," three words that in the twenty-first century can be misinterpreted two ways. The intercourse in question simply meant routine interaction, while the "Orientals" were not Chinese, Japanese or Korean, but residents of Eastern Mediterranean countries such as Turkey, Egypt and Syria, among others. The Baedeker said of them, "Many are mere children, whose waywardness should excite compassion rather than anger, and who often display a touching simplicity and kindliness of disposition."

Still, Baedeker guides were also capable of shrewd observations that hold up well. The 1907 Baedeker on Canada, written when my hometown of Vancouver was just decades old, reads, "The chief attraction of Vancouver for the tourist is ... the beautiful Stanley Park, 960 acres in extent which, with commendable promptitude, the young city has laid out on the wooded peninsula." And after mentioning the deep national love of ice hockey the Canadian Baedeker guide adds, "Curling is seen at its fullest perfection in Canada." How many international visitors have understood us so well and so quickly?

A typical Baedeker packed in enough historical, cultural and geographic knowledge to let you bluff your way through a doctoral thesis, a novel—or a military campaign. Perhaps inevitably, Baedekers published in peacetime were eventually put to use by visitors who were not just shooting pictures. Baedeker would eventually go to war. After all, if Homer's *Odyssey* was a travel story, so was the *Iliad*.

T.E. Lawrence, later to be immortalized as Lawrence of Arabia, had used the company's Middle East edition when touring the region before the Great War, noting in his diary about a particular spot, "It is a magnificent view, one of the finest in Syria, according to Baedeker." Later Lawrence convinced the British War Office to print out copies of the guide for military use. The 1940 German invasion of Norway was reportedly planned with the help of a Baedeker. Most notoriously, spring 1942 saw the Luftwaffe's "Baedeker raids" on British targets, so named after a German spokesman said bombers would attack any British target that earned multiple stars in the Baedeker guide.

By that time the Baedeker firm itself had been enlisted in the Nazi cause, with edits made in German editions to conform with Hitler's ideology and racial theories. After the invasion of Poland, the Reich encouraged Baedeker to publish a guide to that country titled *Generalgouvernement*, perhaps intended for a new German population. The book now stands as an artifact of Nazi rule in occupied Europe. It featured an introduction by Governor Hans Frank, later sentenced to death at Nuremberg, and offered information about areas that were now "free of Jews."

Another bombing run would ultimately bring disaster to the House of Baedeker. On the night of December 3, an RAF raid on Leipzig destroyed the company headquarters and much of its archive. As a result old Baedeker editions are now relatively rare and valuable.

Baedeker did manage to revive itself after the war, joining brands like Volkswagen, Hugo Boss and Fanta in shaking off their Nazi taint. But the guides would never regain their commercial or cultural dominance.

Travel itself, though, was entering a phase old Karl could never have envisaged. Postwar tourism was about to take wing. Air travel was on the threshold of achieving Brobdingnagian size, both in terms of passenger numbers and the aircraft themselves. According to United Nations figures, in 1950 international arrivals were equivalent to roughly 1 percent of the world's population. By 2000 that figure was 11.5 percent, and by 2018, an astonishing 18 percent.

That is not to say that 18 percent of the world was on the move in 2018— only that the number of trips taken was equal to almost one-fifth of the population. Your Facebook friend Sally with all the lovely photos from Hong Kong, Singapore and Bali might have counted as three or more of those trips.

That question of just who is doing all the travelling drives some fierce debate about class. Is modern tourism a populist phenomenon? Or does it still retain some vestiges of the elite grand tour?

"Most flights are by a minority of frequent flyers," says TU Dortmund University's Giulio Mattioli. "There is a substantial minority of the population that never fly at all. So it remains very unequal, almost the pre-serve of a minority."

Paul Chiambaretto of Montpelier Business School begs to differ. "Actually, air transport is not a transportation mode only for wealthy people," he says. "In 2020 we studied this in a report. We looked at the two groups of the French population, ones that travel by plane and ones that do not. You can divide the population of any country by social/professional categor-ies—workers, executives and so on. The share of these categories is more or less the same in the two groups. Meaning people who travel or don't travel are more or less the same. It completely changes the idea that air transport is only for the rich."

And yet when it comes to greenhouse gas emissions, research sug-gests the economic imbalance is real. In 2020 Stefan Gössling, professor of tourism studies at Lund University and Linnaeus University, released a study of pre-pandemic air travel. It found only 11 percent of the world's population used air transport in 2018, less than 4 percent on international flights. Unsurprisingly, industrialized countries had much higher percent-ages of flyers. But overall a small elite accounted for more than half of the total carbon dioxide emissions. It was, as US senator Bernie Sanders likes to say, the 1 percent. One percent of travellers contributed emissions of up to 7,500 tonnes of carbon dioxide every year. The average traveller contributed 130 kilos per year. Many of these one-percenters, Gössling says, are frequent first-class flyers. But others—the elite of the 1 percent—disdain to line up with the merely wealthy. They have their own reserved seats, and pilots too. The modern grand tourist flies in a private jet.

Some of them also sail international waters in yachts the size of extinct volcanoes. But the über-wealthy are not alone on the high seas. The hoi polloi have some big boats of their own. If your idea of maritime adven-ture includes drinking rum, singing "Spanish Ladies," but also sliding down a hot-pink waterslide after bowling a few frames, good news: The cruise industry has you covered.

The Seven Pools of Leviathan

My friend Dave Verinder was murdered on a cruise ship. He was thrown over the railing in the dark of night by persons unknown. Cameras captured it all.

I am pleased to report that Dave was able to tell me about this in person, as he was acting in an episode of Amazon Prime's *Cruise Ship Killers* at the time. "I did my own stunts," he says.

Although Dave's dramatic expulsion was a speculative recreation, his episode of the true crime series was based on the real case of Andy Wallis, who disappeared from the *Grand Princess* in 1999 after winning ten thousand dollars at the onboard casino. His body later washed up on the shore of a small Greek island. Wallis's family accused Princess Cruises of a lack of prompt action (the family themselves hired a helicopter to search for Wallis). The cause of Wallis's death was never determined. In a later blog post Wallis's daughter wrote, "It is clear that the cruise lines have no regard for human life and take absolutely no responsibility for their actions or lack of action."

While cases like Wallis's get more attention, at sea, death by cardiac arrest is more likely than homicide, just as it is onshore. Considering the millions who answer the call to climb aboard every year, the cruise ship death rate does not seem to be high, though specific numbers are hard to come by. Pre-pandemic figures estimate that 623 people, passengers and crew, died on cruise ships between 2000 and 2019. A great many more lose their lunch than their lives.

I have never been aboard a cruise ship myself, but I do have a sort of family connection to the industry—I was born in Norwalk, Ohio. That's the town that gave its name to the norovirus, the gastrointestinal invader that has spent more time at sea than Jack Sparrow. If I ever get really famous, my dream is that they'll put both me and the virus on a "Welcome to Norwalk" billboard on the outskirts of town.

A cruise ship is an awe-inspiring spectacle up close. I have stood on Vancouver's Lions Gate Bridge watching a monster vessel slide underneath, seemingly close enough that I could leave my bicycle behind and step on board. In fact, the very largest ships afloat cannot dock in Vancouver because of the bridge clearance. One behemoth, the twenty-deck, 4,200-passenger *Norwegian Bliss*, twelfth-largest cruise ship in the world as of 2019, did stop by a couple of times. But in order to do so it had to wait for a seasonally low tide in order to squeeze under the bridge deck.

Cruise ships also make for fat targets—nautical wedding cakes laden with tubs of lasagna and limp nachos and sunburned flesh, widely reviled as emblematic of grotesque overindulgence and bad taste. Stereotypes like that are often evoked by people who have never been on board—people like me. Giulio Mattioli says those who criticize suffer from something of a double standard. "Certain social milieus certainly look down on cruise ships," he says. "When people dunk on cruise ships there's probably more than one thing going on there, not just the environmental impact, but also they're stigmatized, considered uncool as opposed to air travel which is much more glamorized. That doesn't make cruise ships any less environmentally damaging. But it's always good to separate these kinds of social tastes from what the actual environmental impact is."

People who actually cruise, on the other hand, often gush about the experience.

My building caretaker, Ken, for instance. When COVID restrictions lifted he wasted no time in signing on for a Vancouver to Alaska trip on Holland America's MS *Koningsdam*. He loved it. A single gay man, Ken noted that there were special social events for singles and also Pride-themed gatherings (although Ken declined to attend either—no *Love Boat* for him). There were quarantine areas too, and with reason—the *Koningsdam* had recently been refused docking in Puerto Vallarta after twenty-one crew members tested positive for COVID. All was well on Ken's voyage though. He has since taken another cruise, this time in the Mediterranean.

In addition to the themed mix-and-mingle events, cruise organizers might want to create Republican and Democratic quarantine sectors. What is the political breakdown of typical cruise passengers? If the cruiser stereotype suggests you have a greater chance of sharing the hot tub with a Trump supporter, a 2023 study backs it up. Conducted by YouGov for the *Washington Post*, the survey found that pre-pandemic cruisers broke down as 26 percent Trump voters and 17 percent Biden voters in the 2020 presidential election. But after the pandemic, the political gap widened. Only 11 percent of Biden voters said they would be comfortable taking a post-pandemic cruise while 32 percent of Trump supporters were fine with it. COVID denialism, generally a feature of Republican politics, also shows up at sea.

If the pandemic did nothing else it proved this: for many people the appeal of cruising is durable. Cruising was hit hard by the pandemic, with an 88 percent drop in revenue in 2020. But it appears to have resurfaced just as strongly.

Spring of 2022 also saw Vancouver merchants cheering the announcement that the port would soon welcome its first cruise ship since 2019, the *Caribbean Princess*, scheduled to arrive April 7. It didn't happen—the ship would get no farther than San Francisco before being halted by a COVID outbreak. No matter: less than a week later the *Koningsdam* docked in Vancouver. No one wanted to call a halt now. Even the passengers who had endured the hellish confinement on the *Diamond Princess* in 2020 were offered a free cruise for their trouble, and most of those interviewed later seemed happily inclined to accept.

But COVID did not simply admit defeat and disembark. In November 2022 yet another floating princess, the *Majestic*, was wheezing into Sydney with a boatload of disease, roughly eight hundred passengers out of 4,600 down with COVID. Vaccines at least had helped blunt the impact of the disease among those infected.

Once upon a time ocean liners were the way one travelled abroad. World War II was not kind to the dominant mode of overseas transport. There were torpedoes. Also, getting a ticket for an international sea voyage usually required a preliminary stretch in boot camp. In the postwar period the leisure travel business discovered that airplanes had more than one way of destroying industries—the rise of rapid jet travel appeared to be sending luxury liners to the scrapyard.

Ship travel still occupied an elevated place in the public mind, as exemplified by the 1957 Hollywood hit *An Affair to Remember*. Cary Grant and Deborah Kerr fall in love aboard the ss *Constitution* in the middle of the Atlantic. Everybody is dressed to the nines, and they are all bound for New York. Luxury notwithstanding, the ship is primarily a means of transportation. That practical aspect of the passenger ship trade would soon fade from history.

By the 1960s liners had re-emerged as pleasure craft, often cruising the south seas with a cargo of well-off clientele. Cruising remained a niche business though, until the arrival of the titan who would save—if not essentially create—the modern cruising industry: Gavin MacLeod.

Better known as Captain Merrill Stubing of *The Love Boat*, MacLeod began sailing the seas in 1977 with his lovable crew and a rotating cast of special guests that at one time or another included the stars of nearly every television series that had ever existed. The show's popularity led to an explosion of interest in cruising. Passengers flocked to their travel agents, perhaps in hopes of experiencing wacky misadventures involving Eva Gabor and a missing tiara. Carnival Cruise Line dominated the early cruise trade, with Royal Caribbean eventually becoming a major rival. Business grew exponentially. In 1970 half a million fun seekers had boarded cruise ships; by 1980 that number had almost tripled, and by 1990 the annual total of cruisers was approaching four million.

Ralph Waldo Emerson wrote, "It's not the destination. It's the journey." What Emerson meant was that Venice is not the real treasure—it's the unlimited drinks and spa packages you enjoy along the way.

There are now cruise ships with ten times the capacity of *The Love Boat*'s *Pacific Princess*. Recent innovations in onboard entertainment include skydiving simulators, glow-in-the-dark laser tag, multi-deck go-kart tracks, ten-storey waterslides and sex robots. (I made up that last item. But there are bartending robots on Royal Caribbean ships, and considering what tends to happen when liquor starts to flow, some human-machine indiscretions seem inevitable.) Up at the very high end, cruising departs the world of tourism and enters the realm of lifestyle. A July 2022 *New Yorker* story reported that 887 superyachts (of over ninety-eight feet) were sold in 2021, and over one thousand were on order. Jeff Bezos, who is rumoured to have developed a long prehensile tongue that laps up money, famously has a half-billion-dollar superyacht that has its own support yacht where he can land his helicopter without hitting the main boat's high-tech sails. (Go to Amazon.ca and Bezos will happily sell you a copy of this book, in which it is spuriously suggested that he possesses a dollar-lapping tongue like some sort of currency-adapted anteater. He doesn't care.)

Cruising has proved to be an irresistible subject for drama, fantasy and reality programming, from *An Affair to Remember* to *The Love Boat* to *Cruise Ship Killers*. I was surprised to find myself captivated by the Bravo reality series *Below Deck*, which typically follows a season onboard a luxury charter yacht. The focus is mostly on the crew, with the rotating clientele as a sideshow, often providing an ongoing demonstration of how money cannot buy class. The real drama, though, usually comes from drunken staff hookups and constant power struggles. The battle between a chief steward and the third stew who simply refuses to take direction on how best to fold a towel can be remarkably compelling.

There's dramatic footage from the big boats too. In October 2019, phone video captured a near mutiny by passengers aboard the *Norwegian Spirit*, which had been forced to cancel port calls in Iceland and Scotland due to weather. Ordinary cruisers, transformed into a mob of Fletcher Christians, surrounded crew members and howled for refunds and a return to London. Norwegian Cruise Line responded by offering passengers a 25 percent discount on their next cruise. "That set everyone off again," passenger Cody McNutt told the *Washington Post*. "None of us want to get on their ships ever again."

The incident ended without the loyal crew members adrift in a small boat and the ship bound for Pitcairn Island. Nor were any mutineers hanged from the yardarm. Captains do not get the respect they once did.

YouTube also offers a wide range of cruise ship brawl videos. The balletic violence of Hollywood has no place here—cruise ship fights typically feature the improvised choreography of drunken swings, general flailing, thrown chairs, awkward dog piles, exposed butt cracks and high-pitched screeching. Somewhere out beyond the narrow scope of the iPhone screen lies the moonlit ocean, the timeless romance of the sea. But that's a different show. As a *Carnival Legend* security staff member is seen repeatedly kicking a prostrate passenger in a 2018 video clip, a narrator for Australia's *A Current Affair* intones, "This was not in the brochure."

More serious is the incidence of onboard sexual assault. According to a 2015 report by Ross Klein of Memorial University and Jill Poulston of Auckland University of Technology titled "Crime at Sea: A Comparison of Crime on Carnival Cruise Lines, 2007–2011," "Incidents of sexual assault and sexual victimization are significantly more common on cruise ships than on land." The US Department of Transportation reported 101 sexual assaults onboard US-based cruise ships in 2019, roughly three-quarters committed by passengers.

The most common concern for passengers on an economy cruise is money. Budget-minded cruisers who have signed up for an economy package do not always factor in service charges, and not all tips are included in the price. Then there are onboard impulse buys, impulses that are relentlessly encouraged. "It was sell, sell, sell," one Alaska cruise passenger told me. "And they gave you casino coupons. But you had to make your own bet in order to use them."

For climate change activists, the passenger experience is less of a concern than the environmental impacts of cruising. In 2016, Princess Cruises, a division of Carnival Corporation, was fined forty million dollars by the US Department of Justice for illegal waste dumping and an attempted cover-up. Carnival Cruise Line was assessed a twenty-million-dollar fine in 2019 for illegal dumping of plastic and waste. The company also admitted to other crimes such as falsifying records. Carnival CEO Arnold Donald told a Miami judge in 2019, "I sincerely regret these mistakes." In 2022 Princess Cruises was fined another one million for violating their probation.

Smokestack emissions from heavy fuel have long been a problem for cruise ships, one that the industry has dealt with via scrubbers, which remove carbon from ship exhaust. There are two types of scrubbers, open loop and closed loop. (Memorize this part to amaze and entertain friends at dinner parties.) Closed-loop scrubbers are the most environmentally friendly option. They use chemically treated water to extract and neutralize pollutants. Residues are collected on board and the treatment water is reused rather than being released into the ocean. Predictably, they are relatively rare. Far more common are open-loop scrubbers, which use seawater that is then dumped into the ocean, contaminants and all. According to the Clear Seas Centre for Responsible Marine Shipping, most ships operating in an ocean environment use open-loop scrubbers.

"A typical seven-day cruise voyage produces five tonnes of scrubber sludge and about 75,000 cubic metres of open-loop scrubber wash water," says Andrew Dumbrille of the World Wildlife Federation (WWF) Canada. "Open-loop wash water contains heavy metals and polycyclic aromatic

hydrocarbons that, when accumulated in the environment, have carcino-
genic effects, and can cause mutations and impact marine life." (Imagine
nailing that sentence in casual conversation. Your friends will gaze at you
with new admiration and respect.)

"In general, scrubbers are a stopgap measure," says Edward Downing
of Clear Seas. "LNG [liquefied natural gas] is definitely a lower carbon fuel
option, lower in CO2 emissions than heavy fuel oil."

LNG ships currently make up a small fraction of the global cruise fleet.
According to ship certification experts DNV, about a dozen LNG-powered
cruise ships were expected to be afloat by the end of 2023, with twenty-
seven more expected to be in service by 2028. Cruise Market Watch says 322
cruise ships were in service around the world as of 2023.

Retrofitting older cruise ships is no picnic—to operate on LNG, ships
need a particular type of engine as well as larger fuel tanks. Another barrier
to LNG cruise ships is one that will be familiar to the owners of electric
vehicles—at present the refuelling infrastructure is lagging. For an LNG-
powered ship low on fuel, there are large stretches of coastline that are the
equivalent of a desert highway with nothing in sight but the odd lonely
tumbleweed. And no one wants to send three thousand passengers rowing
to shore carrying LNG gas cans. Thus, LNG ships are currently being built as,
in effect, hybrids, capable of running on diesel if LNG is unavailable.

Even LNG is no magic solution. One potential problem with some
types of LNG engines is methane slip, an issue that can allow methane to
escape into the atmosphere. Methane has twenty-five times the climate
warming effect of carbon dioxide.

Grey water is another issue. Black water, including sewage, oil and oily
water, cannot legally be dumped. But grey water, the outflow from sinks,
showers, laundry, is treated and dumped. New cruise ships boast more
advanced treatment systems, but according to WWF Canada's Dumbrille,
grey water is still a problem. "The vast majority of grey water produced by
ships off the BC coast comes from the cruise sector, 1.37 billion litres in 2017,"
Dumbrille says. "We know that grey water contains nutrients such as nitrogen and phosphorus; oil and grease; detergent and soap residue; metals

such as copper, lead and mercury; bacteria; pathogens; hair; organic matter including food particles; suspended solids; bleach and pesticide residues."

Underwater noise is a serious issue for whales, disrupting their communications and impairing their ability to hunt. New propellers that reduce cavitation (the production of small bubbles that actually cause much of the noise) are coming into use. But Dumbrille also believes that cruise ships need to slow down. "A 10 percent operational speed reduction equals a 19 percent reduction in CO_2 emissions," he says.

Even better, studies suggest a 20 percent reduction in ship speed would reduce underwater noise levels by 66 percent and whale collisions by a whopping 78 percent. "It's possible to reduce impact from the sector," Dumbrille says, "but regulators need to step up with ambitious absolute greenhouse gas and black carbon emissions targets, stringent controls on pollution like grey water and sewage, and enforcement and policing of current rules."

What of the economic benefits generated by cruise ships? Industry boosters suggest that when a large vessel docks in your home port, your ship has truly come in. Tourist dollars will flow into town like a mighty bow wave.

Others beg to differ. Most modern cruise ships are self-contained accommodation, dining and entertainment complexes—tourists need not search for any of that onshore. Souvenir tchotchkes and T-shirts do not add up to the kind of money earned by hotel stays and restaurant meals.

Charmian Nimmo is a ceramic artist who sells her work on Vancouver's Granville Island. She says cruise ships can bring in crowds but sales tend to be modest. "They'll say they have several stops ahead and only so much room in their luggage," she says, "so they tend to buy smaller items."

A 2022 study of Victoria, BC, commissioned by environmental organization Stand.earth reported that local cruise tourism spending totalled $137.1 million (CAD) while non-cruise tourism added up to nearly three billion dollars. While cruise tourists made up about 12 percent of visitors, they contributed under 2 percent of total revenue.

In Victoria, cruise passengers are estimated to have spent $87.36 per visit. Regular tourists who book accommodations typically spend seven times more per visit, and 2.7 times more per day. Even day trippers who arrive in Victoria on their own spend on average about one-and-a-half times more than cruisers. Non-cruise tourism, the report said, generated over thirty times as many jobs and nearly twenty times as much tax revenue.

Industry boosters suggest that a cruise stop in a particular destination can be a kind of sampler that will pay off with return visits. Donna Spalding of Cruise Lines International Association says, "Many cruise passengers visit Vancouver for several days either before or after their cruise. They take trips to Vancouver Island, Whistler and on the Rocky Mountaineer, to name a few. They stay in hotels, eat in Vancouver restaurants and shop for Canadian souvenirs. They return to visit Vancouver and other areas of BC on land-based vacations."

Cities such as Vancouver that are home ports for a variety of cruise ships will typically do better than places like Victoria that are only ports of call for Alaska-bound cruisers. But the general principle holds: people who pay for a cruise are buying an all-inclusive vacation. That often leaves relative crumbs for businesses onshore. Over the years major cruise lines have made the problem worse by giving passengers lists of "approved" onshore businesses (which usually pay kickbacks to the cruise line) and issuing warnings about dealing with random merchants who do not possess their coveted seal of approval.

All the same, a 2021 American effort to bypass Canadian West Coast ports of call entirely drew howls of outrage in BC. Annoyed at stringent Canadian vaccination requirements, US legislators proposed to allow Seattle-based ships to go straight to Alaska non-stop. "It could be very damaging," Ian Robertson, then-CEO of the Greater Victoria Harbour Authority, told the CBC. "We need to take this legislation very seriously."

If there is any one character who has summarized the agenda of the cruise industry, it would have to be Amity Island's Chief Martin Brody. As played by Roy Scheider in the 1975 movie *Jaws*, Brody delivered the immortal line: "You're gonna need a bigger boat." The cruise industry seems to have adopted this as their mantra.

In Florida, March 2022 saw the maiden voyage of what was then the largest cruise ship ever floated, Royal Caribbean's *Wonder of the Seas*, capable of carrying almost seven thousand passengers and 2,300 crew. The ship had been ordered in May of 2016, when pandemics were still just frightening movie fodder, like giant homicidal sharks.

Wonder of the Seas' reign would prove shorter than Anne Boleyn's. A new queen of the oceans was announced for a January 2024 launch—the LNG-powered *Icon of the Seas*, another Royal Caribbean vessel, ten feet longer and about fifteen thousand tons heavier. Photos of the ship circulating online show a floating funhouse, a cartoonish stack of carnival midway attractions in a colour scheme even Barbie might consider a bit much. Chief Brody didn't say "You're gonna need seven pools, six waterslides, fifteen bars and a waterfall," but perhaps it was implied. *Icon of the Seas* would never fit under Vancouver's Lions Gate Bridge. It would swallow the bridge and spit out six new waterslides.

When contemplating *Icon of the Seas*, cinematic comparisons come naturally. Ships like this have given *over-the-top* a maritime meaning that has nothing to do with *The Poseidon Adventure*. If James Cameron were to remake the movie *Titanic* on *Icon of the Seas*, Jack and Rose would have to be on their way to clown college.

Perhaps movies are the reason it is difficult to see ships like *Icon of the Seas* without imagining disaster. But it's not just movies that inform our perception—real-life incidents play a role as well. In 2012 we saw the *Costa Concordia* on its side in the Tyrrhenian Sea, and the *Diamond Princess* (with its various contagions) still casts its shadow over the industry. Still, ships like *Icon of the Seas* are state of the art. They have an emphasis on safety that means you would likely be safer onboard than on a local ferry. The real issue is not so much one of looming disaster as the continuing emphasis on excess they represent. When the drive is always toward bigger and more spectacular, other considerations become secondary at best. The cruise industry is not selling sustainable.

That may explain why Amsterdam passed a proposal in July 2023 to close down the city's cruise ship terminal. A local politician told CNN that "polluting cruise ships do not fit with [Amsterdam's] sustainable ambitions."

A shot fired across the bow. And perhaps a preview of tourism battles yet to come.

Meltdown in Shibuya

My television career in Canada is moribund. The lively little CBC talk show I hosted has been off the air for twenty years, too old even to be memorialized on YouTube. But I did experience a brief international career renaissance. For a fleeting moment I was a TV star in Japan.

During a 2016 visit to Tokyo I was wandering through the Sugamo neighbourhood when a reporter for Tokyo's Fuji TV stopped me. He showed me a picture of a pop star. Did I recognize him? Alas, I did not. Perhaps, the reporter suggested, I knew his movies? "Clint Eastwood," he hinted.

"Ah," I answered, remembering one of Clint's directorial efforts, "*Letters from Iwo Jima?*"

Correct! The star in the photograph, Kazunari Ninomiya, had played a Japanese soldier in that Eastwood-directed flick.

Later when the interview segment aired, my friend Ren watched and explained it to me. It turned out I was participating in a little game show, part of a prime-time program called *vs Arashi*. Mr. Ninomiya was back at the studio with another Japanese star. Every time a pedestrian recognized one of them, they would score a point. Unfortunately, correctly naming his movie was not enough—although Mr. Ninomiya, seen watching my street interview from a little box in the corner of the screen, suggested he should get half a point for my half-bright response.

I had let Mr. Ninomiya down. But the important thing is, I looked great.

Later I imagined the effect had I replied to the reporter and camera crew in perfect Japanese. "*Sugoi!*" they would have cried in unison, lost in surprise and admiration. But even after numerous visits over many years, my Japanese was limited to a handful of phrases and useful questions. I took a beginner Italian course, but retained little. I have a smattering of high school French. But honesty dictates that I must still check the box marked *unilingual.*

"A different language is a different vision of life," filmmaker Federico Fellini once said. If I seek to be a more engaged traveller, one who does not merely pass through a country but immerses himself in its culture, language would seem to be essential. But do I take the necessary step of learning languages? I do not. Another entry on my rap sheet—I stand accused of being a lazy dilettante, unwilling to do the work required to truly engage.

How best can you engage with another culture? Inability to speak and understand a native language is a serious impediment. So a traveller like me must seek shortcuts.

Supermarkets are a great entry point. I love to go shopping in other countries, finding culinary mysteries and making discoveries both tasty and vile. But watching TV can be surprisingly illuminating as well. Television can offer glimpses of local culture, albeit often reflected in a funhouse mirror. One would not want to draw too many conclusions about America from bingeing *The Price Is Right*, but it wouldn't be a complete waste of a sociologist's time either.

On my first trip to Japan I often watched baseball. Here was something I could follow. One evening I settled in to watch a game between the mighty Yomiuri Giants and the Hiroshima Toyo Carp. Naturally I was cheering for the Carp since they were the underdogs and had such a stupid name. The broadcast started at seven p.m., even though the ball game itself had started at least an hour earlier. By airtime the feisty fish had already built up a six-run lead. The Giants fought back, narrowing the gap to only two runs. And then it was over. Not the game—just the broadcast. It was 9:30 p.m., and the programming period reserved for baseball had ended. Japanese TV, like Japanese trains, always ran on time.

Sumo was another watchable event. I came to enjoy the sport, and was able to read up on it in the English-language *Japan Times* newspaper. One day I found myself on a Tokyo sidewalk with a small crowd of Japanese men, staring at a TV in a shop window. It was showing a much-anticipated match between two titans of sumo: long-time champion Asashōryū and his rising young challenger, Hakuhō, in a contest that would decide the tournament winner. Hakuhō triumphed and spectators threw seat cushions into the air, a traditional sign of either enthusiasm, shock or dismay. Watching on the sidewalk in that little group reminded me of the days when a friend would sneak a transistor radio into class so we could surreptitiously listen to the World Series. It was sport as ritual bonding.

Japanese TV tended to get a little strange after midnight. One night I watched *Geki Susure Garage Sale*, which appeared to be a kind of game show featuring a female street gang (apparently called *Pucchiibo*, meaning a small wart) as contestants. Hosted by the comedy duo Garage Sale, two smiling young men wearing *Clockwork Orange* Droog outfits consisting of bowler hats, makeup and white jumpsuits, the program pitted gang members against others in a series of contests—brawling, trash talking, elbowing each other in the ribs until somebody said "Ow." On the episode I saw, an angry gang member in a red silk gown suddenly attacked one of the hosts, flailing at him with a windmill of kicks and punches. He came out smiling and moved right along to the next event. Jeff Probst couldn't have handled it better.

TV has offered me windows into other cultures as well. Language was not really a barrier during my 2008 visit to Manila, but the programming was still surprising. When I checked into my hotel room and flipped on the TV, I found the prime-time sports event of the evening: cockfighting.

The broadcast came from a fancy-looking venue with plenty of seating and a cockpit surrounded by Plexiglas. Handlers held the contending birds together to establish some initial animosity—and suffice to say no two cocks ever decided to let bygones be bygones and go grab a beer—then placed the antagonists down. The cocks strutted around a bit in seeming indifference. Then they flew at each other. Beautiful creatures when simply taking the air, on the attack they became truly impressive, with flaring collars of bright orange or yellow feathers, and wings spread to assist quick aerial attacks. They looked like small dragons. "Look at those feathers fly," droned the announcer, shifting from English to Tagalog mid-sentence as locals typically do, even when writing in Manila's major newspapers. "One has to go," he muttered. "One has to go ..."

And quickly one bird did indeed go limp. The defeated bird was dropped once, twice, three times to confirm the obvious. The fight, and the losing bird, were finished. Fights generally lasted no more than a minute. It's tough to work up a fan club in a game where you're either undefeated or stew.

The broadcast was being presented by Speed Super Premium Conditioner Concentrate (for birds) and Honeymoon Love Potion (for bird fanciers). Viewers were also urged to try Mite-Free Extra-Strong Gamefowl Shampoo and Feather Conditioner, so their birds would look their shiny best while possibly being clawed and pecked to death on national TV.

Later that week I would appear on Filipino TV myself, interviewed by a reporter at Manila's Quiapo Church, scene of the annual Black Nazarene parade. Being a conspicuous Western face can earn you airtime, or at least notice. That was something I learned when I was interviewed in Sugamo. But it was also evident on my very first day in Japan, back in 2001.

While Kyoko and I were planning our trip I had expressed an interest in seeing a Japanese game show I had heard about. It focused on the peculiar Japanese tradition of "drunken salarymen"—teams of mostly male white-collar workers who toil long hours, then go out together every night to get blotto before staggering home to their families. In pre-recorded clips, a quizmaster on a Tokyo street snagged two sozzled office blokes and asked them a pop culture question. Each man could then weave into a nearby phone booth and call home to get either the correct answer or, in some cases, a stream of abuse from a lonely, housebound spouse. A celebrity panel then weighed their answers in the studio.

The show was called *Sanma no Super Karakuri TV*. At the turn of the century there were few Japanese stars as popular as Sanma Akashiya. Unlike North American television where performers are featured on one or two shows at the most, Sanma starred in as many as ten different franchises—a role model for young Gordon Ramsay, perhaps.

As a TV anchor herself, Kyoko had connections. Unfortunately the only available taping date of the game show was on the day of my arrival. We went straight from our hotel to the TV studio. Battling jet lag, I joined Kyoko and a crowd consisting mainly of young women filing into a warm, unadorned studio. Two comedians, stylish young Japanese men, came out to warm up the crowd and tell them when to ooh and aah. Suddenly, everyone was looking at me. The comedians had spotted the foreigner in the crowd and were addressing me. "They're asking how you are," Kyoko whispered. I mustered up my phrase-book Japanese and replied "*Genki desu*"—I'm fine. There was a roar of laughter from the crowd. Either my pronunciation was ludicrous or my attempt to speak Japanese had made me the proverbial dancing dog—the dog doesn't have to dance well. The fun is in watching it try.

Soon the curtain pulled back to reveal a wood-panelled set. Sanma stood at a podium on one side, his celebrity guests seated opposite. At one point Sanma took a break from the game to work the crowd and, like the warm-up comedians, quickly spotted my sore-thumb white face in the throng. Once more I was being addressed in Japanese. It's a good thing I was unfamiliar with the pantheon of Japanese celebrities—Ren told me later that for the average Japanese citizen, such an encounter with Sanma would be every bit as intimidating as an unexpected chat with Oprah.

I turned to Kyoko for a translation, causing another outburst of laughter from the crowd. He asked what I was doing here. Deciding that my only hope was to speak up boldly in English, I offered the rather inflated explanation that I was a Canadian TV host, here to observe and learn from my Japanese counterparts.

It seemed to work. Heads swivelled as a collective *ooh* went up from the crowd. For all they knew I could have been a Canadian Letterman and

Leno combined. At any rate, I was off the hook, far too important to pick on anymore. The show went on with various street interview segments, eventually reaching the one featuring soused salarymen. This episode even featured a couple of drunk female contestants, one of whom was flirting with the sidewalk host. "Who's better, me or your girlfriend?" she asked.

How do you engage with another culture? A savvy local companion can help. But that approach can also bring major complications.

Kyoko and I hit the ground running in Tokyo. Every day we took the then-new Yurikamome Line train (it is elevated, boasts huge windows and runs on rubber tires) to Shimbashi where, as Kyoko had learned, I had to begin the day with espresso. Then we were off on one train or another, at level or below ground, visiting Shibuya, Harajuku, Shinjuku, Shimo-Kitazawa, Ameyoko market, Ginza.

One day, I think Kyoko may have taken me for lunch at the legendary sushi establishment of Jiro Ono, later made internationally famous in the documentary *Jiro Dreams of Sushi*. But it is indicative of the whirlwind the week was that, to this day, I am not sure. Both Jiro and the restaurant looked familiar when I eventually saw the film. The neighbourhood, Ginza, and the fixed lunch price (three hundred dollars US) were both the same. But the truth is I simply don't know. At the time it was all tumbling past in an impressionistic, badly translated jumble.

Tokyo. Automated voices everywhere—escalators and elevators talking to you. On subway platforms, a bewildering array of privately owned lines, stations often identified by particular little snippets of music played in a warbling electronic tone. (Ebisu Station on the Yamanote Line is announced by the theme from one of my all-time favourite movies, *The Third Man*.) Standing in a packed subway car rattling down the track, you can look to the right and left and see competing trains keeping pace, barrelling toward the finish line in a never-ending Tokyo derby.

I was feeling stressed. It wasn't simply a byproduct of my introduction to the hyper-urban world of Tokyo. Jet lag was surely playing a role, though never having experienced it before it was difficult for me to understand just what it was doing to my mental state. But there was more going on. I was becoming increasingly worried about what I had signed on for.

Kyoko had left her job. It made sense—her plan to study overseas would require a sabbatical at the very least. But there was more to her decision. Kyoko had applied for three weeks' holiday to coincide with my visit and been denied, even though she was owed far more by the company. So she resigned a few weeks before my arrival, the better to devote herself to our holiday happiness. Kyoko had been diligent and determined in planning our trip, sparing no expense. My attempts to suggest cheap hotels were rebuffed—we were going first class. I was paying for our Tokyo hotel—more than I expected—but could hardly complain as Kyoko was paying for everything else. She had insisted on making arrangements for remarkable accommodations and experiences elsewhere that were frankly beyond my means. I was her guest, she said. "This will be the great adventure of my life," she had written to me as we planned the trip.

Was I really the stuff of a great adventure? Our three-month email courtship had indeed offered indications of the importance our trip would hold for Kyoko.

There had been linguistic and cultural glitches, sometimes combined. In one email I casually referred to Kyoko as *babe*. Her reply, after an unusual period of silence, was cold enough to cause freezer burn. Had I taken too great a liberty? Several emails were required to reveal the problem: for Kyoko, *Babe* was only the title of a movie about a pig. Explanations and apologies followed.

As emails continued, biographical details were revealed. And I came to realize that Kyoko's history with men had been limited.

Throughout Kyoko's high school years her parents would not let her associate with boys, nor even go out in the evenings. The failed romances she described to me never got to the stage where they really qualified as relationships. It was beginning to dawn on me that there was more significance attached to our trip than I realized. For me, it would be a first overseas trip. For Kyoko, it promised a more momentous kind of first. Although she was approaching thirty, she had never really been in a relationship.

Our first day in Tokyo, then, came with some added weight. As I emerged from the baggage area at Narita, she came toward me holding a video camera. She wore a silky, zebra-patterned top, kelly green pants and a grave expression on her lovely face. Our hotel room was the first private space we had shared alone. We were due at the TV studio soon but first, here we were. An urgent embrace, questions about whether this hurried lovemaking was really best suited to such a significant milestone in Kyoko's experience, then questions discarded in a heated rush. Kyoko and I were lovers now. "I still feel you here," she told me later.

For Kyoko then, this trip truly was a once-in-a-lifetime experience. Perhaps that was why it felt less like a vacation and more like a honeymoon. I felt there were implications to our great adventure, promises I did not feel ready to make. Perhaps this was routine stuff for a man like me—the standard commitment phobia that makes any over-forty single man appear to wiser female onlookers like a bright-orange poisonous toad. All the same, I was starting to sweat. Engagement with a culture is all very well, but there is engagement and then there is *engagement*. I was not ready to be engaged.

I had no one else to blame for this. Martin and Laura had warned me. But I had been caught up in the endorphins and romance of it all. And now Kyoko had quit her job and was planning to study English in Vancouver. I felt I was being carried along on a bullet train and did not know the Japanese words for "slow down."

If I was feeling stressed, what about Kyoko? She was essentially baby-sitting a giant, babbling three-year-old. One day on the Yamanote train I was looking around and asking questions: What's that ad say? What does that one mean? What's that one selling? What does that symbol mean? Why are the trains different colours? What's that building over there? Where is everyone going?

Kyoko was quiet. When I looked over there were tears rolling down her cheeks. It was too much. Kyoko was determined to be a worthy guide of her homeland, and my relentless questions had surely left her feeling helpless and inadequate. It seemed our mutual adventure was proving more difficult than she had envisioned. The linguistic and cultural gulf that separated us was not so easily bridged as the Pacific Ocean.

Our final day in Tokyo. I had a mental map of urban islands, enchanting spots reached via mystifying subway connections, but I had no geographic sense of how these places related to each other. "I want to go back to Asakusa and Ueno," I announced. "And Shibuya. And some other places if we have time." That this would require a subway version of the Bataan Death March, I did not understand. Kyoko, dutiful guide, was not about to complain.

By evening we reached Shibuya, hungry, worn out from walking and jostling. After wending through the narrow streets we climbed some stairs to a glass-walled restaurant and parked ourselves on the floor beside the table, Japanese-style. Without warning, I began to weep.

Not counting movie theatres, I could not recall the last time I wept in public. Too late to stop now. Like the awful dream in which a loose tooth finally lets go and pulls all your other teeth out like a pearl bracelet, everything must come babbling out. I started to talk.

I don't remember the entire torrent. Fitting, since Kyoko must have perceived it like a faraway radio signal—a few intelligible words, a lot of static. "I'm afraid I am going to make you unhappy," I said. "I feel as though I have been lying to you."

Kyoko looked calm. "Steve, I must tell you that I am not thinking about our relationship after this trip. I thought only of our trip. Nothing more. So it's OK."

After dinner we strolled through Shibuya. I felt tremendous relief. Communication had solved everything.

Next day we were to catch the Shinkansen bullet train to Kyoto before switching to the regular rolling stock for the trip up to her home in Kanazawa, near the north coast. We sat in a Starbucks, waiting for our train. My earlier sense of relief over unburdening myself had since given way to a feeling of unease. Kyoko was wearing the expressionless face I had first seen the night we met. I was starting to realize I had underestimated the consequences of my public meltdown. "Before we leave," Kyoko said suddenly, "I offer one more chance to get rid of me. I go home alone. You stay in Japan without me."

I was aghast. "Why are you saying this? Why would I want to get rid of you?"

"You lied."

"When?" I asked. "When did I lie?"

"You said to me yesterday. At restaurant, you had your shameful time. You cried. You said to me, 'I lied.'"

"No, no, I said, 'I feel as though I am lying to you.'"

"So you lied."

It's when fights begin that language must be wielded with a surgeon's precision. Kyoko and I had nothing but hand grenades. My Japanese vocabulary, consisting of "Thank you, "Excuse me," and "I'm fine," was not much use now. How could I explain the difference between "I lied" and "I feel as though I've been lying to you by omission?'" Kyoko stared at me coldly as I struggled, and the more I talked the more weaselly I felt. Why had I used the word *lie* if I hadn't meant it? Was I lying then or lying now?

My tears in the restaurant had stunned and embarrassed Kyoko. I had punctured her dream, confirmed her fears, shamed her. I had essentially vomited fear and uncertainty from my queasy gut and felt much improved for it. Now it was Kyoko's turn to feel sick.

We still had a train to catch, but it seemed our great adventure might be going off the rails.

Balcony Seat in Magaluf

That first visit to Japan held many challenges. Few were as daunting as the toilet slippers.

Japanese bathrooms could be a puzzle at the best of times. There were still plenty of old-school squat toilets, hooded porcelain floor sinks designed to strike terror into every Western sphincter. But modern toilets had proliferated after World War II and in the early 1980s came the Washlet toilet, a purely Japanese creation featuring a bidet-like spray nozzle. Today Japanese toilets come with control panels worthy of small aircraft, and offer heated seats, a variety of spray functions, fans and sometimes music. But it was the slippers that left me flummoxed.

They sat at the door of every private and hotel bathroom. I did not notice them at first. But Kyoko soon made me understand my breach of etiquette. The idea that one might traipse into a potentially germy bathroom with the same footwear that would subsequently track filth all over the room was distasteful to Japanese sensibilities—rather like strangers sharing a single toothbrush. You always slipped off your own shoes and donned the provided slippers when entering the bathroom.

But I kept forgetting. I would barge in, look down, remember and go trade my shoes for the slippers, too late to serve their prophylactic purpose. It didn't help that the slippers were generally four or five sizes too small.

The slipper awkwardness stood in for a number of issues. Japanese etiquette seemed an unsettling mystery to me, and I went through my days with a vague sense that I was blundering through invisible guide ropes left and right, leaving locals quietly appalled. At times my transgressions were more obvious: I once mortified Kyoko by stealing a wanted poster for members of the Aum Shinrikyo poison gas cult from the wall of a Tokyo subway station. The next wanted poster, she feared, would surely feature my smiling face.

Near-constant background anxiety came from immersion in a different culture with unfamiliar mores. It is a feeling some tourists prefer to avoid. A sense of insecurity about appropriate behaviour can be a hindrance when one simply wants to kick back and relax. Why must one worry about the etiquette of leaving chopsticks stuck in the rice bowl when one is simply trying to eat lunch? Isn't it better to avoid such aggravation by going abroad, yet essentially cocooning with one's own kind? A great many do. It's a phenomenon sometimes referred to as enclave tourism.

One such enclave is the Spanish city of Magaluf. Located on the island of Mallorca, Magaluf has long been tagged by young Brits as "Shagaluf." High season is by all accounts a free-range frat party. The popular strip called Punta Ballena has been described by one local as a "street of shame." Authorities attributed three 2017 Mallorcan tourist deaths to the practice of "balconing," jumping from a hotel balcony into a swimming pool, a stunt made popular in part by YouTube videos. There are other extreme balcony sports as well—in 2018 a twenty-year-old UK tourist was seriously injured in a fall from a balcony while attempting to take a shit over the railing. In May 2022 a man fell to his death from a seventh-floor balcony at a Magaluf hotel, apparently while trying to climb down to a lower floor. Later that summer a British man died after a scuffle with police outside a Magaluf bar. And just one day after the coronation of King Charles III, Magaluf hosted another public spectacle, as a massive brawl involving almost fifty combatants broke out on Avenida S'Olivera. "The youths started hitting each other," said *Euro Weekly News*, "reportedly due to an excess of drugs and alcohol."

That's mere speculation, of course.

To be fair to the Brits, this particular brawl seemed to be an international event involving youth of many lands. It's another example of how travel can bring the peoples and trash bins and patio chairs and broken bottles of the world together.

A particularly infamous episode took place at a club called Playhouse. In the summer of 2014 a drunken eighteen-year-old from Northern Ireland was immortalized on video performing brief acts of fellatio on a row of bar patrons while a well-lubricated crowd cheered. In exchange for servicing twenty-four barflies she had been promised a "free holiday." Unbeknownst to her she was the victim of a hilarious little joke—Free Holiday was actually the name of a cocktail on the bar menu, at five-pound value. The video, recorded by an employee of a tour company called Carnage Events Magaluf, subsequently went viral as the young woman's parents conducted sorrowful telephone interviews with a stream of reporters. The owner of Carnage Events later told reporters he felt no need to apologize to the young woman's parents and that the existence and dissemination of the video was the young woman's own fault and no one else's.

Others disagreed. The video spurred local outrage and changes in the regulations surrounding tour companies. Eventually Carnage and Playhouse were both fined, and the club was forced to close. Magaluf, however, rolls on.

In the late 1990s Dr. Hazel Andrews from the Liverpool John Moores University spent time among the tourists in Magaluf, subsequently publishing *The British on Holiday* in 2011. She found that here at least, travelling to a Spanish resort seemed to inspire an enhanced sense of British identity, or at least the expression of it. The idea of travel as a means of exploration and engagement with other cultures was simply inoperative. "In the late 90s the majority of the tourists were white, working class," Andrews says. "There was a lot of flag-waving, a lot of what I describe as effervescent expressions of Britishness, a kind of coming together. Of course that happens in the UK as well—take for example the death of the Queen. But this was a different kind of Britishness. People would talk about problems with migration and immigration in the UK and about how you couldn't say certain things. They felt that some things couldn't be expressed as clearly in their home world as they could in Mallorca."

Brexit, the 2016 British referendum that led to the withdrawal of the United Kingdom from the European Union, would seem to have been a triumph, albeit a narrow one, for the brand of nationalism Andrews documented years ago. Today Andrews believes Brexit may have affected international opinions about Britain more than the other way around: "The hostility that Brexit gives out, the chaos that has ensued since." But she notes the global tourism industry did attempt to respond to the event. "It's interesting that the Australians, in the aftermath of Brexit, tried to capitalize on that. There was an advert featuring Kylie Minogue saying, 'You don't want to engage with the Europeans? Come to Australia instead.' The Portuguese put out an advert saying 'We still love you.' It's interesting. It's still not really settled."

Brexit notwithstanding, Magaluf remains a British tourist enclave.

Enclave tourism has been defined as taking place in a relatively confined geographic space, allowing tourists to avoid engagement with local populations, often at resorts regulated by external corporations whose profits do not stay within the country.

If tourism styles can be plotted on a spectrum of desirability and benefits for the locations themselves, enclaves (and large cruise ships, the enclaves of the sea) would be at the low end. What's at the other?

Shortly before the pandemic an organization called Wonderful Copenhagen set out to define the ideal traveller. They called this magical being the "mindful tourist." As part of a larger tourism initiative called 10x Copenhagen, they sought first to identify what qualities make for a good visitor, and second to find out how many of them there are.

To qualify as a mindful tourist, a visitor needed to prioritize environmental protection, spend money with an eye to supporting local business and interacting with local residents, attempt to move beyond typical tourist sites to explore low-traffic areas of the city, and adhere to local norms (points surely deducted for trying to take a shit off a balcony). Over 4,500 visitors were surveyed to determine how many fit roughly within those parameters. Their finding: the mindful tourists represented about 13 percent of the total, or roughly one in eight.

Safe to say the figures would look a lot worse in Magaluf. In fact in Europe the reputation of hard-partying young Brits is so bad that in the spring of 2023, Holland launched what was in effect an anti-tourism campaign. Online ads were triggered when UK web surfers entered search terms like "stag party Amsterdam" or "pub crawl Amsterdam." Featuring images of young men being arrested and handcuffed, the ads carried a slogan that must be unique in the history of travel marketing: "Stay away."

Tourists get a bad rap. No one ever glowed with secret pride after being called a tourist. So those who go abroad often struggle to redefine themselves, often in opposition to others who go abroad. Tales of obnoxious party resorts and boorish foreigners barking at beleaguered local service staff inspire many to make distinctions between "travellers" (themselves) and "tourists" (those other assholes). British author G.K. Chesterton described regular tourists as "trippers" and he too distinguished between them and more enlightened voyagers. "The traveller sees what he sees," Chesterton wrote. "The tripper sees what he has come to see."

Are the distinctions legitimate?

Environmentally, perhaps not. Long flights are heavy in emissions regardless of who is aboard. A traveller from St. Louis or Nashville might feel like an intrepid adventurer when trekking in the wilds of Panama. But in terms of environmental impact, that person might have been better off driving to Graceland and visiting the Jungle Room.

In *The Tourist: A New Theory of the Leisure Class*, Dean MacCannell suggested that attempts by some travellers to elevate themselves above others was a form of prejudice, redirected from racial groups to a new category of exclusion. "Tourists dislike tourists," he wrote. "God is dead, but man's need to appear holier than his fellows lives."

Snobbery aside, there are legitimate economic issues at play. Enclave tourism tends to shut out local businesses at the expense of resort owners and tour operators. Just as cruise ships often attempt to discourage passengers from patronizing unaffiliated merchants, tour operators have an interest in keeping their clients on the beaten track. "A lot of the time it's a mediated experience," Andrews says of Magaluf tours. "And the travel companies, through their reps, try to control as much of that experience as possible. I sat in on what were called 'welcome meetings.' The tourists arrive, the first day they have a meeting with the rep, who is selling them packages to go on a bar crawl or an island tour or something like that."

"One thing the tourists could do was visit the leather market in the centre of the island. And they are warned, 'You better not try to do this trip on your own because of the difficulties in getting the train home. You better not get on the local buses because of the danger of pickpockets.' Now, I frequently got on local buses and the only place I've ever had my pocket picked was back in London."

British holidaymakers are certainly not the only ones who favour party destinations that offer the comfort of familiarity. "I think Americans do the exact same thing British travellers do," says travel writer Alex Temblador. "Mexico is the biggest example of Americans going to resorts to be around more Americans. A lot of Americans are very scared of getting off the resorts and the hotels. They go back to the same places that feel comfortable. My parents, for instance." She laughs. "If they go to Cabo one more time, or Vegas one more time, we can't be family anymore."

There are good reasons why tourists would choose destinations that offer a degree of comfort and familiarity, Temblador points out. "Mexican Americans will often go to Mexico. Part of it is seeing family but it's partly about speaking the same language. Or they'll go to Puerto Rico or places where other Latinos are at."

Once upon a time in America, enclave tourism was the law. The famous *Negro Motorist Green Book* was a necessity for Black American travellers to avoid segregated and hostile establishments in the Jim Crow era. Temblador believes a vestige of that desire for travel security survives today. "I think it's a safety thing. I've spoken to different travellers of colour and they've said, 'I want to go somewhere and learn about something similar to my history and my culture. I want to see a tour guide who looks like me and can tell me whether it's safe to go to a particular part of town.'"

"I think that's a general statement for most of my clients, of every kind," says Shalene Dudley, owner of Ontario travel agency Latitude Concierge Travels. "I do have people who will openly say, 'I want to go somewhere where everybody speaks English.' So you just want to ask people what their purpose is for the travel, even if it's a wedding. Are you going somewhere where you want it to be culturally immersive? Do you want to learn about where you're going?"

"How much of the responsibility is on the travel advisor to make sure that their client can actually learn about the world they're travelling through," Dudley asks, "instead of just plopping yourself in another environment, and then taking it over? Because those are the sins of colonialism, right? We don't want to do that anymore."

There is some evidence that a willingness to engage with a destination can lead to a new sense of community—in effect, the discovery of a new place to feel comfortable.

Among the fascinating elements of the Wonderful Copenhagen study was the difference between visitors' expectations and reality. The study separated first-time and repeat visitors, and found first-time visitors were drawn to the prospect of seeing the usual highlights: famous attractions, castles, historic churches, the usual checklist items. But when those who had been to Copenhagen before were asked about the city's main selling points, they did not emphasize the major attractions. Rather, they cited its widespread bicycle culture, canals and the small, manageable size of the city. (Bicycles scored 40 percent higher than any other element of Copenhagen life for return visitors.) So repeat travellers were returning not for what they had initially seen in the brochures, but for the experience of Copenhagen life they had discovered at ground level.

"Tourists don't return to be tourists," says Greg Oates, vice president of travel consulting firm MMGY NextFactor. "They return because they want to be part of the community. They identify with that community. That's how you drive loyalty, by saying, 'This is what we are about as a community and we want you to be part of it.'"

"San Francisco is a good example," Oates says. "They've been very intentional about selling the city as a network of neighbourhoods. You want that overarching, iconic experience—the Golden Gate Bridge, Fisherman's Wharf and so on—but then you also find your unique identity and the unique neighbourhood that you align with, whether it's the Castro District or the North Beach district. It's about self-congruency—we want to patronize the places that we identify with."

Ultimately, tourists go abroad with very different agendas. Successful trips can thus take a wide variety of forms. "I am not judging the tourists in Magaluf," Andrews says. "It's not my kind of holiday. But if people want to go lie in the sun, have drinks, engage in sex with people they don't know, that's their holiday. It may be the only week or two weeks of the year they get. I spoke to one man who was quite depressed about his life back home. His phrase was 'I've been digging shit all my life.' We need to remember what people are coming from and what the expectations of the holiday are."

"Tourism gets blamed for lots of things but I think it's not fair," she says. "There are lots of ways that cultures travel. For me the bottom line is the role of business. Would the experience in Magaluf be different if the tour operators weren't interfering and trying to cajole people?"

"It's not fair to say there's never any kind of cultural exchange, because I think there is," Andrews says. "There are friendships produced."

Can there ever be a perfect tourist? If so, I may have met him.

In spring 2023 I was staying at an *agriturismo* (farm-based inn) called Il Torrione, located just north of the Tuscan town of Certaldo. Il Torrione is run by a brother and sister team, Salvatore and Lucia, and may boast the loveliest setting I have ever had the pleasure of staying in—a hilltop perch with green pastures and hillsides rolling and rising in every direction.

Late one afternoon, after a stop at Caffè Solferino to sip rich, dark espresso under the gaze of the Boccaccio statue in the town square, my rented bike and I laboured up the steep slope I had dubbed Murder Hill and rolled into the grounds of Il Torrione. There I found a young man setting up a tent and a little cookstove beside a bicycle. He had asked Salvatore if it would be OK to camp here overnight and, in stark contrast to the usual North American attitude to such requests, Salvatore was happy to oblige.

The young man's name was Victor Dumoulin; he was a twenty-eight-year-old from Nantes, France. With dark hair, moustache and goatee, he was the kind of guy who you might think resembles a movie star, but you can't quite nail down which one. He had taken the train to Marseille and from there had pedalled his way down the Italian Peninsula. I watched as he fired up his little burner and prepared a lentil stew I would have been proud to produce in my own kitchen. We chatted about our respective travels, admiring the evening vista of olive groves and grape orchards below a sky flecked with clouds and swallows.

Victor was aware that not everyone could travel as he does. Nor do his flightless methods permit him the exploration of, say, Australia. Still, it occurred to me that travelling like Victor answers every concern raised against modern tourism. No emissions, save the truly unavoidable ones (Salvatore even kindly offered Victor use of the bathroom facilities), no over-consumption, no disruption of local landscapes. His was travel in its purest form.

Victor's plan was to head to Siena the next day, about forty-two kilometres southeast. Mine too, but one of us would be taking the train. Murder Hill was enough exercise for me. It turned out our paths would cross again on the streets of that ancient Tuscan city. Heading back toward the train, I bumped into him near the old city gate called Porta Camollia. Victor told me he would soon be headed south again, describing a long loop that would eventually take in Puglia, Calabria and Sardinia. As for me, my little train hop to Siena had been a day trip in search of the past.

It was perhaps fourteen years since I had last been in Siena, but once upon a time it had been a regular destination. Over a number of years I had been engaged in a quixotic attempt to make common cause with an ancient fraternity that existed in Siena centuries before the arrival of tomatoes. It was on my very first visit to Italy that I had plunged headlong into the chaos of the Palio.

Riding Out the Palio

My first trip to Europe is made in 2002 with three good friends—Martin, Laura and her husband, Ren. After a spell in Paris and a couple of Italian stops, we arrive in Siena. It is the end of June, just a couple of days before the summer's first running of the Palio di Siena.

Strictly speaking the Palio is a horse race, a three-lap, bareback careen around the Campo, Siena's ancient town square, held on July 2 and August 16 of each year, a galloping free-for-all that can leave riders broken and horses destroyed. In practice the Palio is considerably more—eight centuries of ritualized combat, an all-consuming goal, an organizing principle that has gerrymandered Siena the way high school football carves up Texas. Each race lasts under a minute and a half. But in old-town Siena, the Palio defines every day of the year.

The first known running of the Palio has been variously marked at 1187 or 1283, possibly inspired by Roman military training. Originally a long run through the streets of town, the (relatively) modern *palio alla tonda*—three laps around the Campo track—was inaugurated in 1633.

For the people of Siena the Palio overrides all other considerations. In their definitive 1975 book on the race, *La Terra in Piazza*, authors Alan

Dundes and Alessandro Falassi describe how, in April 1919, Italy descended into violent clashes between leftists and Mussolini's Fascists. But not in Siena—at least not right away. It was decided that political riots could wait. First, the Palio.

In the twenty-first century the Palio is also a tourist attraction, seen in the opening sequence of the 2008 Bond movie *Quantum of Solace* (sharp-eyed locals will note actual footage from the August 16, 2007, race, won by the Leocorno—or Unicorn—*contrada*). I once took a picture, from the piazza below, of Tom Hanks and Rita Wilson watching the race from a high window. But how many visitors grasp the immensity of what they are witnessing? Imagine strolling into Waterloo, sitting down beside Napoleon with a picnic basket and a pair of binoculars, and you have a sense of it.

In Old Siena, seventeen different flags mark the turf of the *contrade*, the little neighbourhood states that have dominated Sienese life since medieval times. Each *contrada* has its own brilliantly coloured uniform and flies its own banner. Most *contrade* have several allies and, more importantly, at least one bitter enemy among the other groups. At Palio time, roving gangs of young men will shout songs of challenge to their crosstown enemies, occasionally coming to blows. Visitors to Disneyland will note that Mickey and Minnie rarely get into punch-ups with Donald and his nephews.

A few days before the race, a lottery is held. Ten worthy horses are selected, and each in turn is assigned to one of the participating *contrade*. Not every *contrada* runs every Palio—the Campo track will not accommo-date seventeen furiously thrashing beasts, so ten participants are selected. Those *contrade* not blessed with a mount will have their chance next time.

It is in the lottery that the true genius of the Palio is revealed. It determines who will have a legitimate chance of victory. Big money is powerless here.

Although ten horses run, ultimately two will be remembered—one winner and one loser. The loser is the horse that finishes second. The ration-ale for this can be surmised. Since Palio horses are assigned by lot, finishing dead last probably indicates nothing more shameful than drawing a bad ticket. But to finish second suggests a good horse and a bad ride. That may not always be the case, but this powerfully entrenched tradition is by now too well accepted to respond to logic or reason. Finishing second in the Palio, whatever the circumstances, earns a *contrada* nothing but disgrace. In fact, tradition holds that the losing *contrada* should undergo a physical purge using castor oil.

To win the Palio is every *contrada*'s dream. To lose the Palio is a nightmare of shame that drives each team to furious plotting and desperate deal-making in the days before the race. Almost sweeter than victory is the ultimate finesse—to manoeuvre your enemy into second position. Teams will spread money around via a complex series of agreements called *partiti*, arranging for friendly jockeys to impede rival horses by whatever means possible. One Palio saw Aquila with a good horse and its rival, Pantera, stuck with a no-hoper. At the start, the Pantera (Panther) jockey simply reached out and grabbed the reins of the Aquila (Eagle) mount, preventing both horses from moving. The illegal tactic earned Pantera a ban from the next Palio, but no matter. Their jockey was feted as a hero.

Once the lottery has been held and the horses selected, each team must decide on its course—to strive for victory with a likely mount or, cursed with a nag, to accept near-certain defeat. (The horses are well known—one horse, Urbino de Ozieri, was actually retired from competition because he was too damn good.) If you get a bad horse, you throw all resources toward defeating the foe. Those resources can be considerable. An insider who witnessed the accounting session that followed one Palio victory told me that, when all the bribes and banquet expenses had been tallied, success had cost the *contrada* well over half a million dollars. Bribes become payable only in the event of victory, so triumph often leaves a *contrada* destitute. It is exactly the opposite of a standard horse race where the winner is enriched. In the Palio the winner is financially devastated, having sacrificed everything for glory. Thus a *contrada* seeking to deal its way to victory will usually target last season's Palio winners—they'll always be desperate for money.

July 1, 2002, one day before the Palio, the Campo teems with the usual assortment of tacky souvenir stalls perused by crowds of people in socks and sandals. The magic of the Palio has yet to stir in the midday heat. Then a singing crowd of teenagers rounds the corner, decked out in the yellow-and-green *fazzoletto*, or scarf, of the Contrada del Bruco. It is a song I will hear many times over the next two days—stately, almost hymnlike, the verses punctuated by thrusting arms and rhythmic clapping. For every *contrada* the melody is the same. Only the lyrics are altered, each team delivering its particular version of the basic message: You suck. We rule.

Meandering through the side streets I meet Laura and Ren on the Via Duprè, a long lane that empties into the Campo (and incidentally, the street Daniel Craig would later drive down as James Bond's Aston Martin entered Siena). This is the home turf of Onda, and their blue-and-white flags adorned with dolphins hang from each side of the narrow passage. The social centre of this *contrada* is a little coffee bar, Bar L'Onda, run by a man named Gianni and his brother. It's a busy place today. In a scene being echoed in sixteen other neighbourhoods, the people of Onda (Wave) are setting up for the massive outdoor banquet that will celebrate the eve of the Palio. Tourists are quite welcome to pony up thirty-five euros for a seat at the table, if space is available.

The people here in Onda territory seem friendly. We buy tickets to banquet with Onda. In my case at least, it's a little like getting drunk and joining the Navy—the depth of one's commitment does not become clear until later.

Joining a *contrada* is simple. You merely have to be born there. Babies born to Onda parents will be baptized swaddled in the *contrada* colours, lifelong members of the tribe. Once upon a time this meant being born at home, in the actual neighbourhood. But eventually hospital births became the norm. Problem: Siena's hospital was located in the territory of the Contrada della Selva (Forest). Would every Sienese infant thus automatically join

Selva? Parents became desperate. Relatives would show up at the hospital with containers of earth from their home turf to be placed under the birthing bed. Alternatively, the newborn might be laid upon a flag of the home *contrada*. Eventually the rules were relaxed so that one could be born into a *contrada* purely via parental lineage.

Shakespeare set Romeo and Juliet three hundred kilometres to the north in Verona, but tell a tale of a Tartuca (Turtle) lad enamoured of a Chiocciola (Snail) girl and the story would play out the same. Intermarriage does happen but it is said that married couples of different *contrade* will separate during Palio week to avoid strife.

These days an outsider like me can pledge fealty to a *contrada* but it will take years of devoted attendance before I might be considered one of the group. Perhaps if I learn Italian, marry a *contrada* girl, and/or get beat up by our enemies, Contrada della Torre (Tower), I might someday be baptized as an official Onda man. (Another option is to become a major star. The Contrada dell'Aquila baptized Palio enthusiast Mel Gibson as an official member, a slavish bit of celebrity ass-kissing that earned Aquila a fair bit of local scorn.)

I do want to be part of it, though, insofar as possible. The Palio has fascinated me ever since I first heard about it via a TV documentary. Now I have chosen a *contrada*. I even buy myself a blue-and-white *fazzoletto*.

Despite having cast my lot with Onda I am still an invisible tourist, free to wander ghostlike among the faithful. That afternoon, Laura, Ren and I head out toward Porta Camollia to the territory of Istrice. The Porcupines are among the most populous of *contrade*. And this year, locals say, they are definitely in the running.

Crowds of young men are drinking and jostling, all garbed in the burgundy, black and white *fazzoletto* of Istrice. Down a little side street the trainer walks a small chestnut horse named Ugo Sancez. Is this the best horse, I ask an old man in broken French—"*Le meilleur?*"

He shakes his head, wagging his finger. Not just the best, he says, in definite language even I can understand. "*Il vincitore,*" he says. The winner.

Two rows of women standing opposite each other suddenly begin to sing, swaying and waving their arms ecstatically as they look up the street toward something not yet in my view. Then he is there, strutting down the lane. Ugo Sancez is on his way to the Campo.

Laura and Ren look around at the roistering crowd and decide they want no part of it. But when the faithful fall in behind their horse, I slip in among them. Above our heads small windows are open, each showing the disembodied grey head of an old woman, watching the tide below. The growing chorus is roaring a challenge to every neighbourhood in Siena. Packed into the narrow street we are carried downhill like scales on a snake.

Where are the tourists now? Still here, I see—a few bob along in the throng, conspicuous by our wide-eyed looks. But everything has changed now. We, the visitors, are an inert force. Something else is moving and it has blown the tourist crowd off the road, dried leaves before a gale. Siena has awakened to the Palio.

North Americans do get worked up at sports events, when the jumbotron tells them to. But you don't often see this kind of coordinated movement in the New World (not since the Salem witch trials, anyway). This river of Sienese is bound together by shared knowledge, rooted in ritual. There is coherency in their actions, something that seems to have never made the jump across the Atlantic to the world of citizen kings.

The mob makes the final turn and faces the Campo. Abruptly, collectively, the voices triple in volume. Arms thrust skyward as the song is flung defiantly into the milling Campo crowd. The hair on the back of my neck stands up. Istrice, indeed.

The grandstands are filled with *contrada* factions, each chanting and swaying in turn. A troop of black-clad riders appears—the Carabinieri, sporting sashes, sabres and plumed hats, trotting past to the applause of the multitude. At a signal from their captain, the riders draw their sabres and charge.

Now the horses are circling the track, carrying the jockeys in their brilliant silks—Torre, Valdimontone (Valley of the Ram), Chiocciola, Pantera,

Oca (Goose), Onda, Bruco (Caterpillar), Lupa (She-Wolf), Aquila and Istrice. This final trial run is a casual lope, and the order of finish is relatively unimportant. Torre, picked by local pundits to do well, crosses the finish line first, and the cannon fires.

The crowd floods onto a track now dented by hooves and dotted with horseshit. By the mouth of Via Duprè a cadre has formed—all young men, wearing the *fazzoletto* of Onda. Their song is a shout, a rebuke. They come to an abrupt halt, shoulder to shoulder, and glare menacingly, expectantly, down the track. But no answering challenge comes. After a moment they break ranks, joining a stream of blue and white that pours down Via Duprè toward the banquet tables.

In the twilight, rows of streetlamps light the long tables that stretch for perhaps a quarter mile. I am seated across from Mario and Lorenza, a married couple in their sixties. I have just purchased a beautiful silk *fazzoletto* from a passing vendor, officially casting my lot with the Wave. But Mario's is hand-sewn. He was born and baptized in Onda country.

And me? Despite my enthusiasm, I am a dilettante. Up and down Via Duprè the songs are joined. I can only listen. *"Abasso le Torre!"* ("Down with the Tower!") they shout. I can manage that one, at least.

Onda has its friends too, including Valdimontone and Nicchio (Shell). Problem is, those two *contrade* are themselves bitter enemies. Socially, it's a little awkward. Following one Onda victory years earlier, our allies showed up at the celebratory banquet bearing the traditional gifts. The Valley of the Ram *contrada* offered up a barrel of wine. Then Nicchio arrived, bearing the carcass of a full-grown ram with its throat cut. "Tongue hanging out and everything," one observer recalls. Dinner was a tad uncomfortable.

Sitting forlornly at tonight's banquet is the father of Salasso, Onda's jockey. Passersby attempt to comfort him. The Palio is a dangerous place for a jockey during the race, and sometimes after. One famous archival photo shows a jockey scrambling into the stands to avoid his own enraged supporters. In one early-80s Palio, the Istrice jockey slipped off his horse early in the race with a little too much ease. His employers suspected a private side deal had been cut, inducing him to betrayal. Moments after the race the Istrice jockey was beaten within an inch of his life. Next day the jockey's mother was heard on local radio pleading, not for justice, but forgiveness for her misguided son. No action was taken against the Istrice supporters— it was considered an internal matter. (Only one woman has ever run in a modern Palio—Rosanna Bonelli, a.k.a. "Rompicollo" (Breakneck), who rode for Aquila in August 1957. Like many riders before and since, she was unhorsed during the race. A horse can still win without a rider, and it does happen, though it didn't that time.)

I wander off to seek a public toilet. A man emerges from a side door. "Is this a restroom?" I ask in English and halting French. The man's eyes light up. He nods vigorously and waves me in. The door closes behind me. I am in absolute darkness. Fumbling for a light switch, I find myself standing in the hallway of an apartment building. A man comes down the stairs. "Is there a toilet?" I ask. "No, no," he says, alarmed. "This is a residence."

Back on the street, my helpful friend looks at me with wide-eyed innocence. "No luck?" He smirks. I return to my seat. Onda? No. I belong to the *contrada* Turista. It is my birthright.

You can't just parachute into a sacred fraternity and blend in. Not even movie stars can truly pull that off.

Mario and Lorenza are kinder. They invite me to return to the neighbourhood tomorrow for the blessing of the horse, just up the street at the Church of San Giuseppe. And after the race, they say, we will return here to Via Duprè—"*Lacrime,*" Mario says. To shed tears.

Our little European tour had included the obligatory stop in Venice. It proved as pretty as advertised but otherwise somewhat disconcerting, even depressing. If there is indeed a Paris syndrome, it surely has a Venetian counterpart. Venice is a city with a grand history, and that remains in the art, architecture and canals. But to a modern visitor it has all been subsumed by the city's new theme park identity. There is almost nowhere you can go, with the possible exception of the university area, to feel yourself in the city proper and away from the tourist track. The tourist takeover of Venice has been completed.

By contrast, Siena has achieved something almost miraculous. In *The Tourist*, Dean MacCannell wrote of what he called "staged authenticity." But the Palio is not a performance of an ancient tradition now restaged for the benefit of tour bus crowds. It may be a major tourist draw but the city has never surrendered ownership of its civic obsession. Over the centuries its power has not faded or diminished. The Sienese welcome tourism, but there is a limit to how far they will go to accommodate the looky-loos. In Siena, the Palio is more important than the crowds that come to watch it.

The tourists putzing around Siena this week cannot destroy something older than Protestantism, and just as insanely complex. The volcanic flow of pop culture cannot burn away everything it meets—some traditions are strong enough to survive, drawing tourists and yet resisting them. The Palio will remain beyond the reach of its observers. Its roots run too deep.

July 2—race day. Martin, Laura, Ren and I meet for lunch at a pizzeria named for New York, featuring pizza that is Sienese right down to the local pear slices in olive oil. "You seem to have slipped into a parallel universe," Laura remarks to me, to general nodding agreement.

It's true—I have gone to a place where my friends are unwilling or unable to follow. Sensing the genuine fervour beneath the rituals, they have reacted by backing away. I have tried my best to dive into the madness.

The people of Siena have been depicted as lunatics. A story is told that Pietro Leopoldo, eighteenth-century grand duke of Tuscany, was asked by the Sienese to build an insane asylum in their city. He is said to have replied, "Shut the city gates and you will have your madhouse ready-made." Tellingly, it is the Sienese themselves who recount this tale.

In a courtyard near the Church of San Giuseppe stands Zilata Usa, the beautiful grey-and-white animal who will carry the hopes of Onda today.

A large crowd waits in the hot sun to enter the church for one of the most important of all Palio rituals.

Zilata Usa is led through the solemn crowd inside the church. As the priest begins to speak, the horse answers with a long, frightened whinny. The cross is thrust against the horse's lips, then the jockey's, then the trainer's. The priest shouts, *"Vai e torna vincitore!"* ("Go and return a winner!") It is considered good luck if the horse takes a dump on the carpet, but through the crowd I can't see whether they scored that particular four-leaf clover. Zilata Usa departs from the church, and it's prickly neck time again as the assembled faithful burst into song, loud enough to blow the toupée off old San Giuseppe.

It is just after four o'clock. If I'm to find a good place in the Campo, now is the time.

Money may not buy you a good horse in the Palio, but it does buy you a good seat. There are bleachers around the Campo and above them the windows of those lucky residents who can rent their premises as luxury boxes (like the spot where I saw Tom Hanks and family sitting in comfort). But these choice spots, even the bleachers, require money and pull. For the rest of us, attendance is free. All we have to do is empty our bladders as best we can, file into the central piazza hours ahead of time and stake out a spot. It's the peasants' option. The central area of the Campo is colloquially known as *il palco dei cani*—roughly, the dog park.

Some camp out overnight beside the railings to preserve their place. But at around 4:20 p.m. I'm pleasantly surprised to find that I can still comfortably slide in about three rows back from the rail, near the final turn, known as Casato. Not too bad.

It is close to 5:30 when the pre-Palio parade begins. By God, it does go on. For the next two sweltering hours, thickly costumed representatives of Sienese glories past and present file past. By the time 7:30 rolls around you'd think they were pulling *contrade* out of Sweden. So far one woman has been hauled out of the Campo on a stretcher, but that's a minor miracle—if the sun hadn't gone behind merciful clouds, they'd be relaying limp bodies out of here like a bucket brigade. I get down on my knees, balancing on an empty water bottle to keep the bricks from cutting into my legs. The trick is to properly hydrate yourself without overdoing it and suddenly requiring the kind of facilities you can never access. Near me, one desperate young American woman attempts to climb over the railing onto the track. No escape is allowed. Soon she's looking for an empty bottle, pleading in vain for privacy.

The Palio itself, a giant banner bearing a likeness of the Madonna, enters on a giant cart laden with three wooden thrones and drawn by white oxen.

At last the horses enter the track. As the riders emerge from the enclosure each is handed a *nerbo*, a whip made from a stretched calf penis. Jockeys often smack each other with these during the race. The horses gather near the starting line, and locals urgently call for silence. It is time to inaugurate the final, crucial preliminary to the Palio—deciding the lineup. There is room on the line for only nine horses. The tenth will be the *rincorsa*, allowed to get a running start behind the others so that it is in full stride when the rope drops. To be the *rincorsa* gives no real competitive advantage. But politically, the *rincorsa* is king. By choosing his moment to hit the starting line, the *rincorsa*'s jockey can help decide the early positioning. That makes him the man to talk to. In addition to seeking deals with the *rincorsa*, jockeys will attempt to strike deals with the riders positioned directly beside them, bargaining for a little open space at the start. Thus, it is only when the starting lineup is announced that the real deal-making can be finalized.

Any network executives in the crowd are beginning to realize why this ain't no Kentucky Derby. The Palio is not made for TV. It's made for local politics. The lengthy start process is a last-minute bargain fair, a senate cloakroom on horseback where riders attempt to cut deals until the last possible moment.

This time, Lupa is *rincorsa*. It's a bad omen for Lupa's rival, Istrice. The *rincorsa* will always attempt to hit the starting line when it sees its rival in an awkward position. Onda has scored the place along the rail. The blessing of San Giuseppe may yet pay dividends.

There's a sudden roar from the crowd—a horse has thrown its rider. It was Ascon, the Lupa horse, rearing to slip his burden. Remounted, Ascon gallops to the line. Crowd noise rises. The rope drops, the horses leap forward—the cannon fires. False start. The horses circle the track and the sorting begins anew.

The rope drops again. And again. Three false starts. The crowd is growing testy. Almost half an hour and at least one more tourist-laden stretcher has gone by since the horses first approached the line.

The rope drops again. The horses surge. There is little reaction from the crowd, but as the horses reach the first turn and no cannon fire is heard they respond at last. The race is on.

Bruco's Urban II takes the early lead. But the *rincorsa*'s gambit has failed—Istrice has started well, running near the front of the pack. The horses pile into the sharp-angled San Martino turn that leads to the straightaway. Looking down the track, the horses seem to round the turn and disappear as if they have all run straight into the padded walls. As they bounce back into view heading straight for my position, I'm amazed to see that no one, horse or rider, has been scattered on the track in their wake. And as they pass me into the Casato corner, Zilata Usa is tantalizingly near the lead. It's early, but the hopes of Onda are alive.

As the horses round into the third and final circuit, Onda slips into the lead. By the next turn Istrice too has sliced past the fading Bruco mount to draw a bead on Zilata Usa. Now they are angling into the final turn. As the group approaches my position, the leading jockey is still Onda's. Istrice's horse Ugo Sancez is a length behind. I am screaming myself raw. Onda is just a home stretch from victory.

They flash past and disappear behind a sea of heads. Something has happened—I can sense it, I can hear the roar, but see nothing but the haunches of trailing mounts. Cannon fire indicates the finish. I have the impression that Onda's horse has fallen, and turn to those on higher ground for a clue. No, the horse did not fall. Who has won? There is no consensus.

"Onda!"

"Bruco!"

Confirmation comes via the flag that is unfurled from the Palazzo Pubblico. Heads turn and the banner drops—white, blue, black, burgundy. Istrice. A mob has formed around the victorious jockey, pulling at his clothes as he sits astride Ugo Sancez. As the old man told me—*il vincitore*. The winner.

There is worse to come. Zilata Usa, running ahead of all expectations, met with misfortune on the very Casato turn where I stood straining to see. The video appears to show Salasso clipping his leg against the railing as he makes the turn. The next development is obvious to all—Zilata Usa veers off to the outside, allowing Istrice's champion to blow past on the rail. And yet it was tantalizingly close. At the finish, Zilata Usa was edged out by only a head. All around me men and women in blue-and-white *fazzoletti* stand dumbstruck. It is a disaster—Onda has finished second.

Mario and Lorenza had invited me to join the crowd after the race for *lacrime*. Clearly they had not understood the kind of *lacrime* they were in for. Up and down the Via Duprè people sit with heads in hands, sobbing as though their pudgy little Sienese dogs had been chewed up under the galloping hooves. A lone teenage girl weaves down the street, wailing to the skies—"*Ondaa ...*"

I want to commiserate, prove I'm one of the gang, share the bad times with the good. But in the depths of this genuine bitterness I'm a wannabe sufferer, a Munchausen's syndrome schmuck faking symptoms for sympathy. I have not earned the right to share in this moment of tragedy. It occurs to me that my continued presence might not be looked upon kindly. I slip away, pulling the *fazzoletto* from my neck as I follow the celebrating mob toward Istrice territory.

Partiers jam the route of yesterday's Istrice parade. I have no heart for this—even if Onda does not want my sympathy I can't pretend to jump on this bandwagon. Apparently others don't share my delicate scruples. Istrice flags are blossoming from every public building and souvenir stand. I half expect to see hapless little Sienese dogs dumped for an army of hedgehogs on leashes.

Drumming and singing fade behind me. It's like waking from a vaguely disquieting dream. The passion that suffuses the Palio defies easy celebration—it demands more than mere tourism.

This would not be my final Palio. Over the years I have returned many times. I've made friends and spent brutal sun-baked hours in the Campo guarding a spot by the rail. Onda has won the coveted Palio three times since I became a follower, most recently in August 2017. I have not been there for any of those happy moments.

I have solid excuses for my absence of course—an intervening ocean, other places to be. And it's the latter that really damns me. I want to belong. But do I want it enough to forsake all others? Is my commitment sufficient to move heaven and Earth so that I will be in the Campo, decked out in my Onda *fazzoletto*, at the renewal of each ancient cycle? That is the price of true belonging. Short of that, I am a dilettante. Worse—I am a tourist.

Err-bnb

It was a lovely day in early May. I was sitting in a comfortable rattan chair beside open sliding doors, perusing a three-day-old copy of the *International Herald Tribune*. My second-storey vantage point overlooked a stone walkway that ambled alongside the Asano River in Kanazawa, Japan. A Californian couple paused as they strolled the stone street that passed by the traditional houses of Kazue-machi, Kanazawa's historic village named for the samurai who once owned it, now surrounded by the modern city. They gazed up at my comfortable perch. "That's a great spot," the woman said. "How can we get a reservation?"

Now there was a question. A proper reply could take a while. I kept it simple. "It's a private residence. I know the owner."

This was Kyoko's house in Kanazawa. Kyoko's house is famous, but nobody knows that. It had stood on this spot for four hundred years, gradually renewing itself, the original materials replaced piece by piece over the years like the legendary Ship of Theseus, or the cells in a human body.

Over a hundred years ago, Kyoko's little house had been home to one of the most famous of all geisha—Michiyakko. The writer Izumi Kyōka used Michiyakko as the model for his tragic story, "Giketsu kyōketsu" ("The Righteous and the Chivalrous"), later made into a play and movie, *Taki no Shiraito* (*The Water Magician*). It tells of a young apprentice geisha (known as a *maiko*) who helps put her boyfriend through law school. A crime is committed—the young woman accepts responsibility to spare her lover. When at last she is brought to justice, it is her beloved who sits on the bench and passes the sentence of death.

The real-life Michiyakko met no such terrible end. She and Kyōka were neighbours. The writer was born near the Shinto shrine where Kyoko now parks her car. There's a little museum dedicated to his work nearby. Michiyakko's house—Kyoko's house—is registered as a historical treasure, but happily for Kyoko, few are aware of its touristic value. It sits there, as anonymous as a former child star riding a desk in the loan department.

Kyoko's house was narrow but three storeys high. Two white cloths were hung to screen the sliding front door. A little vestibule held racks of shoes and parasols and led to the door of the house proper. The ground floor was cluttered and unpretentious—a low table and couch faced the TV set, a desk faced the wall and there were shelves full of plates, dolls and personal treasures. The ceilings were low. By the end of the week my forehead would be tattooed with the imprint of wooden archways.

Kazue-machi is one of two geisha districts in Kanazawa. At least four geisha lived on the street, and there was an *ochaya*, a place where geisha entertain their clients. Kazue-machi was featured on the official promotional poster of Kanazawa, available for free at city hall. Pasted onto a pink background illustrated with cherry blossoms, Kyoko's house nestled unobtrusively amid the picturesque wooden houses, fronted by the broad river and flanked by a wide stone bridge. Along the sides of the poster Japanese characters spelled out a message: "Perhaps a beautiful woman lives there."

Indeed. And I was her guest. I don't blame the American couple for seeking out such cozy personal accommodation. But I could never have foreseen that their question to me would one day reverberate through the realms of both travel and real estate.

In August 2008 two San Francisco residents would launch a modest rental operation named for the air mattress they were offering to guests. In the years that followed, Airbnb would inflate an entire industry.

Of all internet-generated travel phenomena, Airbnb may be the most contentious. The company facilitates private rentals of homes and apartments for travellers who prefer to avoid hotels or are simply looking for a better deal. Users swear by it as a service that democratizes hospitality and puts money directly in the pockets of locals. Urban planners point to unbalanced domestic rental markets, and frustrated clients point to scams, scams, scams. As Airbnb's popularity grew, online travel advice listicles like "10 Best Ecotourism Destinations" and "10 Best Island Getaways" were joined by "10 Airbnb Scams That Will Ruin Your Vacation."

The reach of Airbnb is stunning. According to AllTheRooms, a site that offers data analysis for the home rental market, in the summer of 2023 there were almost twice as many listings for Airbnb (and its more upscale competitor, Vrbo) as there were homes for sale in the United States.

Airbnb began as a useful online tool for budget travellers and a way for cash-strapped homeowners to pay off mortgages. But as with plastic bags, a useful convenience can metastasize into a global scourge. The company grew into a largely unregulated, room-devouring colossus. Airbnb removes units from the long-term rental market as landlords go for the higher profits of short-term tourist stays. The result is scarcity and higher rents. "It's complicated and contentious," says travel consultant Greg Oates, "particularly in resort towns. You have young people who say 'I want to live in the community I grew up in, I want to work as a hostess, a waiter, a bartender.' If they can't afford to live there now you are diluting the character of the community. You're starting to mess with the DNA of the destination. And if the DNA is what destinations are differentiating themselves on, then you have some problems."

Airbnb—scourge or blessing? "In places with little housing that are typically static for a historic reason like Venice it seems to harm a residential area," says Santa Cruz housing policy analyst Darrell Owens, "but otherwise Airbnb has addressed a market deficit in family or large group lodging that hotels have not."

Airbnb offers something certain travellers treasure—family-friendly accommodations. Few hotels cater to families that want adjoining rooms and full kitchens. Airbnb rentals often check those boxes.

Jeroen Oskam, director of research at Hotelschool The Hague, is the author of *The Future of Airbnb and the "Sharing Economy."* He says the company's overall impact has been decidedly mixed. "Airbnb has contributed to the growth of city tourism, which is judged as positive by some and negative by others. The main problem of Airbnb is the negative externalities it is causing in those cities. My opinion is that the effects of Airbnb have been plainly negative."

Airbnb has been heralded as a way to funnel money to people in desperate straits. Claire Newell of Travel Best Bets points out it came in handy for residents of Ukraine after Putin's invasion. "Airbnb was a perfect example of something really great in Ukraine, where people would rent their houses, with no intention of staying," she says. "That was how they were getting money to people who needed it. They were renting through Airbnb for twenty dollars a night or whatever, getting money into people's hands."

"After Hurricane Maria, Puerto Rico came back twice as fast as they expected because of Airbnb," says Oates.

Oates counts himself among the service's biggest fans for a number of reasons. "One is because it lets me experience the city in a unique way," he says. "I don't want to be around a bunch of other visitors. Another is that it has allowed me to visit places I wouldn't have gone before because it would have been too expensive. I started going to [Austin, Texas, music event] SXSW every year. It would have been too expensive to stay in hotels. Airbnb let me go to tourism conferences in Europe. So it's the sharing economy helping drive the knowledge economy."

The response of many municipal governments to Airbnb has evolved over time. The provincial capital Victoria, BC, has gone from one extreme to the other, first encouraging Airbnb rentals and then attempting to forbid them.

Before August 2008, Airbnb did not exist and many cities were facing issues with decaying downtowns. As Paul Nursey, CEO of Destination Greater Victoria, recalls, restoration of downtown heritage properties was a cherished goal. "The city wanted to bring more life to downtown," he says. "Developers said 'We need more flexibility.' Liberal zoning regulations allowing for short-term rentals helped make these projects more attractive. The idea was to attract people and visitors downtown and make the area more vital.

"Then Airbnb exploded."

Like cane toads in Australia, a solution rapidly became an even bigger problem. Oskam estimates that Airbnb has claimed approximately 14 percent of the accommodation market, the vast majority of it in leisure rather than business travel. Victoria eventually reversed course and moved to shut down the short-term rental market as it spread through the available housing stock.

My own experience of the service has been limited to a trip down the US Pacific Coast several years ago. An Airbnb accommodation in Portland, Oregon, was my first, followed by another in Oceano, California. It was certainly a change from hotels—I had never previously been tempted to take sides in a feud between two guests over who should get a particular bedroom. I had never been delayed in departing because the owner of the vehicle parked behind me in the driveway had locked their keys inside. And until using Airbnb, I had never before stayed overnight in an RV. It was OK. Having to bag and dispose of used toilet paper was a novelty, to be sure.

My accommodations were not misrepresented, at least. Journalist Allie Conti's 2019 investigation for *Vice* magazine revealed an American bait-and-switch scam so widespread it led Airbnb to make changes to its corporate policy. Following publication of the article, Airbnb CEO Brian Chesky announced a year-long project to verify listings and eliminate the issue of glamorous-looking digs that are then swapped for rancid dumps after the renters are told of unexpected problems.

Airbnb hosts are victimized by scams too—big ones. In May 2023, Toronto police arrested forty-two-year-old Jay Allen MacDougall and charged him with five counts of fraud over five thousand dollars and one count of laundering the proceeds of crime. Police said MacDougall used fake names to rent Airbnb homes, then searched them for personal information he then used to take out home mortgages with private lenders. He's alleged to have pulled the scam at least five times and received $2.5 million Canadian in mortgages.

Meanwhile Conti's article underlined another reality about Airbnb: what had begun as a way for people to make money renting out their own homes and apartments had inevitably morphed into a parallel lodging industry run by large companies controlling dozens or even hundreds of properties, a dark, untaxed and largely unregulated competitor for the hotel and motel business.

Nursey believes what's happening in BC cities like Victoria is nowhere near the situation being experienced by some major European destinations. "In places like Barcelona, Paris, Prague, they've seen the rise of the mega-hosts, with eleven or twelve thousand properties," he says, "the mass commodification of residential areas. We want to avoid that."

Cities from Vancouver to Barcelona have attempted to regulate Airbnb rentals via required registration with civic authorities. In 2018 Vancouver signed an agreement with Airbnb requiring licences for all short-term rentals and requiring hosts to rent space in their primary residences only. As of January 2024 the annual Vancouver licence fee was increased from about a hundred dollars to a thousand.

This drew a rebuke from Airbnb. "The dramatic and unnecessary fee increase hurts regular Vancouver citizens who are trying to make ends meet in an already expensive city to live in," said Nathan Rotman, policy lead for Airbnb in Canada.

To those who insist short-term rentals are a key reason for the increasing expense of housing, Airbnb's response might seem like an arsonist complaining about the price of gas.

At any rate, the situation for Airbnb was about to get even worse as civic regulations were succeeded by new province-wide rules. In October 2023, the BC provincial government stepped in with new legislation to take effect in May 2024, mandating similar primary residence rules for the entire province and increasing fines for illegal rentals to three thousand dollars per day.

But previously, enforcement has proven difficult. In Vancouver, an online watchdog who goes by the name of Mortimer believes illegal operators are thick on the ground. "It's more widespread than some would think," he says, "and it is being done by a wide array of people. I've seen illegal Airbnb listings from various professionals, including lawyers, accountants and real estate agents."

The issue came tragically to the fore in March 2023 when a deadly Montreal fire claimed seven lives in an 1890 building that was revealed to contain a number of illegal Airbnb operations. Whether the true culprit was Airbnb or inadequate civic fire-safety regulation and enforcement was fiercely debated—Airbnb or not, the building should have had fire escapes, working alarms and sprinklers. On the other hand, Airbnb customers ought to have some assurance that they are not booking an illegal fire trap. Airbnb subsequently announced they would be delisting thousands of Quebec properties.

In the land of the free, regulating Airbnb tends to be even tougher. American states that protect your right to carry a concealed Glock in a grocery store are unlikely to try to tell homeowners what they can and cannot do with their property. "In the US it's problematic," says Oates. "You have property rights laws that state if you own a house, the government can't tell you anything you can do with it."

"It's going to be here to stay," Newell believes. As proof, she cites the effect Airbnb has had on the hotel industry. "Many of the major chains, including Marriott, are now moving to that type of stay, where you can have a kitchen and have a bigger living space, do your own wash. Because people are moving to that. Hotels around the world are feeling the pressure and many of the major chains are putting in accommodation that will be direct competition to Airbnb."

"Part of that is the whole COVID situation," Newell says, "where people can now work from anywhere. Even large corporations are giving people the option to go away for a month a year, because people can work from anywhere in the world. That could be a week in Mexico, a week in Thailand, whatever. Or it could be a month-long stay where people typically want something like an Airbnb because they want to live there. It does let people live more like a local."

Even if it prevents some locals from doing the same.

Airbnb is large enough to be a potential danger to the economy. In June 2023 AllTheRooms reported a major crash in Airbnb revenues in markets like Phoenix and Austin. Airbnb itself disputed those figures, as did other industry observers. But there were other warning signs. European data from Airbnb, Booking.com, Expedia, and Tripadvisor indicated a serious drop-off in private rentals for summer 2023 in European cities such as Dublin (down 59.4 percent), Amsterdam (down 54.5 percent), Prague (down 52.4 percent) and Berlin (down 38.6 percent). *Business Insider* reported that high- and low-end booking remained strong in the US as people paid for luxury digs or searched for bargains. It was the middle ground that suffered, with property owners scrambling to attract dwindling bookings.

The reports were enough to start a discussion of the effects an Airbnb collapse might have. With almost a million American Airbnb listings nationwide, a serious revenue downturn could lead to a wave of property sales with the potential to crater the US housing market in a way comparable to the subprime mortgage debacle of 2008. Everyone would be paying for Airbnb then.

The appeal of Airbnb is understandable. One of my travel goals, however quixotic, is to experience everyday life in a foreign place. "Live like a local" was one Airbnb slogan. That's the dream. Kyoko let me live that dream in Kanazawa. But I experienced complications the average tenant does not.

Five By Ten-Out-of-Ten

My 2023 Asian tour has a stop in Singapore. Accommodations in Chinatown were booked months earlier with the online travel agency Agoda. Reviews of the hotel were stellar: "10 out of 10." "Great!" "Exceptional!" "Best best best!" Etc.

Coming out of the Outram Park transit station I get lost—I always get lost. I pass a Hindu temple with stacks of brightly coloured figures gazing down from its roof, but sightseeing brings little joy when dragging a heavy bag (no wheels) and trying to figure out where in the name of all the gods Teck Lim Road is. Finally reaching the hotel, I hump my bag off the elevator at the second floor. I open the assigned door to find myself, essentially, in jail. Aside from a bed, there is no furniture—nor would there be room for any. The dimensions of the windowless rectangle are roughly comparable to a bisected badminton court. A phone sits on the floor, and a safe in the corner. There is a shelf with a kettle, and an attached bathroom of the sort that requires you to remove all the toilet paper before showering. It isn't the first such room I have encountered on my travels. It's just that not a single Agoda review had prepared me for it.

Singapore is an unusual city for accommodations. It offers a wealth of great hostels for young backpackers, some of the finest high-end hotels on the Asian continent, and a yawning chasm in the middle. There are precious few mid-range options. Hospitality expert Edward Koh of Bangkok University says it's not the result of some grand tourism strategy. "It's market forces at play," he says. "It probably makes more sense to invest in a five- or six-star hotel than a mid-range, while backpacker hostels require less land, less manpower and less prestigious addresses."

Singapore is actually the sort of place where Airbnb could make a positive difference by providing an array of mid-range options. But the city state has banned rentals of less than three months for Singapore condos and apartments (though enforcement does not appear to be strict).

On previous visits I did what many budget-conscious visitors to Singapore do, at least the ones who want a private bathroom—I relied on what are essentially sex work hotels. There are some reasonably priced establishments in Geylang, the red-light district, places that usually cater to, shall we say, short stays. On one visit years ago I was lying in bed making some notes when I dropped my pen down beside the bed. Leaning over to search around on the floor, my hand found instead something soft and squishy with a silky latex cover. I'm not the squeamish sort, but after depositing the used condom in the trash and washing my hands thoroughly, I did ask for a different room. They were very nice about it.

So when planning this trip I was pleased to see Agoda cough up something in centrally located Chinatown, a reasonably priced hotel with nothing but glowing reviews.

My turn next. Asked for a review by Agoda, I submitted one. I was polite. The staff was helpful and friendly, I said. The location was excellent. The room, however, was an air-conditioned prison cell. As such, it had come as an unpleasant surprise.

As of this writing, my review has not been posted by Agoda. The top reviews are still the ones that lured me in.

So now I am the one levelling a charge—one count of dishonest solicitation.

A week or so after leaving Singapore I am in Bangkok, at a little restaurant beside the Chong Nonsi transit station. Over bowls of ramen, I am chatting with Franco, who worked in Agoda's Bangkok office until massive pandemic layoffs forced him to look elsewhere for employment. He left with no hard feelings. "They treated us very well," he says. "Agoda was a great place to work."

Around the turn of the twenty-first century the travel industry experienced something like a secular Reformation. The original one is said to have begun on October 31, 1517, when, legend has it, Martin Luther nailed his *Ninety-five Theses* to the door of the All Saints' Church in Wittenberg, Germany. Ninety-five is a lot of theses. For some it was TL;DR (too long; didn't read) and for most, TB;CR (too bad; can't read). At any rate, the document was only the beginning. While Luther's original attack on the Catholic Church focused on corruption and the blasphemy of selling indulgences, what ultimately emerged from his defiant stand was a spiritual DIY movement. Ordinary sixteenth-century folk did not have Bibles, and the only ones around were written in Latin anyway. People relied on priests and clergy to select, recite and interpret scripture for them, which was how the Church wanted it. Now new voices began to insist the Gospels belong to everyone and lay people should be able to read scripture for themselves in their own languages, without church intermediaries. A proliferation of new religious sects followed. This was the Reformation.

It was succeeded, roughly four and a half centuries later, by the internet.

The travel industry too had its priesthood—travel agents who would organize trip details for you, make bookings, arrange itineraries. Then came the travel reformation. As in the Garden of Eden, knowledge came from an apple (or for the budget conscious, a Dell). Online booking became the norm as the web blew holes in the established hierarchy of tourism.

Agoda was just one of many companies that emerged to service the newly empowered traveller. It began life in the mid-90s as a modest agency called Precision Reservations based in Phuket, Thailand. By the time it was purchased by Booking Holdings (formerly the Priceline Group) in 2007 it was a monolith, and, give or take a pandemic, it has continued to grow since.

A company like Agoda reserves a block of rooms at a property and then markets them, taking a hefty commission. "Hotels hate companies like Agoda," Franco says, "but they need them. In the early days of the online reservation industry there was no standardization. It was confusing for people because unless the hotels were part of a big group, no two had the same booking experience, even in the same country. Companies like Agoda simplified and streamlined everything and really came to drive the industry, just at the same time that people were becoming comfortable with putting their credit card into a website to book a room."

"Agoda is not a travel company," Franco tells me. "Agoda is a tech company that operates in the travel industry. They have elite tech people, NASA-level brains, people who have worked with companies that are on the cutting edge of science, technology and engineering."

The current CEO of Agoda is Omri Morgenshtern, co-founder of an Israeli company called Qlika that pioneered the creation of localized web displays, sometimes referred to as "micro-marketing." Morgenshtern entered the Agoda boardroom when Priceline (which also owns Booking.com and Kayak) bought his company. "Agoda got the Qlika team, and those guys are smart," Franco says. "They're the best. In the Agoda/Priceline partnership, Agoda is really the tech leader. Agoda is known for its tech savvy, and plays a big role in developing the tech that the group uses.

"When you search for a reservation on Agoda, you're not just landing on a web page. It's not the same as if I have a blog or something, you click on it and there it is. The Agoda page that loads on your device is an agglomeration of data points and elements from servers located in widely scattered places, and the page you see is created on the basis of a vast array of parameters that depend on you, your location, your searches and so on. Every element of that page has been tested to death. For instance, if testing reveals that a blue button gets, say, 0.07 percent more clicks than a red button, then you get a blue button."

The conspiracy-minded will tell you that online booking companies jack up prices when they see browsers returning to a particular property or ticket. That bit of paranoia seems unfounded. Google is sometimes fingered as the culprit, with some advising you to disguise your browser history or use incognito mode. But Google merely aggregates results—it has neither influence nor any economic interest in affecting prices.

Franco doesn't think price fluctuations are the result of snooping. "I definitely think prices can fluctuate depending on where you are and what you are looking for. But it's an incredibly complicated jumble of variables that fluctuate and change and move around thousands of times a day based on tens of thousands of data points."

Reviews are important for sites like Agoda. The consumer feedback loop is key to establishing the credibility of any online reservation service, be it for accommodations, dining or services. Why did it fail me?

Franco can only speculate about the fate of my Agoda review. "I don't imagine they are individually checked anymore," he says. "But their algorithms will definitely flag certain words and phrases."

It is possible, then, that my review was spiked by the phrase *prison cell*. And yet it remains suspicious to me that none of the posted reviews saw fit to mention the dimensions of a room that would be considered small for a janitorial supply closet.

Gaming the review system is an issue for any online service. Consider Le Nouveau Duluth. For a brief halcyon period, this remarkable restaurant was Tripadvisor's number one recommendation for Montreal diners, boasting no fewer than eighty-five five-star reviews. One competing Montreal restaurant owner complained to CBC News: "They do everything: they deliver, they do takeout, reservations, outdoor seating, buffet, private dinings, private parking, they have a full bar, wine and beer, waterfront, live music, jazz bar, it's a drive-through, they're on the beach, they have a playground."

But no place is perfect. Le Nouveau Duluth's biggest flaw was that it did not exist. The mythical Nouveau Duluth was in fact the creation of Quebec comedian Charles Deschamps.

When it comes to online reviews, Airbnb has the potential for double trouble since both hosts and guests are rated, with the outcome affecting the ability to either continue offering rentals or continue renting them. Complaints and confusion about the system have been rampant from both sides, and so have questions about the inherent motivation for both host and guest to protect each other's reputations regardless of the actual situation.

Nor has Airbnb escaped the pranksters. In early 2021 Londoners Archie Manners and Josh Pieters listed a lovely Airbnb property, a classic English home described as a luxurious eighteenth-century London town-house, that drew over three thousand US dollars in reservation requests. It was elegant, it was refined—it was a dollhouse. (One of the online photos included a full-sized water bottle beneath a miniature spiral staircase.)

Booking services must establish trust with consumers. When does the system break down?

Unfair and malicious one-star reviews can destroy businesses. Yet a systematic winnowing out of any negativity leads to experiences like mine, which make me less likely to trust future reviews. Or to put it in academic speak, from a Boston University and MIT study of Airbnb reviews, "An upwardly biased reputation system can cause buyers to unexpectedly transact with low-quality sellers, which in turn makes them less likely to transact on that platform again in the future."

Like I said.

Perhaps trust issues help explain one rather surprising post-pandemic development: a travel agent renaissance. You might call it a travel counter-reformation. Many agencies closed as COVID-19 raced through the travel industry like the Black Death. It was a macabre consequence of that fourteenth-century plague that after a third of the European population died, survivors reaped the rewards of a sudden labour shortage. So it seems to have been for surviving travel agencies. Not only have they benefited from pandemic attrition among other agencies, they have profited from labour shortages all through the industry. Staff cuts at airlines, hotels and booking services have led to greater public uncertainty about travel arrangements, inspiring some to hand things off to professionals.

One Vancouver agent (who prefers to remain anonymous) told me, "The chaos at the airports last summer and the problems with Sunwing and Flair [small Canadian airlines that ran into difficulty in 2023] have brought in people who just want someone else to take care of things."

These days his company also thrives on corporate work: "Mining companies moving workers to work sites, cruise ships transporting staff—jobs like that make up most of our business."

Oakville travel agent Shalene Dudley says a new variety of requests started coming in as soon as the pandemic hit. "I had a lot of Americans still travelling but they didn't know all the rules under COVID. I said, if you want me to do this for you, I need to charge a fee, because I now have to keep up to date on changes for your travel, I need to know if you need your second vaccine, if you have to fill out a passport document, and then if they all have insurance and so on."

When travel resumed in Canada, Dudley's services remained in demand. "I honestly have been shocked at how many people I thought would turn away because I had a fee, will pay it immediately. I'm so busy I had to hire more agents."

There are other questions that a well-heeled clientele might want to know. "How would you know whether Aruba has a casino where you can bring in ten thousand dollars?" she asks. "Or should you go to Costa Rica and find out that dogs are going to chase you? And I tell you that because it's happened. You're a lesbian couple—do not go to this resort, but there's another one up the street that I think would be good for you. You tell me your family needs to bring their support animals, and I tell you where you won't be able to go. There's a lot of things we as travel professionals know, and that's why people pay our fee."

I didn't do much investigating before my first trip to Japan. Kyoko was puzzled by my own seat-of-the-pants approach to travel. "I thought you would do more research," she told me.

Nope. It's a style difference to go along with the linguistic and cultural ones. There is a great deal for Kyoko and me to discover, and not many communication skills to help discover it. But people reveal themselves in many different ways. A person's home can tell you a lot. Kyoko's house holds treasures and mysteries both.

Kyoko's House

Who is Kyoko?

Figuring out one's romantic companion can be difficult under the best of circumstances, and ours were far from optimal. Couples in arranged marriages get more lead time than we had. Our ongoing efforts have had to overcome her rudimentary English and my almost complete lack of Japanese.

But Kyoko's house offered tantalizing glimpses of her life, and what they suggested was wondrous. For all the history it embodied, the wooden house was perhaps more remarkable for its contents. It was hard to escape the conclusion that Kyoko exuded some sort of mystical aura that drew eccentrics and artists toward her, bearing gifts—even though Kyoko often reacted to these offerings with indifference.

"What are these?" I asked, picking up two carved wooden figures from a table.

"Do you like?" she said, bemused. "They are from the island of Yakushima."

The dolls were of petrified cedar, carved by an island hermit named Gakunan. He had first arrived on Yakushima as an ordinary Japanese salaryman on holiday. Then, he explained, he heard the wood speaking to him. Abandoning his former life, Gakunan remained on Yakushima, digging up the cedar logs like a pig hunting truffles, carving them into small dolls and sculptures. One time the Japanese prime minister visited the island and asked to purchase some dolls. Gakunan refused. He sells only to those he deems worthy. Kyoko met him when her family visited the island years ago. Later the dolls arrived in the mail, addressed to her. She doesn't much care for them.

On Kyoko's shelves were antique plates, one of them a family heirloom three hundred years old. She also owned plates made by Shimizu Kosho. Kosho was the head priest of Tōdai-ji in the city of Nara, one of Japan's most famous temples and one of our scheduled destinations. He had lived well into his nineties. More than just a revered cleric, Kosho was a beloved artist and philosopher. A Kosho painted plate could easily sell for over ten thousand US dollars. One of them was holding detergent above Kyoko's washing machine. "I met him because my friend is a potter who fired his plates," Kyoko explained. "He gave me a set of his plates. I didn't think about it too much. My friends said, 'Are you crazy?' They are worth big money!"

And you use one of them to hold detergent?

"It's suitable," she replied.

The staircase is of a traditional style called *hako kaidan*, or box stairs, cleverly constructed from ascending blocks of cabinets and steep enough to give the sense one is climbing into the upper room on a ladder. Emerging on the second floor, one can imagine the geisha Michiyyako entertaining her guests here on a warm evening. In the front room is a low, polished wood table, sitting on dark floorboards and surrounded by cushions. The sliding screens that close off each room are decorated with colourful stylized fish painted by Chingyo, an artist friend of Kyoko's. He has contributed some framed nudes as well (Kyoko is unimpressed). At the front of the room are the small table and two cushioned rattan chairs, the sliding doors that open to create my charming balcony café.

Two colourful baby kimonos hang in the front room, handed down from Kyoko's grandmother. Just below them sit a couple of large, three-stringed lutes. These are shamisen. Every aspiring geisha must learn to play these ancient instruments. The strange, discordant twang of the shamisen and the haunting songs it accompanies are integral to any *geiko*'s party entertainment. (Young geisha apprentices are called *maiko* while the established members of the sorority, Kyoko informs me, are often referred to within the profession not as geisha but as *geiko*). These particular shamisen are not Kyoko's. They belong to Ms. Hanabishi Asamichi, who owns Kyoko's house.

Kyoko first met Ms. Asamichi when interviewing her for a story about historic Kanazawa. No one was renting the little house on Kazue-machi then—Ms. Asamichi was afraid to let anyone move in. After the interview, Kyoko began to pack even though the owner had not yet invited her. She knew, Kyoko told me, that this small place would be her home. The invitation came a few days later.

Kyoko slept on the top floor, a glorified attic that sported bare earthen walls when she first moved in. There was space for a net-shrouded bedroom just large enough for its mattress and, in the small adjoining room, a little sauna bed.

The stress of Tokyo was behind us now. Kyoko was home and thus relaxed, and in relatively slow-paced Kanazawa I felt myself decompressing as well. She treated me like a visiting dignitary. Kyoko was an excellent cook, serving up the kinds of meals I did not think existed outside Japanese restaurants. Even my standard Vancouver breakfast of peanut butter and banana sandwiches was reinvented here as something softer and sweeter. The jet lag was gone, and Kyoko and I seemed to be hitting our stride.

I didn't need to see the contents of her house to know Kyoko was a remarkable person. She was talented. In addition to her broadcast career, Kyoko, along with her mother, had started a business making handbags from old kimono fabric (Kyoko's dresser drawers contained thousands of dollars' worth of her mother's valuable old kimonos). Kyoko was a risk taker. In a country that for all its charms tends to be somewhat provincial and prone to groupthink, Kyoko strived to develop an international world view. Pursuing an education and perhaps a career beyond the confines of

Japan meant leaving behind the considerable advantages of her established Japanese position to prepare instead for a course of study where she would be at a distinct disadvantage, linguistically, culturally and even emotionally. She was courageous.

We still had issues though. One day Kyoko suggested we give each other some space. "Go and explore," she said with a laugh. "Don't come back till nighttime."

This is the way I was used to travelling—serendipitous wandering, ducking down narrow streets, seeking out little restaurants. Kanazawa is no Tokyo, but it's far more manageable for a pedestrian adventurer. Shrines and gardens, street vendors peddling *okonomiyaki* to the lunch crowd, the sprawling Omicho Market with rows of exotic seafood and new treasures like the fruit tomato, heart-shaped and sweet, ready to eat like a peach.

At the end of the day I got a little lost and headed for the river, following the stone wall until the houses looked familiar. It was about nine when I walked in. Kyoko was red-faced from crying. "I thought you were dead!" she wailed, throwing her arms around me.

"But you said don't come back till night."

"I was kidding!" she cried incredulously.

One evening I went for a walk on my own and headed straight for a nearby pay phone where I navigated the complicated routine of an international call. Back in Vancouver, Martin answered and heard me launch into a frenzied, frustrated tirade. "I'm going crazy," I said. "I can't get a moment to myself."

In the years to come, Martin would often remind me of that phone call.

Kyoko's landlady was something of an enigma. In addition to Kyoko's house, Ms. Asamichi owned her own *ochaya* across the river in Kanazawa's Higashi Chaya District. At her establishment the *geiko* of Kanazawa, diminished in number but still active, entertained their guests in the evening. A serene, elegant, almost severe figure in her late forties, Ms. Asamichi was a master of the shamisen who had spent years training *geiko* and *maiko* in her art.

Although not a *geiko*, she was constantly dressed in traditional garb—a blue kimono tied with the formal waistband called an obi. On her feet were *geta*—wooden platform sandals with two little slats underneath.

Just what *geta* were designed for is hard to figure, since slipping them on is like accepting two coupons for a free sprained ankle. But bad as they are for walking, their ancient inventor clearly did not foresee the rise of the automobile. Driving while *geta*-shod is considered so tricky it's illegal. Thus, when Ms. Asamichi was spotted driving in her formal Japanese attire by Kanazawa police, she was regularly pulled over. The Japanese cops could never seem to give Ms. Asamichi a ticket. She listened politely to their stammered cautions, responding with a lilting "*Sou-desu ka?*" (meaning, roughly, "You don't say?") Then she thanked them and drove on. Kyoko and I struggled for a few minutes to find the proper English word to describe Ms. Asamichi. We settled on *imperious*.

Nonetheless, her *ochaya* was a changed and somewhat humbled place by the time I visited. Twenty years earlier it had been the sole preserve of political and business leaders who gathered in the upstairs rooms for private parties with Kanazawa's leading *geiko*. But on the afternoon we visited, the dark, once-quiet rooms were crawling with Japanese tourists, parading up and down stairs, sipping green tea at low tables. Recession and the fading of the *geiko* tradition in modern Japan had led to new revenue strategies for Ms. Asamichi and her peers up and down Higashi Chaya. Bus tours did not pay as well as the elite. But this industry, like Japan itself, had come through hard times before.

For ordinary Japanese the *geiko* world is as remote and strange as it appears from Des Moines or Sudbury. On this day troops of them filed through Ms. Asamichi's *ochaya* with video cameras. The empty rooms with their dark wood and opaque screens gave little hint of what intoxications a night with *geiko* might hold. Keepers of this tradition are frequently at pains to point out that the lurid sexuality so often imagined to lie within these walls represents a fundamental misunderstanding of the *geiko*'s art. That's no doubt accurate, but a sharp-eyed tourist might find salacious evidence in one particular room.

There on an upstairs wall was a print depicting a relaxed social gathering. Closer inspection revealed that the guest of honour, reclining on central cushions, was a giant penis equipped with arms and legs (you've probably worked for a few). The young women who lounged around him all had vaginas where their faces should be. It was a definite conversation starter, unless your heart was set on talking baseball.

Kyoko's house had a secret, too. It was one she considered disgraceful.

Our final morning dawned on Kazue-machi. At the big low table on the second floor, Kyoko had laid out another of her insanely huge breakfasts. Cereal, fruit salad, rice, an omelet, peanut butter and banana sandwiches.

"What do you want on your last day in Kanazawa?" she asked.

"A parade," I said.

Within the hour my wish would be granted. While I dressed, Kyoko ran up from the ground floor in a state of agitation. "Please do not go downstairs," she pleaded before running down again.

I couldn't stay upstairs all day. As I came down the stairs the front door stood open. A long double line snaked from the wall, over Kyoko's couch, across the floor and out the front door to the walk, where the inching black segments suddenly took flight, a smattering of shiny wings disappearing on the breeze. Termites. "It's shameful," Kyoko sighed.

It took about an hour for the last of the little marching band to straggle across the floor and float off in the wind. The parade of doom was a little early this year—Kyoko had not been expecting the termite colony's annual migration for a couple of months yet. But she was used to it by now. Around the ground floor she showed me spongy beams, eaten away from within. This four-hundred-year-old national treasure was dying slowly. "Have you told Ms. Asamichi?" I asked.

"Of course," Kyoko said resignedly. "I will tell her again today. But I know what she will say."

Ridding the house of termites would cost money. Ms. Asamichi had a new boyfriend—they enjoyed travel and the finer things.

Over at the *ochaya*, Ms. Asamichi served us red bean sweets and *matcha* tea. As Kyoko recounted the morning's termite parade, Ms. Asamichi raised her eyebrows in a polite show of interest. "*Sou-desu ka?*" she said sweetly.

Year of the Cattle

On the northwest coast of Sicily, facing the Tyrrhenian Sea, is the city of Palermo. It has been here since the days of Homer. No one is exactly sure when the blind poet first told the tale of Odysseus and his crew battling gods and monsters along the coast of this Mediterranean island. But estimates have dated the *Odyssey* to the eighth century BCE, roughly the time Phoenicians founded the city of Ziz. Over the centuries it would pass through the control of Greeks (who renamed it Panormus), Carthaginians, Romans, Vandals, Ostrogoths, Byzantines, Arabs, Spanish, Austrians and Normans. Palermo has seen more turnover than a college dorm, and remnants of each civilization can probably be found hidden somewhere in its streets and laneways.

One summer day in 2016 I am sitting outside Bar Genovese, not far from Palermo's Capo Market. I'm at a plastic table with a few stacked chairs and an umbrella, hard against the wall across from the café. I felt drawn to this place, a hole in the wall where the coffee is served by an old woman who treats your cheery greeting as though you just insulted her dog. Repeat business does not seem to improve her mood any more than persistent ants improve a picnic. As for the street, in a more recently planned city Via Sant

Agostino would be called an alley. This part of Palermo brings to mind the medinas of Morocco, whose Islamic history it shares. Shimmering textiles hang nearby, and pushcarts full of melons or fish bump past. Perched on my plastic chair I watch them go by on their way to the Capo, one of several lively markets that dot the city.

With espresso of the darkest and most powerful kind coursing through my circulatory system, a magical light descends—the world appears at its most intoxicating. I am seized by one of those unexpected moments of euphoria. Al Stewart's 1976 hit "Year of the Cat" starts to play in my head.

It is perhaps the most epic ballad ever sung about a bus tour. Stewart sings of a man—it is implied that he's part of a tour bus group—who encounters a mysterious woman. She leads him away through the twisting paths of a teeming marketplace and through a secret door where, presumably, she ravishes him. In the end he languishes in exotic torpor, contemplating a future beyond this ancient world but powerless to break the bewitching spell of his captor.

When it was first released I thought the song was a bit cheesy. How many men who grew up hearing it later got propositioned by some professional siren on a foreign sidewalk and thought, *Wow, Al Stewart was right?*

Now in my espresso-fuelled vision, I feel differently. I have become that intrepid traveller—an outsider perhaps, but one at home in this or any world, no matter how strange and unfamiliar. A Bogart, a Charles Boyer, a suave *flâneur* navigating my way through a foreign landscape.

As if on cue a tour group turns onto my little street, led by a woman holding a paddle aloft. There are a couple of cruise ships in port and this bunch must be fresh off the boat. It's hard to believe an alluring temptress would want to grab any of them. None seem like potential love slave material.

As the guide and her obedient followers shuffle by, my little reverie evaporates. I am no longer a romantic figure, worthy of comparison to Peter Lorre, as Stewart put it. The tour group might just as well have turned toward me to begin chanting, "One of us! One of us!"

Their presence is yet another indictment. I am not who I pretend, they say. I am what I behold, what I was in Siena, in Rome, in Kyoto—a tourist.

Attempts to distinguish myself by my style of travel, my dedication to solo wandering and the pleasures of serendipity rather than the spoon-fed coddling of the package tour, don't really change that.

How do I differ from the cruise ship gang? I did not reach Palermo across the Strait of Messina in a small, storm-tossed boat, followed by a perilous trek through Sicilian bandit country. I flew. Ultimately I am just another twenty-first-century beneficiary of cheap air travel, lodging not in a smoky attic with a languorous local but in a well-kept B & B highly recommended on Tripadvisor, my return ticket paid for. And then one day at a plastic table, I encounter my nemesis—the Pied Piper with her paddle. For me the paddle is a mirror: *Look, fool. See who you truly are. Join us.*

Seventy years earlier I might have indeed made for a rare and unaccountable sight, an inscrutable foreigner sipping espresso in a Palermo alley. But then, seventy years earlier only two people had ever climbed Mount Everest.

Certainly the Palermo residents who pass me by on the way to peddle fruit or do laundry are unlikely to think of themselves as pursuing a romantic adventure, any more than I do in my day-to-day Vancouver existence.

Romance is a matter of perspective. While at my Palermo B & B I met a mother and daughter from Belarus. "Canada?" they said. "Wow! Exotic!" Well, why not? Canada has bears and mountains and waterfalls and such. You could think we are exotic, as long as you never meet any actual Canadians.

While in Bhutan I took many pictures of monks in their scarlet and saffron robes. A young staffer at my hotel was puzzled. "Why take pictures of them?" she asked. "They are everywhere."

Travel ads may sell us fantasies but we also sell them to ourselves. There is almost always something constructed about the travel experience, something manufactured. The sense of being on an adventure demands an element of self-consciousness. Look at me—I am Leo DiCaprio on the secluded beach. I am Gregory Peck in Rome. I am Robert Mitchum in Acapulco. I am Tintin, bold explorer. And over the years I have sold myself the fantasy of belonging, assuming the role of man of the world. A unilingual man of the world.

Karen Stein, author of *Getting Away from It All: Vacations and Identity*, feels the pain I felt in Palermo. "There's that perception of being a traveller, having a real, authentic experience, versus being a tourist who is having this more superficial experience," she says. "Both groups have their pretensions and their presumptions. Is either of them more valid?

"I too was someone who wanted to identify as a traveller, not a tourist. Seeing those other people who remind you of home yanks you out of that. It's like an aspect of yourself that you're trying to leave behind. But it follows you in a way that you can't control.

"What is an authentic experience, and is it possible to have one? You've always got one foot in your everyday life and one foot in where you want to be."

If we lie to ourselves a little, is it so bad? So much bullshit is winked at every day as essentially harmless—astrology, juice cleanses, people saying "Everything happens for a reason." But is this gateway bullshit that can potentially lead to worse? The tendency to believe whatever one pleases has led to some hellish outcomes. How many pandemic deaths were caused by lies about vaccine plots and horse dewormer? A willingness to acknowledge reality, unpleasant or not, ought to be an essential tool for life. "Seeking what is true," said French philosopher Albert Camus, "is not seeking what is desirable."

Does that leave no place for romance? If you make it your priority to look at the world with objective clarity, what do you lose? Even Camus confessed, "It is almost impossible to be logical to the bitter end."

I stubbornly hang on to at least some illusions. I couldn't cheer for the Vancouver Canucks otherwise. And some of what I call illusion is simply a sincere attempt to bring meaning to my personal experiences—to some of my most cherished rituals, performed in my favourite places like Rome and Tokyo and Bangkok. Perhaps I don't really belong. But I can still form a relationship with faraway destinations that is mine alone.

I once interviewed Al Stewart. In the mid-80s he visited the Edmonton radio station where I was working as a disc jockey, an amiable Englishman who would have looked at home in a Cambridge library. Some time after my "Year of the Cat" moment in Palermo I dug up the interview and listened again. I realized I was not the only one who had been temporarily derailed by his beguiling 1976 ballad. Stewart too had found himself temporarily wearing a new and unfamiliar identity.

"I was a pop star for about six weeks when 'Year of the Cat' was in the top ten," he told me then. "It gave me an insight into a lifestyle which I had previously seen only in *People* magazine. It was the only time in my life I was invited to Hollywood parties."

At one of those he happened to be standing near *Charlie's Angels* star Cheryl Ladd. A photographer came over and stuck the two together. "She didn't look at me," Stewart recalled, "and as soon as the camera flashed she immediately turned back around and continued her conversation. She never actually saw my face, heard my name or knew who I was. I realized that this was going on all over the room."

Even the hit record itself was not really in line with Stewart's previous self-image. "I never had anything against 'Year of the Cat,'" he told me. "I thought it was rather a good song."

But Stewart was not really focused on crafting irresistible radio candy. His first love was writing interesting lyrics. "By far my favourites are the ones that have intricate phraseology," he said.

"Year of the Cat," however, burst out of mid-70s radio speakers largely on the strength of a memorable saxophone part played by Phil Kenzie. That idea came not from Stewart but from his superstar producer, Alan Parsons. "It wasn't the way I saw my music." Stewart shrugged. "My intention was to let Alan put the sax solo in and realize it was a bad idea."

It wasn't. But it wasn't Stewart's vision either. And for a while the record's success put him into new and unfamiliar pop star territory. "I was stunned by 'Year of the Cat,'" he said. "It was so ridiculous."

We borrow the veil of glamour from cinema, novel, legend and song. Had I miscast myself as a romantic figure, humming "Year of the Cat" in a crowded Sicilian alley? Perhaps. But I was not alone. Stewart too had found himself in a charade, ill-suited to the new identity success had shaped for him. Mystique and illusion, stacked up like so many plastic chairs in a Palermo laneway.

Moral Hazard

In 2009 I travel to Kathmandu. At one end of the sprawling temple complex known as Durbar Square, there's an open plaza where merchants spread their handicrafts on the ground. At the end of the row is a final blanket, belonging to the Khambu family. Kwina Khambu is there helping her father Prakash hawk curios to tourists. I am hell-bent on reaching the temples beyond, but she snares me. Her open smile and sincere enthusiasm will not be denied. The temples will have to wait. Soon I am sitting on a little three-legged stool, listening. Kwina attends Jubilant Higher Secondary School in Kathmandu. She comes here to help the family business but, she tells me, she'd rather be in school all the time. "Education is the most important thing to me," Kwina says. She's a great salesperson, and her best pitch is for her own future.

"I have big aims," Kwina tells me, perched beside me in the sunny square. "I will become a doctor. Then I will go back to the mountains and help people for free."

"Many girls do not get an education," she says. "They have babies when they are still young. But I will get an education. I want to go away to school.

I want to go to university in a foreign country. Then I will come home and help people."

She looks at me with a smile that most North American kids would save for a new Xbox. "You are my first foreign friend," she says. "Thank you for talking to me. It is a happy day for me to meet you."

There are plenty of items for sale on the family blanket but Kwina does not seem particularly intent on selling any of them, at least not directly. Nonetheless my eye falls on one offering—a wooden disc with a red metal plate on top, criss-crossed with a grid of lines. In each of the four corners of the grid stands a little brass tiger.

"This is a traditional Nepalese game, Tigers and Goats," Kwina tells me. She brings out a handful of little brass goats and places a few at intersecting points on the grid, explaining what turns out to be a sort of ruthless variation on Chinese checkers. One player gets the goats, which are placed on grid points one at a time. The tigers move in for the kill step by step—jump a goat and you've eaten it. It seems rather one-sided. But with clever placement the goats can trap the tigers, who require an open space to make a jump. Crowd all four tigers into immobility and the goats become the improbable victors. "But it's easier to be a tiger," Kwina agrees.

I buy one. Kwina is determined that this will not be the end of our friendship. "Please come back and visit me again," she pleads. "You can come to our home for dinner."

I return to Durbar Square late on a Sunday afternoon. Prakash spots me from halfway across the square, as if he has been waiting for me since my first visit. "Kwina is not here—she is at home," her father tells me. "She will be very happy to see you."

"She has big aims," Prakash says. "But they are expensive."

When Kwina started attending her English language school, times were better for the Khambu family. Tuition is expensive: "Forty thousand rupees a year," he says (about $633 Canadian). Plus there are three other daughters and a four-year-old son to consider. "She wants to go to university in a foreign country," Prakash says. "But this is for rich people."

Kwina dreams of being a tiger. It's an admirable goal. But getting a shot at earning those stripes is tough when your family tree has generally produced goats.

We set out for the Khambu home but, before we get halfway through Durbar Square, Kwina intercepts us. She is overjoyed. She leads me to a long, narrow laneway made of equal parts bricks and dirt, sloping down to create a little urban valley between closely packed apartment blocks that rise up again on the far side. Near the bottom we turn off into a still-narrower alley populated by a few children and stray dogs. Inside a ramshackle apartment building we step through a hanging blanket into a single room. Kwina calls to her mother in a kitchen somewhere down the hall—there's a visitor for dinner.

The room is painted green and smells vaguely damp. There's a couch, a cabinet full of pictures and books, and a large daybed piled high with blankets. Kwina's brother and a neighbour's boy play on the couch. Kwina introduces her sister Binita. Somewhere in the pile of blankets is Binita's two-month-old son. "When things got harder for our family," Kwina explains quietly, "she decided that she should help out by going away so that my dad would not have to look after her. She had a boyfriend and then she had a baby. But he is not around now—he was no good. My dad took her back in with the baby. Now the neighbours say this and say that. Nepal is not like Canada. She cannot go out and find another man. Everyone talks."

Kwina fetches a brochure from the bookcase and sits down beside me. The brochure describes a media studies course she is eager to take. But it's expensive, and, as it is, the schoolmaster is nagging Kwina's dad for payment of back fees.

I'm uncomfortable. I wish it wasn't so, but I can't deny it—I am squirming. Kwina is clearly hell-bent on achieving her goals and it's a wonderful thing to see. But tigers need goats. I begin to wonder if I'm being fitted for a pair of horns.

There can be no doubt about Kwina's sincere desire for education. But the suddenness of her affection has made me nervous. "The day I met you is my lucky day," she says. "You are my first friend from a foreign country. You are in my heart forever."

Am I really that charming?

A recent edition of the *International Herald Tribune* had contained an interesting letter from Lawrence Bohme of Saint-Jean-de-Luz, France. He described a visit to an Ethiopian town where children have developed an interesting routine for tourists: "Boys accost them, not asking for money, but for one of several schoolbooks displayed in a nearby shop window. Could the kind visitor buy this geography or history textbook for the child's schoolwork, since his own parents are unable to? Quite a few tourists ... buy the book and place it in the child's hands. Later, of course, the boy returns the unopened book to the conniving store-keeper who splits the profit with him."

It will soon be dark. In Kathmandu, that means something. To say the city suffers power outages would be misleading—better to say that sometimes the power comes back on. Dinner is not yet ready, but I make my apologies. I should start back while some light remains.

Kwina and her dad escort me back down the narrow, rutted lane and on toward Durbar Square. "You have a Nepalese family now," Kwina assures me. At the door of the apartment I had given her a thousand-rupee note (about fifteen Canadian dollars), agonizing over the amount like a yokel in a fancy restaurant trying to figure the appropriate tip. I watched Kwina's face for signs of disappointment—fifteen bucks won't pay for much tuition—but perceived none. Leading back to the square, she seems as warm and enthusiastic as ever. "Send me emails, don't forget," she says. "I hope I will see you again."

I slip into the evening crowd, walking past open fires, heading back toward the Thamel district. There is a knot in my gut. What was that all about? Was Kwina simply a seeker of friendship and the broadened horizons it can bring? Or was she playing me? And does it matter? I may not be well off by Canadian standards but I definitely have more money than the Khambu family. It feels good to help.

There is a thriving industry devoted to altruistic travel. It's more commonly known as voluntourism. Voluntourism feels good. *Getting Away from*

It All author Karen Stein did some of the research for her book in Xi'an, China, where she was attached to a group of travellers who had paid for a tour that included volunteer work. "You can pay these organizations to have a volunteer experience," she says. "They came with the idea of helping, engaging with the community on a deeper level than a tourist would."

But even though the tour company was still looking after their needs as they would with any gaggle of tourists, Stein says her group still carried a sense of moral superiority. "Whenever we would see other people from the West, our group wanted nothing to do with them," she says. "Something about those other people's presence was almost polluting."

⸻

Following my return to Vancouver, Kwina sends emails. She talks of school and says she misses me. One early letter mentions financial trouble—a bit of foreshadowing, I am sure. Finally the other shoe drops.

"[M]y dear steve namaste!!!!!!!!!!!!!" the email begins. Kwina goes on to say that financial problems might mean the end of her high school education, and asks for my help. "[M]y family send you big namaste and they bow down their head for you in respect."

I wrote a magazine article about meeting Kwina. I was paid for it. I don't feel I can afford to support her on an ongoing basis. But it seems fair to share the proceeds. I send her a cheque.

More emails follow, sometimes with more requests. I send money by Western Union a couple of times. Then I stop. The emails continue, some telling me of Prakash's failing health. "My family they send you big namaste and they bow down their head for you in respect," Kwina writes again.

Minutes before noon on April 25, 2015, a massive earthquake strikes Nepal, with an estimated magnitude of 7.8 to 8.1. It is followed by a major aftershock May 12. Buildings collapse, hillsides give way. Almost nine thousand are killed and twenty-two thousand injured. The casualties range from Mount Everest to Durbar Square, where historic temples lie in ruins. I receive a desperate email from Kwina. "Many people died in front of us, many people are injury many houses are break this is a very bad condition for Nepal, we are very sad that everything is destroy we have nothing more left you seen in the news that durbar square everything is broken where we live the house is also crack, we don't have anything more left me and my family we alive thank god, we are right now in a village and i come to mail you by walking two hour from my village to find the network and computer to mail you."

I have seen images from Durbar Square on the news. It has been hit hard. I send money via Western Union.

On May 18, Kwina writes: "Thanks a lot for your help." The money I sent, she tells me, helped other families as well as her own.

I send another money transfer. Kwina replies, "[I] travelled with a doctors to rural area to help the injury people, and it is a very good experience for me to achieve my goal, to become doctor is my very big dream … by your kind of help we are getting food and water and shelter otherwise we even don't get it, you are so great to us, you are a god to us."

The impulse to help is laudable. But when on unfamiliar ground, how can a random visitor truly know the score?

Over the years the United Nations has sounded multiple warnings about the children of Cambodia. In a 2021 report, UNICEF and a coalition of other organizations reported that 7.2 million Cambodian children are "deprived of liberty every year." Some of those children are in orphanages.

Tourists are often moved by the plight of Cambodian orphans. In her 2016 book *Overbooked*, Elizabeth Becker described scenes where children from local orphanages in Siem Reap were paraded through tourist zones banging drums, blowing horns and encouraging tourists to visit their orphanage. Those who did got to interact with the children and then leave donations. When Becker visited one such orphanage she found living conditions dire, the promised school facilities non-existent, no supervision, and absolutely no process in place for adoptions.

It's not just that the orphanages aren't good places to be. Many of the children in them are not orphans. "In Cambodia, the number of orphanages has increased by more than 75% since 2005," writes Tara Winkler of the

Cambodian Children's Trust. "Over 80% of the children in these orphanages are not orphans, they are children from poor families. The orphanage boom in Cambodia has been caused by foreign funding, generated by voluntourism. 100% of the orphanages in Cambodia are foreign-funded and almost all are in tourist hotspots."

When I ask Winkler about phony orphanages, she corrects me. "*Phony orphanage* is not the best term to use," she says, "as it suggests there is such a thing as a *legitimate* orphanage. All orphanages are harmful, no matter how well they are run and no matter whether they are full of children with or without parents. Even orphans should be raised by families in their community of origin."

In economics, the concept of "moral hazard" refers to a situation where a financial institution lacks the incentive to avoid risky behaviour because they know their losses will be reimbursed regardless of how recklessly they behave. Perhaps the travel industry version of moral hazard can arise when charitable impulses are successfully harnessed for profit, thus providing an incentive to create even more artificially generated hardship. If sob stories sell, why not manufacture more of them?

In 2012 I visit Luang Prabang, Laos, and meet a woman named Sheila who runs a shop. The topic of voluntourism comes up. "Don't get me started," Sheila warns. Then she starts.

"The government organizations; the UN organizations; the NGOs— they come to Laos, piss millions of dollars against a wall. They bring their families, they have their four-wheel-drive vehicles, and they drive around visiting Vietnam and Cambodia and Thailand and have a wonderful time. Then they go home. And they're useless. Countries are starting to tell them to stay away. These organizations are now paying countries to let them in so they can do their great work. Now they're all leaving Laos for Myanmar— that's their next big project.

"NGOs send kids over here, lots of good intentions, but without any of the skills or talents that might be of some use. My friend Jane calls them 'blancmanges.' They're just bland, ordinary kids with none of the abilities they require to make a difference—especially in a country like this one that has essentially jumped from the sixteenth century to the twenty-first. And the kids don't last—they're gone in a hurry."

"If you aren't qualified to do the work in your home country," Winkler says, "you really shouldn't be attempting to do it in a developing country either."

Shelley is an Australian expat in her fifties who has been living in Luang Prabang for fifteen years. Upon learning that she is conversing with a Canadian writer, she asks not to be identified. "I have to live here," she says. And she has plenty to say about some of her imported neighbours. "All of these businesses started up by expats that promise to 'give back' to the community," she scoffs. "Please. Almost nobody gives back. There are perhaps a couple of good organizations here and the rest are lining their pockets. Like those 'Western guilt' tours, where people pay money to come and paint an orphanage. Does the orphanage get the money? No. The tour company pockets the money. And I talk to the orphanage workers—they say, 'How many new coats of paint do we need?' They ask for money to feed the kids instead. But no. They get more fresh paint. And the tour company gets paid."

"I don't believe that voluntourism does any good," says Tara Winkler. "It is an illusion that white people from the global north are suited to lead the development of the global south. As foreigners, they lack an adequate grasp of local culture and overlook the unique strengths that exist within local communities. All forms of voluntourism stem from the white saviour narrative, which infers an inherent lack of capacity in populations in the global south and is therefore disempowering.

"When you make mistakes in humanitarian work, you're making mistakes with people's lives. All people who participate in the helping sectors should uphold the Hippocratic oath to do no harm."

The way to help, Winkler says, is to give. "Populations in the global south have all the capabilities required to solve their own problems, they just lack the resources to action their own solutions. The donations we give to the global south should not be framed as an act of generosity but as an act of justice to compensate for the capitalist systems that continue to siphon wealth from the south to the north."

I have sent money to Kwina's family. And I know the earthquake devastation in Kathmandu is real. Still, as emails from Kwina continue, I am once again forced to ask myself the depths of my commitment. I stop sending money.

Then in December 2016, another message arrives, this one with a photo attachment. This email arrives from Kwina's email account but apparently comes not from Kwina but from her father, Prakash. He has terrible news to impart. Kwina has been struck by a car and is in the hospital. The attached photo apparently shows Kwina—her face is not visible—in a hospital bed with many tubes attached.

"Her condition is very bad i cannot afford for her operation," the email says. "She can die anytime if she cannot have this operation i am very very worried for my daughter … please mail me after you read this … you are always in my heart i am thinking about you. my family send you a very big namaste and happy new year of 2017. thank you. prakash."

Could it be? The email read suspiciously like every other email I had received from the same account. And until now I had never had any indication that Prakash could write in English. But a fake car accident? Really?

Maybe the "you are a god to us" thing was a bit much, but still—I did think we were friends, sort of. It is hard to accept that the situation has descended to this. I ask a few friends for their opinion. Could the story be true? Their verdict is unanimous: highly unlikely.

I do not reply to the email.

Whatever I conclude about the email and photo, Winkler suggests I shouldn't judge. "People who are struggling to meet their basic needs for survival are often faced with impossible decisions," she says. "Perhaps you could've told her that she didn't need to lie because you would've been happy to help her meet her basic needs or find an organization that could. Generally, people will only give when faced with stories of people in crisis. Distressing images of children and families in desperate situations pull on the heartstrings and donations flow in."

A great deal of restoration work has been done in Nepal since the terrible earthquake. But there have been delays and setbacks as well. Some of the issues had to do with the issue of outside assistance. UNESCO (the United Nations Educational, Scientific and Cultural Organization), which is dedicated to identifying and preserving the world's cultural heritage, became involved in the effort to rebuild damaged sites in Kathmandu's Durbar Square. But they later made the decision to withdraw. "On 10 December 2018, restoration work commenced on-site," UNESCO wrote in a press release. "However, on 23 December, the work was placed on hold, due to pressure citing the wish of some locals for the temples to be restored through local funds alone and without international assistance ... threats were made by some locals a few days later to the restoration workers on-site. UNESCO therefore decided that the project had to be closed."

The politics of rebuilding seem to have been complex—reports from Chinese news agencies have boasted of that nation's participation in the restoration of Kathmandu holy sites, with no mention of local objections. But there certainly appears to have been some local resistance to international help.

On a personal level the disaster served as a reminder to me of the connections travel can establish. Ideally it should not be necessary to have stood in a place in order to have an emotional response to its destruction and the resultant suffering. But it makes a difference. A place and its people become real to you, and their pain has an immediacy that only seems to come via first-hand experience.

In December 2019 I receive another email. This time it is not from Kwina's father but from Kwina herself. A university friend had found the 2009 magazine article I had written about her online. "I really don't like that neither does my family so please it's a humble request for you to delete all of those things you have write about me and my family and everything," she writes.

Lacking outside help, Kwina seems to have recovered. I am glad to hear she is in school. I hope someday her lofty ambitions will be realized.

Disneyland of Death

Near the village of Randan Batu in the Indonesian territory known as Tana Toraja, there is a line of water buffalo standing beside a large pavilion. One man holds the reins of the lead buffalo, while another man lashes the animal's legs to a post. There are perhaps a thousand or more people watching, milling about or relaxing in the shade close by. They have come to attend a funeral. In a few seconds the buffalo will discover this is its funeral, too.

Word of mouth brought me to this landlocked region in the centre of Sulawesi—that, several flights, and a winding nine-hour bus ride from the southern city of Makassar. Although I usually dislike being guided, it's a different situation here. Hiring a guide is pretty much essential if one is to move around the largely rural area, and I have found a great one. Marcus has a small moustache, a wide, friendly face and a motorcycle. He hands me a baseball batting helmet to ensure my personal safety and away we go down the dirt back roads to visit villages and gravesites.

It's certainly not my first time travelling with a guide—Kyoko was as well-connected a guide as any explorer could wish for. One might wonder then why I was so comfortable being guided by Marcus while my earlier trip with Kyoko eventually had me breaking out in a stress rash.

It reminds me of an anecdote I once heard about a friend's father. He was in the habit of buying his paper every day from the same newsstand. Eventually the young man behind the counter began greeting him with "Good morning, Mr. Jones." Mr. Jones then took his business elsewhere— the young man was getting too personal.

Mr. Jones represents a school of thought that one's personal relationships should be walled off from any other spheres of human activity. Of course, my budding relationship with Kyoko was more important than the mere sightseeing aspect of that Japanese journey. But it did add a layer of emotional complexity mercifully absent when bouncing through the Torajan countryside on the back of Marcus's motorbike. The latter relationship was more clear-cut.

Marcus is also an excellent guide, and today he has scored—it's a major funeral. A funeral visit is a coup for any guide in Tana Toraja. February is the rainy season, when funerals are relatively rare. But today the verdant countryside is sunlit and the event is well underway. When it comes to tourism, Tana Toraja is a dead zone—if you're lucky.

Tana Toraja is a world within a world within a world. Located in the middle of this splatter-shaped Indonesian island, it is distinct from the regions that surround it, just as Sulawesi (once known as Celebes) differs from its island neighbours, like the more famous Bali, and they in turn from the rest of far-flung Indonesia. It is certainly unlike any other tourist destination I can think of. Tana Toraja is a Disneyland of death.

Death and its accompanying rituals are the meat of every regional tourist brochure. Where else would you find the sign I saw south of the main city, Rantepao: *Grave of babies in a big tree*, with a helpful arrow pointing the way. Aside from the funerals, tourists flock to the strange gravesites found along little country villages—rotting old coffins that sit on cliffside platforms, spilling their ancient skeletal cargo onto the ground; grottoes filled with bone boxes and dotted with skulls, coffins stacked up like old files, with the occasional fresh one draped in cloth.

Funerals are the biggest blowouts Torajan people throw. For some of the locals it's the only time they really eat well. "Some people never get to eat meat unless there is a funeral," Marcus explains to me.

Visitors are welcome too—the bigger the crowd, the better the party, and the more prestige for the dearly departed. And while it's not exactly a lark, a Torajan funeral presents a spectacle unlike any other.

This event began yesterday with the first animal sacrifice and the carrying of the coffin through a circuit of nearby villages. The deceased, a nonagenarian woman named Ne' Komo', has been dead for about a year and a half. That's a fairly standard time frame here. Torajan funerals are so elaborate that families often have to save for years. In addition, many native Torajans have left the region for larger centres like Jakarta. It is unacceptable that any of the deceased's offspring should be absent. Thus, the children and other close relatives must save up money to return, not to mention coordinate vacation time, before a proper funeral can be held. It takes time.

That complicated reality underlies one of the most distinctive of all Torajan traditions—the *tomakula*. *Tomakula* translates as "sick person" in a Torajan dialect, but theirs is an illness that will admit no cure. A *tomakula* is in fact a corpse, embalmed and often kept in a closed coffin in the family home, but still treated like an ailing relative. Tea is brought to the coffin side, changes of clothes laid out, one-sided conversations held as plans for the send-off are arranged. Until the funeral is held, the death is not officially recognized. And with all the difficulties associated with organizing and paying for a three-day extravaganza, a *tomakula* can hang around the house for years before pushing on to glory.

Eighteen months after her heart stopped, Ne' Komo' finally gets to be dead. Her ceremony is underway at last. A whole miniature settlement has arisen in an open field, with long, sturdy bamboo guest halls constructed solely for the event. Rice barns (far more beautiful and impressive than their name and usage suggest) have also been converted into seating areas for the elite—the village leaders and the local nobility, who comprise about 10 percent of the population. A structure called a *balkon* holds the coffin. It looks like a smaller version of the local houses called *tongkonan*, featuring swooping boat-shaped roofs and a signature four-colour design.

A group of white-and-black-clad dancers form a circle in front of the *balkon*, chanting to welcome new guests. They part for a procession of gorgeously dressed family members, carrying libations into the pavilion. Leading the procession is a small man with a large cane, wearing sunglasses, a head wrap and a large sash. He lets out little whoops and yelps as he walks.

Just beyond this show stands another man in shabby street clothes. He is holding a wad of cash and solemnly turns in circles, presenting the money to the points of the compass, then leaping up and tossing the bills into the air. I lean over to Marcus. "What is that man's role in this?" I ask.

"That guy?" says Marcus. "He's just crazy."

Well, why not? Everyone's welcome at a Torajan funeral. Most are invited, but almost everybody comes. Villages have been informed of the event for miles around.

There's even a face I recognize. A standard-issue Sunday school portrait of Jesus graces a pavilion wall. A priest is here too, wearing a ceremonial gown and carrying a wooden cross. If you didn't know better you'd assume this guy took a very wrong turn on the way to work. But he's not lost. These are Christian people. Whether the Pope sanctions buffalo sacrifice or not, this is a Christian event.

The story of Tana Toraja's progression from agrarian animist society to Christian tourist hot spot is a fascinating and relatively recent tale. Working alongside the Dutch East Indies Company, Dutch missionaries both Catholic and Protestant were at work in more accessible lowland areas of Sulawesi as far back as the seventeenth century. But they did not make a serious push into isolated Tana Toraja country until the 1920s, led by Dutch Reformed Church missionary A.C. Kruyt. Initially there was plenty of pushback. Torajans had traditions of their own and had no truck with the imported Christian stuff. That this eventually changed was not necessarily because Torajans saw the light like Hank Williams. What they saw down the road was trouble. The Tana Toraja region was being attacked by nearby Muslim populations, and converting to Christianity meant gaining the protection of the Dutch colonial government. Many did so.

But it's complicated. For the Torajans, rebranding their long-established rituals as Christianity was rather like changing the name on the sign from Kentucky Fried Chicken to KFC—it was still the same old story for the chickens. The ancient belief that entrance to Puya, the promised land, was achieved via animal sacrifice remains the basis of the Torajan belief system. Only now it is overseen by pictures of Jesus. In fact, the Indonesian government officially classifies Torajans as Hindus due to their animistic practices. These days, though, all the old rituals, known as Aluk To Dolo (the way of the ancestors), are done under the sign of the cross.

The entire island of Sulawesi offers a remarkable mix of ancient custom and imported religion. In the most southerly region of the island, the Bugis people are Muslim but hold beliefs unlikely to be found in any other Muslim society—for example, the concept of five genders. Centuries before US Republicans began howling about the issue on Fox News, the Bugis people recognized that two genders don't encompass all of human gender expression. The Bugis categories of *makkunrai* and *oroani* correspond to what the West considers traditional male and female genders; *calalai* are born with female anatomy but take on traditionally male gender roles; *calabai* are born with male anatomy but take on female gender roles; and *bissu* are androgynous, considered to be a sacred unity of male and female. For many years this traditional Bugis system of belief has been attacked and eroded by Muslim clerics, and today it is considered endangered. But for now it survives.

Another group arrives at the Tana Toraja funeral. They're Germans, here on a cruise ship tour. The emcee has impressively slipped into German, like Joel Grey in *Cabaret*. "*Meine Damen und Herren, willkommen,*" he says.

The German cruisers have only about forty-five minutes scheduled for the funeral viewing, and they want action. Tomorrow is the day when most of the buffalo are scheduled to be sacrificed for the departed Ne' Komo'. But exceptions can be made. Today one animal will be sacrificed for tourism.

When the buffalo's legs are securely lashed to prevent dangerous and messy death throes, the blade man steps up quickly. His action is so swift that I see only the convulsive reaction. The buffalo bounds up and back, rears and twists, and drops to the red dirt to expose a gaping, pulsing gash across its throat. It lies still, and the end has seemed mercifully swift. A false hope—the beast is soon thrashing again. Another buffalo moves forward as if to investigate, but merely dips down to drink its comrade's blood. Some onlookers turn away, but not the cameras.

Minutes later the German tour group is filing out. Back to the bus, back to the boat, possibly off to film the strange rituals of Sydney, Australia.

Switching to English, the emcee intones, "We hope you enjoyed your visit and that you will return and tell your friends to visit Tana Toraja—that they will be completely safe here."

And there is the key point. The Indonesian government had been coordinating with cruise ship tours in an effort to battle some alarming recent developments. At the time of my visit, there had been more violent clashes in the nearby district of Poso. "Do not travel" advisories for Central Sulawesi had been issued by the Australian government. Tana Toraja, while centrally located, actually falls within the neighbouring province of South Sulawesi, and is keen to advise the world that it has been absolutely trouble-free. "In Tana Toraja, it's mostly Christians," Marcus explains. "In the Poso area, it's half-Christian, half-Muslim. So they must fight for control."

Tourism is crucial to the economy of Tana Toraja. But as recently as fifty years ago it was virtually unknown. In 1972 a funeral for a Torajan noble was documented by *National Geographic* magazine, opening a window onto the area's unique rituals and traditions. By the 1980s the Indonesian government was launching aggressive promotion of the region as the next big Indonesian destination after Bali. While Tana Toraja never equalled Bali's status as a standard backpacker destination, it did attract enough visitors to shift the once-agrarian economy toward tourism. In the early twenty-first century political instability and violence seriously affected tourist numbers. Now, in February 2006, Marcus tells me I am his first client in many months.

How has tourism affected the Torajan culture? It's been a mixed bag. One downside is exemplified in the history of *tau-tau*.

For centuries Torajans have been buried in cave tombs that dot cliff walls. *Tau-tau* are lifelike wooden effigies that sit in rows in front of the tombs, usually crafted to look like the departed. Somewhat like Egyptian mummies, it is these *tau-tau* that will serve as the bodies of loved ones in the afterlife. Not everyone gets a *tau-tau*, however—only the nobility. And even then it's only the families wealthy enough to sacrifice at least twenty-five buffalo. No twenty-five, no *tau-tau*.

Of course, you could just steal one. Starting in the 1980s *tau-tau* began disappearing rapidly from their cliff and grotto perches. In response to the chronic thefts the design of *tau-tau* began to evolve, or rather devolve. They became less detailed, more generic, since more skilful examples simply became more attractive targets for thieves.

Coffins too went missing. Marcus tells of guiding a French client to a grotto sepulchre where the ancient peaked coffins sat. "He told me, 'I have one of those at home, Marcus. I bought it from a dealer in Bali.'"

Even centuries ago tomb robbers found Torajan gravesites easy pickings, forcing a change in style. Locals gradually shifted to the more modern custom of building grave houses, like family tombs. Ne' Komo' will lie in one of these. In some caves though, fresh coffins can still be found. Every Torajan village has its ways.

Tourism has arguably had some more positive effects on the region. Aside from the economic benefits, the attention given to Torajan death rituals has helped create a sense of regional identity and pride. Like many other groups—Yankees, Canucks, Christians—Torajans were first named by outsiders before claiming the name as their own. Toraja means "people of the uplands." The inhabitants themselves, though, were more likely to identify with their home villages. A sense of group identity was fostered by the boundaries drawn by the Dutch colonial government, who were the first to identify Tana Toraja as a distinct region. But tourism helped by holding up a mirror to the distinctive traditions that Torajans had practised unselfconsciously for centuries. Visitors made them more aware of the unique nature of their rituals.

And the visitors themselves? They have to make peace with the fact that they are treating the lifestyle and sacred rituals of a faraway land like a Broadway show. Global tourism offers many such opportunities.

Years ago my friend Martin booked a room at a luxury hotel located about half an hour from Chiang Mai in Thailand. From his balcony he looked out over what appeared to be a rice paddy, with thatched huts where people came and went. After inquiring, Martin discovered this was in fact an artificial village populated by people hired from a real local village, so as to create a pleasing pastoral scene that hotel guests could enjoy with their morning croissants and coffee.

On one trip of my own to Northern Thailand, undertaken with a guide provided to me by the Thai tourism board, I left the town of Mae Hong Son along the Thai–Myanmar border and was taken by long-tail boat to a traditional Kayan village. The Kayan are a subgroup of the Karen people, famous for the brass coils women wear around their necks. I wandered about, taking photos. The locals went about their business—one woman worked a loom—and posed for pictures. They knew the drill. The experience left me feeling distinctly uncomfortable. I reminded myself though that the Kayan have agency. Tourism has helped to make them self-sufficient.

Are tourists like me guilty of contributing to the commodification and debasement of traditional practices? I confess I do not feel much discomfort about observing the sights and rituals of Tana Toraja. Perhaps it is because the region is not set up like some sort of human petting zoo—Marcus takes me far and wide on the back of his trusty motorbike, visiting towns and fields and tombs, lunching at a Rantepao restaurant where everyone is served from communal bowls. Perhaps it is because these are ancient rites continuing as they have for centuries. And perhaps it is because not all of the local Torajan rituals lend themselves to scheduled viewing by cruise ship tour groups. Some can only be stumbled upon serendipitously by an intrepid guide and his charge.

"Somebody died here recently," Marcus says. He has come bounding up the steps and into the small living room of the house where I am standing. He is slightly breathless with the news.

"I know," I reply. "I think that's him in there."

Through the bedroom doorway the end of a coffin is visible, draped in bright cloth. On a nearby table a glass of tea sits untouched. An old woman in a patterned blue dress and apron stands beside the door, looking tired and sad but otherwise completely unperturbed by our presence in her home.

Marcus brought me here on his motorcycle simply to show me a traditional Torajan village, one with particularly fine examples of *tongkonan* houses. After Marcus wandered off to chat with someone, an old woman beckoned me into her home. Tourists usually like to look around lovely *tongkonan* homes like hers, and she had a smattering of souvenirs ready to capitalize. But the carved plates and generic *tau-tau* figurines did not hold my attention. That was reserved for the draped coffin in the next room.

As Marcus arrives with his news, the woman points to a picture on the wall, a man Marcus recognizes as Petrus Kamma. "He used to take the tickets at the gate when tourists came," Marcus says.

The woman's name is Ama Mangiri. Marcus asks after the fate of her husband. "He saw a specialist," Marcus translates, a little impressed. "But soon he came home. Eleven days later he died. He was about eighty."

Now he lies, preserved, in the next room—a *tomakula*. He's been there for the past six weeks. He could be there for the next three years while preparations are made for a proper Torajan funeral. In the meantime his wife will continue to bring him glasses of tea and lay out his clothes. Relatives and friends who visit will say hello.

Petrus Kamma's portrait hangs at the head of the long coffin, which is wrapped in the same multicoloured fabric that covers the walls of the small, narrow room. The box is also shrouded in plastic. There is no odour. Torajans make use of modern preservation techniques, and nowhere are they more necessary.

And how long will it be before, through the grace of Jesus and the slaughtering of livestock, Petrus Kamma finally journeys to Puya?

Ama Mangiri shakes her head. "There are ten children," Marcus explains. "Only two are still here. It will probably be over a year, at least."

A donation is typical in such circumstances. I leave mine near the glass of tea, and buy two carved plates for good measure. Marcus hands me the batting helmet and I climb on the bike. The old woman has gone back inside as we drive away.

Since the Dutch brought Christianity to Tana Toraja, it can be argued that the region qualifies as a theological colony of the Netherlands. If so, it exists on a continuum of Dutch Christianity that is almost unfathomably wide, both geographically and ritually. The Dutch religious connection extends from the middle of Sulawesi to the horse-and-buggy worlds of Berlin, Ohio and Lancaster County, Pennsylvania, where you will find the several faith communities sometimes referred to as the Pennsylvania Dutch, or more commonly, the Amish.

Holland and Christianity are not the only connections between Torajan and Amish culture. Another is their increasing reliance on tourism. In the past forty or fifty years both groups have transitioned from agrarian economies to tourist-centred ones. Both now draw visitors to gawk at their unusual traditional practices and leave their money behind. In different ways, both have been transformed by observers.

Witness to Tourism

I ate a lot of popcorn in the 1980s. It may not rank among the better decades in the history of cinema, but we cannot choose the prime years we are given to spend our weekends in movie theatres. There were highlights—I avoided seeing *Footloose*. And I have a fond memory of riding my bike across Edmonton in 1985 to see *Blood Simple*, the well-reviewed debut by a pair of filmmakers named Joel and Ethan Coen.

Also in 1985 was the release of a much bigger box office hit—*Witness*. Harrison Ford and Kelly McGillis starred in this Peter Weir film about a cop on the run who must hide out in an Amish settlement in Pennsylvania. I loved it. I sighed over my large popcorn at the sight of lovely McGillis in her plain frock; I nodded with approval as these trusty men raised a barn, trying not to think about the fact that if I so much as tried to build a birdhouse I'd be charged with cruelty to animals. Almost forty years later it holds up like few of its cinematic contemporaries. *Witness* is still a great movie.

The Amish, at least officially, hated it. A statement from the National Committee for Amish Religious Freedom called for a boycott. They admitted that the movie portrayed the Amish in a very positive light. But, the statement said, "For the Amish, the movie represents immoral and unlikely behavior portrayed for profit and laughter in such a way that it appears sympathetic."

For a people who disapprove of photography to begin with, the whole project was damned from the start. The "Amish" extras in *Witness* were mostly Mennonites, as were the owners of the farm in Strasburg, Pennsylvania, on which much of the movie was shot. (Mennonites and Amish are both Anabaptists, tracing their common religious roots to sixteenth-century Holland. But the two groups split over issues of modernism and technology, with Mennonites taking a more permissive stance.)

Already, the statement went on, Amish country in Pennsylvania was overrun by tourists: "Their voyeurism will be greatly stimulated by national circulation of *Witness*, and the crowding, souvenir-hunting, photographing and trespassing on Amish farmsteads will increase."

They got that right. Just a year later the *Chicago Tribune* quoted an Amish man named Levi: "There's too many of them now. I used to wave to them from the fields, but if I did that now, I'd have my arm in a sling."

Yet if *Witness* put more horsepower behind Amish country tourism, it certainly did not start it. Americans had been fascinated by the Pennsylvania Dutch since before World War II. And reluctantly or not, the Amish have come to rely on it.

"The significance of Amish country tourism on the economy of the Amish is impossible to overestimate," says Susan Trollinger, professor of English at the University of Dayton. Her 2012 book *Selling the Amish: The Tourism of Nostalgia* focuses mainly on Ohio Amish communities in towns like Berlin and Walnut Creek. "Tourism is one of the ways that Amish have been able to stay in those larger settlements and make a living. They have a lot more interaction with non-Amish today than they did twenty years ago. And that's having a real impact."

Thirty years before *Witness*, the 1955 Broadway season offered the January opening of a new musical called *Plain and Fancy*. With songs like "Plenty of Pennsylvania" and "How Do You Raise a Barn?" the show told the tale of two New Yorkers who travel to Lancaster County to sell a property to an Amish man. Tourists had already been visiting Amish settlements in the 1930s and 1940s. While *Plain and Fancy* was the most prominent bit of uninvited advertising those communities had ever received, there were other factors leading more visitors to the area, including the 1940 opening of the Pennsylvania Turnpike. Amish areas were seeing a million tourists by 1960, and four million annually by 1973. Amish country tourism was already a three-hundred-million-dollar industry before *Witness* arrived in theatres. According to Trollinger, economic forces were at work that convinced the Amish to come to terms with the tourist mobs.

Modern mechanized farming practices and rising land prices were gradually making the purely agrarian life less sustainable. "It's very difficult to make a living as an Amish farmer, who doesn't have a combine, and so can't produce as much," she says. "At the same time tourism is picking up in Amish country in Pennsylvania, Ohio and Indiana. And land prices are rising. An Amish farmer can own a farm that is worth millions of dollars but it doesn't do him any good if he can't sell what he grows for enough money to make a living. So people had to take on various strategies to remain Amish. One of the strategies is to plug into the tourism business. You might own a lumber yard, you might make wood furniture, cabinetry, quilts."

"The Amish don't typically own tourist attractions," she says. "It's usually Mennonites. Mennonites and Amish share the same religious ancestry. They all come from the Anabaptists, the early-sixteenth-century radical reformation. They had a big schism over modernity. Mennonites ended up going more with modernity—they drive cars, go to college, use computers and so on. Whereas the Amish went another way, to remain tradition-minded.

"So you have an Amish guy who can't make a living on the farm anymore, he's putting out furniture. He's going to sell it at a Mennonite store. There are some Amish furniture makers who own their own stores but most of the time they're selling to Mennonites who have stores. Because the Amish can't have computers, they can't have electric lighting, so it's harder to have a store."

Even though most Amish (there are at least forty different subgroups) don't allow any electrical or modern conveniences at home, the requirements of tourist merchandising have necessitated adaptation. At a large operation called Keim Lumber in Charm, Ohio, Amish men and women work to turn out fine cabinetry and furniture for tourists. "You go in the back and you see it's Old Order Amish by and large who are working these state-of-the-art precision cabinet-making machines," Trollinger says. "They're all computerized. They have Amish guys and Amish women on computers, handling orders and so on."

Tourism has led to more outside contact, which has led to opportunity, and thus to compromise. "They have to make a living," Trollinger says. "So they'll let the young people go work at Keim Lumber where they'll have access to a computer and the internet, but they won't have it at home. The home is a separate space."

And just what is it the tourists are coming to see? In the movie, Kelly McGillis's character simply says they come to "gawk at us." Was that my crime as well—sitting with my popcorn, objectifying and cutesifying the Amish? Have the Pennsylvania Dutch Amish become a quaint, adorable freak show?

Trollinger thinks there is more to it. "I learned from the late Stuart Hall, a wonderful cultural theorist, that people who watch advertising or look at magazine ads have to have some investment. So I was trying to answer the question, What is it about Amish tourism that works? I'm arguing it's because the Amish seem to authorize the possibility that Americans could return to the kind of lives and values and structures that they had in the 1950s. It's this desire, this nostalgia for a future in which we are not overtaken by technology; we run it, it doesn't run us. Men know their jobs, women know their jobs. Nice and clear. So tourism in Amish country gives them hope that they could reclaim this life that they think they had at some point, even though they never really did."

Trollinger believes the Amish offer a challenge to some modern American cultural presumptions. "They don't let us off the hook by saying, 'Well there's nothing we can do, the digital age is here, so I'm just going to let my kid play video games fourteen hours a day and I'm just not going to worry about it,'" Trollinger says. "They say no, you're choosing that, but it's not necessary. There is another way."

Trollinger points out that using the Amish as shining examples of American values is problematic, as the Amish themselves have emphasized. There's a reason they embrace the New Testament verse 2 Corinthians 6:17: "Wherefore come out from among them, and be ye separate, saith the Lord, and touch not the unclean thing; and I will receive you."

"The Amish didn't come into being to prop up American ideology," Trollinger says. "They can seem to do that, but that's not who they are. On the contrary. They don't fight, they're not going to pick up a gun. That's not very patriotic."

They earned the ire of Eleanor Roosevelt by fighting against centralized public education in the 1930s. In a country that has nearly fetishized individual liberty—even at the cost of public health, during the pandemic— the Amish place severe restrictions on behaviour, on pain of shunning. Individual expression and personal freedom, those seminal American concepts, are a long way down the Amish priority list.

Amish rules can appear extreme to the outside world—their settlements would not be a source of public curiosity otherwise. Yet the underlying principles are not always as mysterious as they might first appear. One of those principles, which happens to align roughly with ancient Jewish law, may shed some light on the official Amish rejection of *Witness* and what they saw as its potential impact.

In many Jewish traditions it is forbidden to speak or write the name of God, except in prayer or ritual. This does not only apply to blasphemous cursing; any use of the holy name is forbidden. A strict interpretation of the Third Commandment, perhaps. But as the Jewish scholar Maimonides explained, "For the verse commands us, saying: 'To fear the glorious and awesome name.'"

To see the wisdom of this prohibition against casual divine name-dropping, you need only listen to certain modern politicians and religious hucksters. Countless TV preachers boast of a personal channel to God—the late Oral Roberts claimed to have seen a nine-hundred-foot-tall Jesus, who naturally advised people to give money to Roberts. (And who's going to say no to a nine-hundred-foot-tall collection agent with supremely powerful friends?) In 2020 Paula White, among other Donald Trump–supporting evangelists, proclaimed that God himself had elected Trump and would smite Trump's enemies.

That buddy-buddy relationship with the Supreme Being is the slippery slope Maimonides cautioned against. Once you get too chummy with the Almighty, you begin to take liberties. The personal relationship with Jesus so often celebrated by modern evangelicals was once widely considered blasphemous. Yet a 2018 Pew Research poll reported 28 percent of Americans not only talk to God but believe God talks back (former vice president Mike Pence among them).

Most Amish subgroups hew closer to the Jewish tradition than the evangelical one. They too disdain the idea of a personal relationship with God and consider it blasphemous. Familiarity, they believe, breeds contempt, arrogance and ultimately the debasement of what is holy. And it is arguably a similar principle that led the Amish to reject *Witness*. It's true that the film offers a positive portrait of the so-called Pennsylvania Dutch. But in so doing it made Amish society seem approachable, relatable, almost cuddly. And thus, as some of the leadership feared, the floodgates were opened to much worse.

Today, Amish cultural products proliferate. The reality series *Breaking Amish*, depicting young Amish in the big city, aired on TLC for a couple of seasons beginning in 2012. Amish romance is now an established publishing genre, right up there with true crime, cozy mysteries and vampire literature. Known as "bonnet rippers," the novels first emerged in the 1990s and have sold in the tens of millions. Most of the books are written by evangelical authors, and tend to reflect evangelical rather than Amish theological viewpoints as they tell stories of forbidden yet chaste romance. But Valerie Weaver-Zercher, writing in the *Los Angeles Review of Books*, found the novels were being sold in Amish-owned bookstores and could claim a significant Amish readership (even though many other Amish she spoke with snickered at the stories, some of which feature plot twists such as fatal horse-and-buggy wrecks).

The popularity of Amish novels, combined with the tide of Amish country tourism, has given rise to yet another form of Amish-themed entertainment: the Amish comedy musical. These productions may be the mutant progeny of *Plain and Fancy*, but none of them are headed for Broadway. They're playing a very different sort of Great White Way.

A company called Blue Gate Theatre, founded in Indiana in 2010, now runs venues in numerous Amish tourist areas. They have taken bestselling Amish romance novels by Beverly Lewis and Wanda Brunstetter and added songs and humour—Blue Gate's stage stories are written by Martha Bolton, a former gag writer for Bob Hope. The Amish themselves, of course, do not appear. "The Amish aren't doing this," says Trollinger. "It's the Mennonites, or somebody. I don't see anything good about that."

Upsetting as the Blue Gate productions might be to Old Order Amish, there appear to be worse options out there. The Amish Country Theater in Berlin, Ohio, puts on shows that have been described as "mixing *Hee Haw* with Amish ways." And that's a boast from the promotional material.

The Amish Country Theater website features a photo of a guy in overalls brandishing a toilet plunger, and another denim-clad guy with big false buck teeth. A video preview shows plenty of comical yokels with glued-on beards, sheepskin-covered guitars and a man who appears to be riding a leprechaun. "You'll laugh with comedian Lynyrd, a spotlight stealin' country bumpkin, who's as unpredictable as an Ohio spring," it promises.

Witness, what hast thou wrought?

The Amish themselves are not stooping to such corny japes. Perhaps there is no way they can prevent them. But are they complicit via their second-hand participation in the tourist bonanza? Modernity is a daily challenge to the Amish. Meeting that challenge has resulted in a fracturing of Amish practice, and tourism has exacerbated the issue. The most obvious issues are technological. Ultraconservative subgroup Swartzentruber Amish will not allow flush toilets, gravel on their roads or any sort of decorative plants or shrubs. Other Amish groups permit tractors, chain saws, powered lawn mowers and washing machines.

"The Amish are always negotiating this stuff," Trollinger says. "It's not absolute. Ever since you've had pasteurization they've had to negotiate. Because they don't have electricity. How are they going to do this? Some do, some don't. Some say no, that's a bridge too far. So they'll sell their milk to cheese houses instead of [selling it] as milk."

But technology is not the only intruder in Amish communities. Evangelical Christianity, a far larger and more powerful force in American society than the Amish, has found itself drawn to the Amish world. Evangelists, by their very nature, are not inclined to merely observe. Star Trek's Prime Directive (a prohibition against interfering with other cultures) is not for them.

Evangelical authors write Amish romances, which are then purchased by Amish customers, who read stories in which the strict Amish theology often gives way to that more personal brand of Christian belief found in evangelical churches. Weaver-Zercher describes the standard Amish romance character arc: "[A] typical Amish heroine travel[s] two vectors as her story unfolds: one from the works-based religion of her people to a more warm-hearted and evangelical spirituality, and another from loneliness to love."

Weaver-Zercher asks, "If Amish readers are encountering fictional versions of themselves in the pages of Amish fiction, will they begin donning evangelical habits of romance and language of faith? How does a culture change when outsiders launder its most cherished values and practices ... and sell them back to the people themselves?"

Nor are the books the only conduit for Evangelicalism. As Trollinger explains, tourist-related businesses that employ the Amish also play a role. "They go to work and a lot of the people around them are going to be evangelical fundamentalists," she says. "Stuff comes into their world in ways it didn't before."

Even if not all these influences are the direct result of tourism, tourism is certainly the economic engine driving the process. Cultural isolation and philosophical purity are tough to maintain when you are up to your plain collars in outside influence.

Whether in Ohio, Pennsylvania or Sulawesi, tourist waves raise issues and questions for distinct societies. These might even be said to resemble the questions prompted by other waves—the kind studied by physicists. In both cases the act of observation may change what is being observed.

Theoretical physicists Werner Heisenberg and Erwin Schrödinger both tried to explain the odd phenomenon of wave properties that are altered merely by the act of observing. In order to make a point, Schrödinger famously posited the thought experiment of a box containing a cat that may be simultaneously alive and dead. It makes sense to me. The unfortunate water buffalo I saw in Sulawesi was alive until Schrödinger's tour group showed up. And there is no denying that the act of observing these cultures, Torajan or Amish, has altered the cultures being observed. Tourism can change communities in other ways too—through the intentional actions of the communities themselves. The quest to find a magic key that will unlock tourism riches has led to both innovation and folly, often simultaneously.

The Ghostly Goddess of Ashibetsu

In the summer of 2016 I rode a two-car train through rural Hokkaido, northernmost of Japan's four major islands, headed for a town called Furano, famous for lavender in early summer and skiing in winter. The train stopped briefly at a small station beside the town of Ashibetsu. Through the window I saw a remarkable sight—what I took to be a massive white Buddha. From my perspective it looked to be the size of the Statue of Liberty. No one got off at Ashibetsu. I was in fact the only one in the train car. After a few moments the little train trundled on and the giant receded from view.

Information about that surreal trackside vision was surprisingly scarce. Eventually I discovered that the statue was not of Buddha, but of a Bodhisattva (an enlightened teacher) named Avalokitesvara, a.k.a. Guanyin, a.k.a. Dai Kannon. The Hokkaido Dai Kannon, as the statue is often called, is in fact taller than the Statue of Liberty—when completed in 1989 it became for a time the world's tallest statue, at eighty-eight metres. It contains twenty floors and an elevator to a viewing platform that reportedly offers spectacular views of the surrounding area. And it is more or less abandoned. The vision I saw from the train is essentially a gleaming white elephant in a town that has become, if anything, a shrine to failed tourist megaprojects.

Almost everything I discovered about the statue came from Tom Royal, a visitor from South London whose lengthy blog post is almost the only English-language information available. Royal visited the shrine in May 2014—at the time his was the only car in the huge parking lot—and found an abandoned ticket gate, dry fountains and a single attendant. Bathrooms were out of order and the place smelled "slightly damp," he wrote, but the elevator worked and the view was spectacular.

Like me, Royal was intrigued by the neglected monument and did some digging. Ashibetsu had been a centre of coal mining, and like many such towns began searching for a new source of revenue. Tourism seemed just the thing. But what particular qualities did Ashibetsu have to offer? Like others before and since, the town opted for the "if you build it, they will come" approach. Construction of the giant devotional icon started in 1975. It opened fourteen years later. There was also a monorail, which has since been dismantled. The company that ran the Dai Kannon went bankrupt in 2013, and the site was taken over by a Buddhist organization called Tentokukan, which has kept it open, barely.

The evident failure of the Hokkaido Dai Kannon to draw crowds was particularly striking to me at the time, since I had just come from the seaside town of Otaru. It's a fine enough Japanese town, despite an absence of waterfront amenities that is oddly typical of urban Japanese shorelines. What struck me most though was one of the town's premier tourist attractions: a short canal. No more than two or three blocks long, it was possible to take boat rides along its length. And people did. Not hordes of them perhaps, but I did see some canal tourist traffic.

Now the sight of the forlorn Hokkaido Dai Kannon made me wonder: Why do some tourist attractions succeed while others fail? Why would a waterway the length of a snail's afternoon stroll draw interest while a Buddhist Statue of Liberty is ignored?

There's a reason the Ashibetsu monument is identified as the *Hokkaido Dai Kannon*. You need to be specific when referring to these giants. Japan has more Buddhist mega-statues than Canada has NHL franchises. Among them are the towering Byakue Dai Kannon in the city of Takasaki, about two hours north of Tokyo. Kaga in Ishikawa Prefecture has one. There's another on Shōdo Island off the south coast of Honshu. Fukuoka Prefecture on the southern island of Kyushu has the sixty-two-metre Guze Jibo Dai Kannon. Tsu City, between Osaka and Nagoya, has a glittering thirty-three-metre gold-covered Dai Kannon in the Hojuyama Daikanon Temple. Wander around the temple grounds and you will find a unique variation on the theme—a karaoke Dai Kannon. This goddess of mercy, donated by a businessman who made his money in the karaoke business, holds a microphone. In a true display of mercy, she does not sing.

Dwarfing all of those in both size and expenditure is the four-billion-yen ($36.4 million Canadian), hundred-metre-high Sendai Dai Kannon, which opened in 1991. This epic figure, looming incongruously over a residential neighbourhood in the northern Honshu city of Sendai, holds a vessel tipped, as though pouring. According to two vloggers named Andrew and Nishant, it is intended to pour the water of knowledge, falling from the heavens to the waiting world. This magical water of knowledge is then meant to be collected in a pool at the foot of the statue. But as Andrew explains, "The pond is closed now, unfortunately."

Explains a lot.

Perhaps the most ill-fated Dai Kannon was built on Awaji Island, near Kobe. Eighty metres tall, the Awaji Island Guanyin statue opened in 1982. The man who managed the monument died four years later—his wife took over but died in 2006 and it fell into disrepair. In February 2020 a man jumped to his death from the viewing platform. That was the final straw—Awaji Island's massive statue was dismantled in 2022.

These newly built Dai Kannons may be attempts by local promoters to connect to a very old and more established Japanese tradition—massive ancient Buddhas that date back centuries and draw reliable crowds to this day.

A ninety-minute drive south of Tokyo, Kamakura is famed for its cherry blossoms and is host to many of the traditional spring picnic parties called *hanami*. My friend Ren lives nearby and one day took me to see the Kamakura Buddha.

The bronze Kamakura statue, a relatively modest thirteen and a half metres high, is a representation of the Amitābha Buddha, deity of Pure Land Buddhism. Visitors can enter, as Ren and I did, though climbing the winding interior passageway is a claustrophobic experience. But then, the Kamakura Buddha was no recent town council tourism scheme. It has been meditating on that spot since the middle of the thirteenth century.

Built at a time when Kamakura was the political centre of Japan, the seated figure was once gilded, and presided over a great hall. The hall was destroyed by a storm, rebuilt, wrecked again, and in 1498 finally washed away for the last time by a tsunami. It seems the Great Buddha craved the open air. Rudyard Kipling wrote an ode to the Kamakura Buddha after visiting in 1892. It remains one of Japan's most famous and revered monuments, and although we cannot access the minutes of Kamakura city council meetings of 1251, it's a safe bet the statue was not a ploy to attract tourists.

Nor was Tōdai-ji. Located in the beautiful city of Nara, south of Kyoto, the nearly thirteen-hundred-year-old Tōdai-ji temple sits in a large park guarded by two fearsome cedar statues, each eight and a half metres high. Kyoko took me there. The wooden temple contains an almost equally massive Buddha, a statue that reportedly drained Japan of almost all its bronze in the mid-eighth century.

For almost as long as the temple has stood, the grounds of Tōdai-ji have been full of free-roaming deer, considered sacred animals for their legendary role in carrying the deity Takemi Kajichi no Mikoto to this spot. To call the deer tame does not do them justice—they are downright obsequious. Over centuries of interacting with temple monks, the deer apparently picked up on their bowing motion and began emulating it to earn handouts. Now vendors sell deer-friendly crackers (made of wheat flour and rice bran) to tourists who wish to reward the gracious ungulates. Gift shops offer chocolate pellets marketed as deer shit.

Not every deer got it right during my visit. Some of them merely flicked their heads spasmodically. But others performed graceful bows worthy of royal courts, inclining their long necks to the earth. It was astonishing to see.

Crackers in hand, I fed deer left and right while Kyoko took pictures. At one point I wandered into a little clearing and was promptly surrounded by deer. The ones in front were bowing. The ones behind me had a different strategy—they were head-butting my ass. It was beginning to seem less like panhandling and more like mugging. Kyoko was wiser than I—she wanted no part of these cracker-snarfing hooligans. In fact, she said her brother was once swarmed by deer and attacked, and she has been frightened of them ever since.

It was almost impossible to avoid viewing the deer metaphorically. Once wild creatures, they were now tame beggars, and if their abject pleading failed, more aggressive tactics were employed. The Tōdai-ji deer are the official mascots of overtourism.

Ashibetsu's giant statue drew no crowds. There is currently no mention of it on the town's website. But the central Hokkaido town made another attempt to create a local attraction that, for a while at least, had more success. This was Canadian World.

For any Canadian, a theme park called Canadian World must summon up a wealth of possibilities: mascots roaming the grounds dressed as bilingual cereal boxes; a chorus of animatronic provincial premiers demanding more health care funding from Ottawa; midway rides that are not only safe but boring; sudden price hikes due to currency fluctuations in American World, the much larger and scarier theme park next door. The possibilities are endless.

But Ashibetsu's Canadian World is not quite what it says on the label. It's really Prince Edward Island World, or even more specifically, Anne of Green Gables World. Anne is massively popular in Japan, and Canadian World was an attempt to recreate the nineteenth-century-PEI setting evoked by novelist Lucy Maud Montgomery. "A visit to Canadian World will bring you back to this romantic period in Canada," a promotional video promised. Instead of Mickey Mouse and Goofy, actors were hired to play

Montgomery's beloved characters. During the 1990s, thirteen-year-old Jennifer Long (who is actually from PEI) landed the role of Anne. In a later interview with CBC she recalled the heyday of the park, which at its peak drew tens of thousands of visitors a day with live performances, concerts, an artificial lake, paddle boats, a miniature train, horse-drawn carriage rides, and the little town itself. "It was pretty surreal," she said.

What happened? Long recalled that it was a seasonal attraction: "The winters in Hokkaido are harsh, they are very much like East Coast winters," she told the CBC, "where you get a ton of snow, and there were days, especially during the winter, where we'd see maybe a dozen people."

There's a certain irony in a theme park called Canadian World being thwarted by too much snow. But there were other issues. In the mid-90s Japan was gripped by an economic crisis that had a serious impact on tourism. Eventually the town took over Canadian World, which is still open to summer visitors as a park, free of charge, with none of the pig-tailed moppets or role-playing Maritimers.

Although a shell of its former self, Canadian World has at least avoided membership in a particular niche category of Japanese tourist attraction— the *haikyo*. The word means "ruins," and scattered *haikyo* sites have become popular with adventuresome Japanese explorers. There are abandoned offices, bridges, apartment buildings, and if you can get in, theme parks. Nara Dreamland was a huge Japanese answer to Disneyland that opened in 1961 and failed in 2006, perhaps due to a steady loss of customers to Tokyo Disneyland, which opened in 1983. It is closed to visitors but that has not stopped some *haikyo* fans from trespassing. The massive popularity of Tokyo Disneyland may also have sounded the death knell for Western Village, a.k.a. Kinugawa Ranch, an American West–themed park about one hundred kilometres north of Tokyo that features a replica of Mount Rushmore and now, abandoned and overgrown, looks more authentically Western than ever.

In W.P. Kinsella's book *Shoeless Joe*, later filmed as *Field of Dreams*, the "if you build it, he will come" theory works out well—eventually a whole crowd shows up. The real-world record is spottier. Over the years the allure of tourist wealth has led town planners to create a field of schemes, some popular, some unsuccessful, some disastrous.

Ashibetsu's giant statue may not draw crowds but at least it doesn't try to steal anybody's lunch. Xianfeng Village, a hamlet in China's Sichuan province, would love to have a benign failure like that. Located in the Yangtze River basin, Xianfeng Village is home to about three hundred people and more than twice that number of monkeys. In 2003 local officials decided to create the Macaque Mountain Resort, and imported seventy-three rhesus macaques. The resort was a big success—not for the humans, but certainly for the monkeys. By 2016 the resort had failed and over six hundred unemployed monkeys roamed the town, grabbing food and sometimes attacking residents. More recent reports from the town have been scarce but if locals were to hold a referendum on building a zoo, it's pretty clear which species would have the votes to put the other primates behind bars.

Many an isolated town searches for some local metal they can alchemize into tourist gold. Pop culture fame is one vein to be mined. Driving east on Interstate 40 years ago I saw a billboard presenting the slogan *Stand on a corner in Winslow, Arizona.*

On the face of it, the lamest inducement to adventure in the annals of public relations. But to anyone with access to a classic rock radio station, the pitch will be instantly recognizable from the Eagles' 1972 hit, "Take It Easy." And why not? I once made a point of stopping to buy a local paper in Tonopah, Nevada, just because the town was mentioned in the Little Feat classic, "Willin'."

Timmins, Ontario, would seem to have a much stronger pop music draw. The town of forty-one thousand about seven hundred kilometres north of Toronto claims a famous former resident, and on this the town worthies decided to make book. Thus was born the Shania Twain Centre. Unveiled in 2001, it cost a reported ten million dollars to build. It's a cheap shot but almost unavoidable to say public reaction to the facility was summed up by Twain's hit, "That Don't Impress Me Much." Twain herself did not visit for several years. She did hit that window of availability, though—you, on the other hand, have missed it. The Shania Twain Centre closed in 2013. Attendance was a fraction of what had been expected, and by the time it shut down a civic report estimated that every resident of Timmins was subsidizing the centre to the tune of seven dollars per year. The building was sold for half its initial cost, and in a moment of irony perhaps a little too on the nose, the new owners demolished it to transform the site into an open-pit gold mine.

Megaprojects intended to draw tourists off the beaten track often prove to be misguided. But the goal is nonetheless worthy—they are attempts to spread tourist wealth that is at present highly concentrated. It is one of the curses of the modern tourist industry that a handful of super-centres gain a large majority of tourists, sometimes to the detriment of both visitors and residents. That's particularly true in Japan.

Most tourist traffic in Japan sticks to what is called the Golden Route—Tokyo to Mount Fuji to Kyoto to Osaka. "Tohoku, the upper half of the main island of Honshu, receives only 2 percent of all tourists coming to Japan," says Wesley Keppel-Henry of the tour company Hidden Japan.

"Anytime you build an infrastructure that is centred on tourism rather than the residents and when the money does not flow back into the community, that can create some cultural tension with local residents," Keppel-Henry says. "Even in Kyoto, the biggest tourism companies are based in Tokyo. The profits go back to Tokyo and that doesn't benefit the local community."

Hidden Japan is based in Yamagata Prefecture in northern Honshu. "In our area there are so few tourists they are welcomed when they do come," Keppel-Henry says, "whereas in Kyoto it's sort of a love-hate relationship. The crowds of tourists ruin the most beautiful temples for the locals."

The idea of building a monster attraction to attract tourists seems reminiscent of the advice so often given to those seeking romantic partners: take a pottery course, join a book club. It's not terrible advice—you might read some great books and turn out to be a wonderful potter. But there is an insincerity to such ploys that tends to spell doom.

After seeing the massive, desolate Dai Kannon in Ashibetsu, I wondered: Why? Why does the dinky little Otaru canal draw business while a Buddhist Statue of Liberty does not? Bangkok University's Edward Koh offers an explanation. "The canals are an important part of Otaru's port history," Koh says, citing their role in the town's commercial fishing history. "The cultural and historical links are inherent. It's a must-visit for Otaru first-timers. On the other hand, the Dai Kannon is a recent commercial structure. It's not unique apart from its size. Japanese have their own religious statues in their hometowns. Foreigners mostly don't decide to go to Hokkaido to visit religious sites."

Furano, just down the road from Ashibetsu, draws visitors with a lovely lavender and flower farm, a facility that fits better with the local landscape. But as Koh points out, "If the canals were in Furano, they could well be a commercial flop too."

A tourist destination cannot be separated from its setting. And even if there is a logical connection, as with the Shania Twain Centre, it helps if the location has an overall curb appeal.

Corny tourist attractions can certainly work, as long as they don't have to carry too much of the load. Not too far from my Vancouver apartment is a popular contraption called the steam clock. Designed by Raymond Saunders and located in tourist-centric Gastown, the clock puffs and toots on the hour and at fifteen-minute intervals. One might think that a steam-spouting timepiece called the steam clock would be powered by steam. But no. With steam power having proved unreliable for accurate timekeeping, the main source of power is now an electric motor. Never mind. It's in the guidebooks and visitors crowd around for photos. Be sure to stop in at nearby shops to commemorate your visit with steam clock souvenirs.

There's another Raymond Saunders steam clock, a sister to the Vancouver version. It happens to be in Otaru. I somehow missed the Otaru steam clock on my visit. Too bad. I would definitely have taken a selfie.

"I've never been to Gastown," says Koh, "but if I do, I will probably drop by to see the steam clock, just to check it off the to-do list. Probably just once, never again."

The Genesis of Tourism

Back in the 1970s the highway served the function now provided by the internet—a place for teenagers to meet strangers. One summer my friend Bob and I hitchhiked from Brandon out to Vancouver and then down the coast to San Francisco. Coming back up the California coast, we got a ride in a Volkswagen Beetle with two young women named Ann and Dorothy. They were born-again Christians on their way to visit a commune near Eureka, California, called Lighthouse Ranch. They took pains not to pros-elytize to us—in fact the great revelation they introduced us to, sheltered Prairie lads that we were, was the joy of bagels and cream cheese. They promised to take us farther north after their visit if we would join them in a visit to the commune. We agreed.

Lighthouse Ranch was quite a place. Perched on a bluff overlooking a wide stretch of Pacific beach, it was largely populated by people who were then known as Jesus freaks, a mix of one-time hippies, seekers and reformed speed addicts, repositioning and reprogramming themselves as devout believers. Many seemed eager for that moment when the corrupt world would slide away and leave them triumphant, rewarded for backing the right horse.

They were not a particularly fun group. There was a game of Frisbee where my comment about a gust of wind drew the response, "That's just the Lord throwing your pride back down at you." One camper waylaid Bob and me as we attempted to sneak down the bluff to the beach. "What good is that gathering," the camper asked, pointing down at a family barbecue, "when they have lust in their hearts?"

One young man was on the lam from the law and argued with his fellow campers. "God wants you to turn yourself in," someone insisted.

"God wants me to go to Mexico," he replied.

When at last the four of us headed north into Oregon, our benefactors were sorely disappointed. Pure of heart and sincere of belief, Ann and Dorothy had hoped to find like-minded souls to celebrate a new life in Christ. Instead they had found Jesus variously running the Anti-Barbecue League, smuggling fugitives to Tijuana, and revelling in that old-time told-you-so religion that would be revealed in the fullness of time when the righteous were high-fiving above a roiling stew of human agony.

Lighthouse Ranch was not exactly a tourist destination. But it exerted a pull for Ann and Dorothy, who sought Christian soulmates. Decades later a similar pull is drawing crowds to Petersburg, Kentucky. An unincorporated community with an official population of about 620, it sits by Interstate 275, the ring road that allows motorists to bypass Cincinnati, Ohio. The little town is home to the Creation Museum. An hour away in Williamstown is its companion attraction, the Ark Encounter.

The Creation Museum is a twenty-seven-million-dollar, seventy-five-thousand-square-foot facility that purports to offer evidence supporting YEC (young-Earth creationism). The museum grounds are about seventy-five kilometres northwest of Williamstown and the Ark Encounter, a reconstruction (let's not quibble) of Noah's Ark from the Book of Genesis.

If nothing else, *Selling the Amish* author Susan Trollinger says, the big boat is an impressive sight. "The Ark is stunning, physically, just walking up to the thing," she says. "And the biggest argument the Ark makes is just by its size, that it makes sense to say that this story actually happened, that you could actually get that many animals on this thing and float around for a year."

Trollinger and her husband, William Vance Trollinger, Jr., wrote the book *Righting America at the Creation Museum*. Operated by a company called Answers in Genesis, the museum posits an intriguing theory known as "flood geology," drawing heavily on *The Genesis Flood* by Henry M. Morris and John C. Whitcomb. "The book argues that Noah's flood created all the geological formations that we see that make the world look old," Trollinger says, "and did it all in a year. The Grand Canyon, produced in a year, don't worry about it."

"If you're going to read Genesis literally," she says, "go through the genealogies. You've got Adam and Eve, historical figures, who have descendants, and you add up all those years, and the universe can't be more than ten thousand years old. So you have to explain that. And flood geology was this scientific intervention that explained it."

Count Trollinger and her husband among the unconvinced. "We walked through the Creation Museum for the first time," she says, "and we passed through the flood geology room. There's very little science. We analyzed every placard and video. Only 2 percent of the placards would count as science, even by their own definitions."

Not that there are no worthwhile exhibits. "They have an incredible skeleton of a dinosaur, really impressive," Trollinger says. "So OK, how does this dinosaur skeleton prove a young Earth, or flood geology? They argue that because this dinosaur was found on the side of a hill, obviously the dinosaur was running up the hill to escape the rising flood waters. But then the poor dinosaur drowned and that's why the skeleton was found on the side of a hill."

The Creation Museum opened in 2007 and exceeded its annual attendance projections in only five months. It has since expanded twice, added the Williamstown ark attraction, and welcomed over ten million visitors.

Why has the Creation Museum been a hit while Japan's giant Buddhist statues earn public indifference? You might call it validation tourism.

"Evangelicals and fundamentalists have felt very much on the margins of US society since the Scopes trial," says Trollinger, referring to the 1925 prosecution of a Tennessee high school teacher who taught the theory of evolution. "They won the case but they lost in public opinion. They were constructed by journalists especially as backwater idiots. They don't know anything, they don't do science, they're stupid. And what the Creation Museum and Ark Encounter offer evangelicals and fundamentalists is this 'science,' flood geology, that justifies an ultra-literal reading of Genesis. And it says, 'Look at you! You're legit! You've got yourself a big-ass Ark and a Creation Museum with animatronic dinosaurs. So cutting edge!'"

In 2014 the Creation Museum invited TV personality Bill Nye, a.k.a. Bill Nye the Science Guy, to debate Answers in Genesis CEO Ken Ham on the topic of young Earth creationism. It was popular—tickets sold out almost instantly, it was live streamed, and later broadcast on C-SPAN. "When Ken Ham did his debate with Bill Nye," Trollinger says, "he mentioned science multiple times more often than Nye did." Still, Ham declared in his opening statement that science "has been taken over by secularists." The debate, moderated by CNN's Tom Foreman, probably changed few minds. But it did have an effect. Ham credited publicity from the debate for generating some of the funds to help build the seventy-three-million-dollar Ark Experience, which opened in 2016. The event also provided a preview of another debate that would soon take centre stage in American politics, courtesy of Donald Trump: whether or not engaging in public arguments over unsupported claims simply helps to boost the credibility and dissemination of those baseless claims.

Many a joke has been made about what sort of reading material would be contained in a Donald Trump presidential library—perhaps stolen documents, Big Mac wrappers and shelves of clearance-priced copies of *Trump: The Art of the Deal*. But whatever else it may mean, the success of the Creation Museum suggests that a Trump library would probably be a big draw. In a politically and culturally polarized country, there is considerable appeal in an attraction that simply lets you gather with fellow believers.

The Creation Museum seems a particularly American phenomenon. Unlike many old-world religious sites it was purpose-built to attract a sectarian clientele, while most popular European religious sites are traditional church institutions that survived into an era of mass tourism.

The annual pilgrimage to Mecca, which certainly qualifies as a major travel event, remains entirely religious in nature. The massive Hindu Kumbh Mela festival, held every twelve years at Prayagraj in Uttar Pradesh, is also primarily religious, though a room full of cultural anthropologists could have a fine time arguing whether or not it also qualifies as a tourist event. Falling somewhere in the middle of the religious event–tourist attraction divide is the Camino de Santiago, the Spanish pilgrimage route to Santiago de Compostela, walked for centuries by the faithful and now attracting a mix of modern pilgrims and secular hikers. Like the Camino de Santiago, Europe's massive cathedrals, from the Monreale Cathedral in Sicily to the Cathedral of Saint Mary of the See in Seville, function simultaneously as houses of worship and tourist draws.

In Kathmandu's Durbar Square, one such holy site offers something more—the prospect of glimpsing a living, breathing deity. The Living Goddess Kumari occupies a temple with a quiet courtyard where she makes random appearances to the public. Like the Dalai Lama, the goddess Kumari is incarnated in many different human forms through the years. Unlike the Dalai Lama, the goddess Kumari does not retain her status until death. Each Kumari hangs onto the role until the onset of menstruation. Then they find a new goddess. Presumably the old one goes off to leave a particularly impressive resume at Pizza Hut. (A former Kumari named Rashmila Shakya published a memoir, *From Goddess to Mortal*, describing her life as a living goddess and the difficult transition back to the outside world. Among other issues, she criticized the lack of education granted to goddesses before their divinity abruptly lapses.)

Each new Living Goddess Kumari is selected based on thirty-two qualities—some physical, like black hair and good teeth, while others include a calm demeanour, a cow's eyes and a lion's heart. For this reason little candidates are placed in a dark little room with slaughtered animal carcasses. The winning candidate, no crying she makes.

The newly selected goddess moves into Kumari Ghar, a ramshackle eighteenth-century temple in Durbar Square. She then commences doing what goddesses do—she *appears*. Some lucky devotees gain private audiences with Kumari, often hoping to be healed of illness. Tourists like me, however, are left with the option of hanging around the temple courtyard, waiting for the goddess to show up. There's no telling when. Never between noon and four p.m., though. Around 4:30 one day in January 2009, I was in the small courtyard with a few Germans and Koreans. Suddenly a man popped his head out of an upstairs window and began speaking, apparently instructing us that no photos are allowed and donations should be stuffed into the nearby box. Then she was there, peering over an upper balcony railing—the Living Goddess Kumari. Four years old at the time, she wore a shimmering orange gown, a red headpiece and a lot of makeup for someone so young. But her big eyes were indeed cowlike. She looked us over for a bit, then retreated from the railing and disappeared. I wish I could say the experience left me quaking like Paul on the road to Damascus but I felt no noticeable spiritual impact.

Religious attractions can be prey to particular dangers. England would surely boast many more historical landmarks today had Henry VIII not ravaged Catholic abbeys and monasteries in the sixteenth century. In March 2001 the Buddhas of Bamiyan, massive stone statues in central Afghanistan dating from the sixth century CE, were blown up by the Taliban in a criminal act of extremist vandalism. Secular attacks on religious sites have occurred as well. Numerous Buddhist temples and Confucian sites were attacked and sometimes destroyed during China's Cultural Revolution, as part of the 1966 campaign against the "Four Olds": old ideas, old culture, old customs and old habits.

Religious-themed sites can also self-destruct. In 1978 evangelists Jim and Tammy Faye Bakker, televangelists and founders of the PTL (Praise the Lord) Club, opened Heritage USA in Fort Mill, South Carolina. It covered 2,300 acres and eventually drew an average of six million visitors per year, surpassed only by Disney World in Orlando and Disneyland in Anaheim, making it America's number one non-rodent-related theme park. Alas, a veritable rat's nest of charges would surface in 1987 as former employee Jessica Hahn alleged she had been drugged and raped by Bakker and another preacher. Heritage USA then transitioned from Bible verses to Chapter 11. In a final display of divine displeasure, Hurricane Hugo slammed into the theme park in 1989. It closed shortly after, a victim in part of the particular PR vulnerability that comes with religious marketing.

Populist figures, religious cult leaders and even celebrities remind us that mainstream faiths are not the only avenues for mass worship. The same is true of religious attractions. While the Creation Museum and Hokkaido Dai Kannon were created to attract pilgrims, some devotional spectacles develop spontaneously. Call them cult attractions. They are not always expressly religious—see Jim Morrison's grave in Paris's Père Lachaise Cemetery and Graceland in Memphis—nor are they always welcome. Years ago I took a journey through a place that had acquired an accidental occult significance, a demonic landscape that no longer exists—at least, not under its former designation.

CHAPTER TWENTY

Highway to Hell (via Shiprock)

It was the summer of 2001. Driving east across New Mexico, I turned my ten-year-old BMW 318 north at the city of Gallup. I was now on US Route 666. It ran just east of Monument Valley, through a Navajo reservation, past the Four Corners region where the borders of New Mexico, Colorado, Utah and Arizona meet, and on up to Cortez, Colorado. Carrying the biblical mark of the beast, it was sometimes known as the Devil's Highway, or the Highway to Hell.

Long before AC/DC released their hard-rock hit, Route 666 had a loose connection to another popular melody. Nat King Cole is among those who crooned "Route 66," an ode to the legendary road from St. Louis to the California coast. US Route 66 is gone now except in the roadside shops and attractions that still capitalize on its fame. But as of the beginning of the twenty-first century, Route 666 remained, its designation derived from the more famous parent route it once joined in Gallup.

Driving the Devil's Highway could make one a little edgy and not just for the obvious reason. An Arizona store clerk had warned me before I headed north. "This is monsoon season," he said. "You can get a flash flood up there that'll wash you right off the road."

Already I had seen what he meant. Not far west along Interstate 40 the heavens had opened for a brief stretch, blinding my fellow travellers and me with curtains of rain that turned road and ditch a level, watery grey. Now as I moved north on Route 666 I could see a roving storm cell scouring the earth, an isolated band of vapour bristling with lightning.

Route 666 had a natural tourist appeal. That much was obvious from the fact that the road signs kept disappearing, stolen by souvenir hunters. You'd think the folks along the Highway to Hell could scrape together enough cash for a little billboard welcoming AC/DC fans. But no such idea seemed to have occurred to local chamber of commerce types. Nor were any residents keen to capitalize on the success of Oliver Stone's 1994 movie *Natural Born Killers*, whose titular figures take their murder spree down this very stretch of road.

The landscape had a spooky beauty that often seemed to defy rational explanation—in particular the local mountains. Mountains tend to be social creatures. They bunch up in ranges and ridges, blocking each other's view and generally diminishing the impact of each individual peak. But Route 666 had mountains the way they ought to be, the way they are in stories with wizards. These mountains rose up from the empty plain and stood alone, like icebergs in a calm sea.

It was the kind of road where you frequently checked the gas gauge. If you forgot to fill up in Gallup you would soon be getting nervous.

Halfway up I came at last to the desultory little town of Shiprock. No evidence of storefront covens here, but there was a convent. Christ the King was home to precisely two nuns, serving a parish of 13,000 square kilometres. The visiting sister who answered the phone was alarmed at my suggestion that locals should play up the Beelzebub angle. "I've been in this area for ten years," she said, "and I've never heard of anyone coming here for that reason. Raising the issue would only draw attention to it."

Precisely the idea, but an understandably tough sell at that address.

I tried again, this time on the other side of the Martin Luther line. A mile north of Cortez in a building that once housed a John Deere dealership, New Hope Christian Ministries served the Pentecostal community along Route 666. My call was answered by Pastor Jonathan Bland.

"I've heard some of the music of AC/DC," Bland allowed. "I used to play in a Christian rock and roll band myself. I'm not against rock and roll music. But I am against what they [AC/DC] play."

Bland grew up in Cortez. "If you were known as a town on the Devil's Highway," he says, "I don't think you'd see that as a positive thing for tourism. No one here would want to cash in on that. The only people interested would be demonically inspired rock bands, and those just aren't the kind of people you want to attract."

These were clearly not entrepreneurs with an eye for the main chance. They might have taken a cue from another isolated town about eleven hundred kilometres northwest—Battle Mountain, Nevada. Located on Interstate 80, Battle Mountain was once awarded the dubious honour of "Armpit of America." In 2001, the *Washington Post* Sunday magazine launched a search for that geographical and/or anatomical not-so-sweet spot. In a fateful moment, a visiting *Washington Post* photographer happened to see the sign at the Battle Mountain Shell station—the S had burned out. Battle Mountain clinched the title. And bless them, they ran with it. Billboards outside of town soon read, *Make us your pit stop.* Festival in the Pit was launched. They had fun. On my own visit in 2008, I was charmed. I was there to write about the World Human Powered Speed Challenge, regularly held on a lonely road outside of town, an event for streamlined, enclosed bicycles to attempt record-setting runs. The *Post* be damned—Battle Mountain is an attractive, old-fashioned town with a beautiful view of three different mountain ranges, a great Mexican diner (El Aguila Real) and a good little espresso café. I even returned a few years later for more beef enchiladas.

By contrast, my drive along Route 666 had not been quite the pitchfork-and-brimstone experience I had craved. I had one last hope. There was a little spot marked on my AAA map, about an hour and a half northeast of Cortez—Purgatory, Colorado.

Heading up a wide, empty stretch of Route 550 north of Durango, I searched for a sign that would tell me I was entering Purgatory. I found only a lush green landscape, a lake surrounded by evergreens and a ski lodge. Purgatory, the woman at the registration desk informed me, was not really a town at all—just a ski resort. Without taking her eyes from the cooking show on the lobby TV, she told me the name's origins are a mystery to her. "Have a fun day," she said. It was at least reassuring to know they were skiing in Purgatory.

The reluctance to take advantage of that devilish highway designation was a harbinger of things to come. Just a couple of years later, US Route 666 would be wiped off the map, renamed US Route 491. Not much to work with there. If you add the numbers together you get fourteen. Apparently, in a Tarot deck, card fourteen represents moderation. Phoo.

One way or another, Christian theology can lend a particular power to potential travel destinations. But for the most unusual Christian tourist attractions you must return to Japan. There you will find Christian-themed sites that, depending on your perspective, either suffer or benefit from a near-complete absence of Christian tradition.

Japan's main religious traditions are Shinto and Buddhist. There are Japanese Christians, but it's not easy to find them. You can find Christ in Japan, though. All you need is a map or a GPS device. He's buried in the northern town of Shingō, alongside his brother. Helpful highway signs point you to *Christ Grave*.

Shingō (formerly known as Herai) is a village in Aomori Prefecture, the northernmost part of the main island of Honshu. Located just east of Lake Towada, the town has been steadily losing residents since 1950, when the population was three times its current size of about 2,200. Local farmers grow garlic, yams, chrysanthemums and tobacco. But about a century ago, one local man claimed that something else had been planted here—the Christian Messiah.

The legend was recounted in a set of documents apparently found by a Shinto priest and conveniently said to have been destroyed during World War II. The story they told was that Jesus first came to Japan as a young man, a period of his life overlooked in the Gospels. Jesus became a garlic farmer and studied Buddhist principles. (According to the same manuscripts, Jesus was following a well-worn path—the Buddha, Confucius and Moses had all previously undergone religious training in Japan.) Eventually Jesus's Japanese brother, Isukiri, took his place on the cross and Jesus escaped back to northern Japan via Siberia. Jesus changed his name to Torai Tora Daitenku (he was on the lam, remember), married and lived to be 106. Members of a Shingō family claim lineage to Jesus. The two graves in Shingō are said to be of Jesus and Isukiri, though the latter contains only the unfortunate brother's ear, saved by Jesus before he fled. Now visitors arrive to see the graves and buy ice cream. It brings to mind what comedian Steve Martin said of King Tut: "He gave his life for tourism."

The story certainly raises questions. For one thing, if it's true, the religion really ought to centre on Isukiri. He's the true hero of the tale. But let's not dismiss the legend out of hand. It's not as though no one else has come up with similar tales, many of them focusing on those gap years in Jesus's Gospel history. Perhaps the most beloved of all English hymns, "Jerusalem" is based on a poem by William Blake that draws on an ancient legend of Jesus visiting Albion: "And did those feet in ancient times / Walk upon Englands [sic] mountains green?" The Book of Mormon claims Jesus came to America. Others have written that Jesus visited India before returning to Judea.

Theologians and historians have argued that the teachings of Jesus could well have been influenced by Buddhism. As for the mysterious disappearing Japanese documents that tell the story—remember, we don't have the original Gospels either. Altogether, there is as much accurate history behind the grave of Christ as you'll find at the Creation Museum.

There are more unusual expressions of Christianity in Japan. Just as Western celebrities have from time to time adopted fashionable paraphernalia from world religions, Japanese culture has taken on Christian forms and symbols as stylistic motifs. In Osaka's Kita-ku district I visited one location of the Christon Café (there is one in Tokyo as well). It's a cozy spot decorated with Catholic iconography—statues of the Virgin Mary, images of Jesus, votive candles—and lit disco-style. It's available for party rentals.

Once you've seen the grave of Jesus and his heroic brother in Aomori, you can head a little southwest to Ishikawa Prefecture to find the grave of Moses. In the town of Hōdatsushimizu, farmer Hiroshi Koshino guides tourists to a spot on his property which, he insists, is the burial place of the Hebrew prophet. The story of Moses's time in Japan makes Jesus's Japanese expedition look routine. Moses and the Japanese emperor's daughter gave birth to Romulus, future founder of Rome. And the Japanese legend also claims that Moses was transported to northern Japan in a spaceship.

What's more, the spaceship story is not particularly unusual for that region of Japan. When Kyoko and I make our own pilgrimage to Ishikawa's Hakui City, it is in pursuit of UFOs—or at least, their terrestrial caretakers.

CHAPTER TWENTY-ONE

Kyoko and the UFOs

Kyoko and I were preparing for a trip to the Noto Peninsula on the northern coast of Japan when the man we were travelling to see called with a friendly piece of advice about our visit. "Don't stay out too late tonight," said Johsen Takano. "Aliens will abduct you."

He was only half joking.

Then Kyoko fielded another call, this one from a concerned friend. "Don't stay out there too late," she said. "North Koreans will abduct you."

She was absolutely serious.

The Noto Peninsula is one spooky piece of turf—Japan's Alien Central, in at least three different ways. A 1997 *Los Angeles Times* story had detailed an influx of people-smuggling boats landing on the largely deserted coastline.

And, hysterical friends aside, residents of the Noto did indeed cast worried looks to the sea as twilight fell—the fishing boats plying the waters off this northern spit were not always what they seemed. Just over the empty horizon lies North Korea. Like visitors from a hostile galaxy, spy boats from this planet's most isolated society, decorated with bogus trawling gear, electronically probed the Noto. Local authorities call them *fushin-sen*, or suspicious boats. Japanese news programs reported cases of Noto residents snatched from local beaches after stumbling upon paranoid North Korean operatives. These particular alien abductions were real.

But neither spies nor refugees made the Noto a magnet for space cases from all over Japan and beyond. Johsen Takano did that. In July 1996, this Buddhist priest, engineer and Porsche racer distilled the Noto's timeless tradition of strange visitors into a single fifty-million-dollar edifice. In the little beachfront town of Hakui City, about an hour north of Kanazawa, Takano created Cosmo Isle. That's where we are heading. Kyoko, who seems to have connections everywhere, has scored me a meeting and interview with Takano. They are old friends.

The highway to Hakui City runs along beachfront property that would make any developer weep—long, sandy oceanfront strands that cry out for multi-storey holiday monstrosities. And yet, despite the reasonably warm May weather and the fact that this is Golden Week—the national furlough when most of this workaholic country drops tools for an orgy of travel and tourism—the beaches are empty save for a smattering of families wading for clams. As we drive, Kyoko assures me the Japanese like a sandcastle as much as the next person. Still, you get the impression this part of the country does not share the North American worship of sand and surf. Lift the Noto Peninsula in a mothership, drop it off on the New York coast, and you'd have the summer headquarters of every Manhattanite important enough to screen calls. But here? Gaze out over the mostly empty sand and you'd be forgiven for assuming *Noto* is Japanese for "godforsaken."

UFO sightings have become pretty common in Hakui City. We drive past the giant saucer that sits above the UFO Pachinko Parlor on the road into town. Plenty of shops and businesses sport alien-derived names, and a big, bubble-domed ship sits perched atop a stolid-looking building that I take to be a hotel. Kyoko informs me it's probably a clinic.

Soon we arrive at Cosmo Isle, marked by a real NASA Mercury-Redstone booster rocket out front, the type that sent the Project Mercury capsules into orbit during the late 1950s and early 1960s. Combined with the building's low dome shape, it gives the facility the look of a science mosque with a single minaret.

Cosmo Isle is the world's biggest self-described "UFO science center and Habitable Zone." Never mind the bus tours—Takano is aiming for the intergalactic cruise ship trade. "Some people do say it looks like a landing strip," he tells me with a shy smile.

Twenty-five years before our visit, Johsen Takano first became interested in extraterrestrials while working as a science fiction scriptwriter for Japanese TV. "I translated books on the UFO phenomenon," he says, naming George Adamski's *The Flying Saucers Have Landed* as the first to grab his interest.

It's not as though Takano was lacking career prospects. With an engineering degree from one of Japan's top universities, a flourishing TV-writing career and his position as a priest at his family's Buddhist temple, Takano hardly needed the aggravation involved in pioneering a rather unorthodox educational centre. Besides, he admits, "I have never seen a UFO." No matter. These kinds of crusades take faith.

He began pitching the project around 1989, and eventually found his efforts dovetailing with a government program designed to rain development cash on disadvantaged areas. Apparently, a UFO museum and landing pad is just what your average Japanese bureaucrat wants to see in a public works project. Cosmo Isle, which opened in July of 1996, ended up costing 52 billion of the taxpayers' yen—a little shy of fifty million US dollars.

Once inside, you'd have to say the government got their money's worth. Takano's facility has drawn tens of thousands looking to take in its canny blend of legitimate space-exploration displays and full-on extraterrestrial theorizing. Among other items, NASA coughed up a spare lunar module, a lunar rover, a Mercury capsule, and the spacesuit of Eugene Cernan, the last man to walk on the moon. The Russians contributed a Luna 24 probe of the type that retrieved samples of moon dust and, most impressively, a spherical Vostok capsule that actually took a cosmonaut beyond the surly bonds of Earth in 1967. "I have many friends in NASA," Takano says by way of explanation, "and a friend who was in the KGB." He must know somebody in Hollywood, too—Cosmo Isle boasts Tom Hanks's prop spacesuit trunk from *Apollo 13*.

All well and good for the human exhibits. But the conspiracy demographic is interested in different species. Takano has that covered, too. Visitors can peruse an actual FBI UFO file, and a thick binder of declassified CIA reports on saucer sightings and their possible security implications. Other Cosmo Isle displays feature the scientific work of the American research organization SETI, the Search for Extraterrestrial Intelligence.

Takano's engineering background is evident in the dry video loops of eminent professors who analyze UFO photos or postulate on the unlikelihood of ball lightning being mistaken for flying saucers. Here the museum takes on the earnest tone of the zealot who buttonholes you at a party to expound on Area 51—at least, until you get into the elevator. As the doors slide shut the lights suddenly snap off, replaced by black light that reveals bright galaxies on the elevator walls. For an engineer, Takano's a fun guy.

Takano clearly wants to keep Cosmo Isle free from the taint of sensationalism. In this field though, you unavoidably end up under the tent with some odd characters. He once appeared on a Kanazawa TV station with Raël, the Frenchman formerly known as Claude Vorilhon who states that aliens wrote the Bible, and whose Raëlian cult is dedicated to free sex, cloning experiments and a plan to build their own alien embassy and landing strip. "He's just crazy," Takano says simply.

As we head back to the parking lot we pass by a little attraction we missed on the way in. Most visitors will. Sitting unobtrusively beside the front walkway is a young apple tree. Although small, its pedigree is impressive—this particular specimen was a cutting that originated in Isaac Newton's garden. And it's no bogus Moses, either—"You can check the DNA," Takano insists, hypothetically.

An apple tree from the garden of the man who invented modern physics—yes, perhaps even a clone of the tree that once dropped an apple onto the noggin that would formulate the laws of gravity, as told in that famous story. A story which happens to be bullshit.

Takano laughs. "Of course it wasn't true," he says of the Newton legend. He says goodbye, and we are left to contemplate his slyest exhibit. The perfect symbol of Cosmo Isle—a living slice of genetic history, taken from the very place where scientific discovery bleeds into myth.

I once visited that other notable UFO museum, located in Roswell, New Mexico, the mecca of extraterrestrial tourism. Far more North Americans have heard of Roswell than have ever heard of Hakui City. But Hakui City's UFO attraction got something Roswell's did not—fifty million dollars. The difference, I can testify, is evident. The most memorable exhibit I saw at Roswell's UFO museum was the alien autopsy display, featuring a mannequin doctor and a green rubber alien on the slab. It did not rise to the level of a window display at Macy's.

But at least the Roswell UFO museum is clear in its focus. Cosmo Isle is different. It occupies a liminal space between science and science fiction. The exhibits are legit—those are real spacecraft on display—but the mix of space exploration artifacts with UFO themes serves as a reminder that the real agenda here is not science. It's tourism.

Cosmo Isle reminds me a little of Shingō's grave of Christ. Be it in science or religion, principles rarely survive the exigencies of capitalism.

At the recommendation of Mr. Johsen, Kyoko and I head off to experience another local attraction—a little restaurant called UFO Ramen. It's a modest little corner shack with a smiling, cartoon alien flying across a patch of bright orange siding. Back home in Vancouver ramen is considered Japanese fare. But tell that to Japanese natives and they're shocked—to them, ramen is definitely alien food. They'll tell you it came from China. (Multiculturalism is more complex than I had realized, especially in the culinary field. Not only does almost every nation have its own unique culinary culture, many nations possess their own unique version of another nation's culture. Vancouver has a great restaurant called Green Lettuce that serves Indian-style Chinese food.)

Chef Satoru Kawara is a wiry, balding bantam whose father had started the restaurant fifty years before our visit. It wasn't UFO Ramen back then, of course—Cosmo Isle, which gave rise to so many other opportunistic UFO-themed businesses, has only been around for five years at the time of our visit. Through Kyoko, I ask Satoru when he changed the little diner's name. When the answer finally winds its way back, I assume there's been a mistranslation. But there's no mistake. Satoru just told me that UFO Ramen has been so called for fifteen years. And now I begin to discover why Cosmo Isle's location on the Noto Peninsula was not merely a matter of government caprice.

Long before Johsen Takano conceived of Cosmo Isle, Hakui City was already UFO town. Satoru produces a leaflet telling of Keta Taisha, the ancient shrine located about ten minutes' drive away, where a twelve-hundred-year-old manuscript speaks of fiery, flying objects—*souhachibon*—heading slowly across the sky from east to west. A *souhachi* is a Buddhist altarpiece that resembles a cymbal or straw hat; *bon* means tray or platter. An accompanying illustration of a strange being is thought by many to represent an alien visitor. Here too is the connection between Moses and UFOS—Hiroshi Koshino cites a 1930s book claiming that the Biblical prophet was conveyed to his patch of farmland on a "heavenly floating ship."

In another long-established local tradition, generations of Noto parents have warned their children (just as Kyoko and I were warned) not to stay out too late for fear that *nabe huri*—roughly, flying pots—would descend and carry them away. Chef Satoru renamed his restaurant after hearing many friends speak of UFO sightings. Although he had not seen one himself at the time, Satoru claims he has since seen two. "One February I saw one in the sky. It raced up quickly," he tells Kyoko. "I cried out to my wife, but it disappeared."

Soon Satoru brings out the UFO ramen itself. This being Japan, where attention to detail is crucial, the chef hasn't slapped a UFO moniker on just any bowl of noodles. Satoru's creation is a miniature Spielbergian epic in a bowl. Every item in the broth represents some aspect of an alien visitation: that large clam is the ship; the baby squid, the alien. A slice of egg is the moon and ribbons of seaweed, the dark night. Even the little bean sprouts are blades of grass blown back by the spaceship's mighty engines (those would be the fish cakes with the pink swirls). All this for a reasonable price, and damn tasty too.

Wherever you go in the country, you'll find the Japanese are serious about food. That means museums. Almost every popular dish will have its own. The Shin-Yokohama Ramen Museum near Tokyo is impressive, offering some history, a recreation of an old-fashioned Japanese village neighbourhood and a lot of great ramen restaurants. Meanwhile Osaka's CupNoodles Museum celebrates Momofuku Ando, the inventor of the instant ramen that has powered a million bachelor degrees. And yes, there's an *okonomiyaki* museum in Hiroshima (where they favour a noodle-based variation on the recipe). It's a great idea. The Smithsonian in Washington would be even more popular if it featured an interactive taco exhibit.

Food museums, impressive UFO facilities, short canals, massive statues—all strategies for diverting some modest tributary of tourist cash to neglected byways. Certain places on the planet, however, have the opposite problem. For some destinations tourism becomes a flood tide, one that threatens the very elements the tourists have supposedly come to experience.

Want to visit that cool spot you saw at the movies? Come for the scenery—stay because you are packed too tight to move your arms.

CHAPTER TWENTY-TWO

Not Now, Voyager

The film *The Beach* arrived in theatres in 2000. It stars Leonardo DiCaprio as a young man who is invited to join friends on a secret, secluded cove—"A paradise few have ever experienced," intones the trailer. Fifteen years later it was probably harder to find a visitor to Thailand who hadn't. Maya Bay on Phi Phi Island, filming site for the movie, was entertaining as many as six thousands visitors per day. The beach is approximately 250 metres long and fifteen metres wide. Tokyo subway cars are less crowded.

Boats clogged the bay to the point where you could almost walk across it. The impact on local marine life was devastating. Thrashing feet and flippers battered the underwater coral formations until an estimated 50 percent were destroyed. Eventually even tourism-happy Thai authorities could not tolerate the situation. The beach was closed for three and a half years starting in 2018, and restrictions are still in place limiting the number of visitors at any one time. Lovely as it is, Maya Bay now stands as a testament to the destructive power of mass tourism. The road to hell is paved with recommendations from Tripadvisor.

To be fair though, Tripadvisor reviews long ago began reflecting the new reality of Maya Bay. In 2017 a British visitor named Olga M. posted,

"Cheek to cheek, so to speak. Selfie sticks ready to poke out your eyes … There are so many tourists, all my pics look like I've photographed ants on an ice-cream lolly."

Ending up in a confined space with six-thousand-odd people seems less like a vacation and more like the consequence of showing up in court with an incompetent lawyer. It is hard to understand how watching a movie about discovering a secluded bit of paradise might inspire someone to sign up for a beachfront Woodstock.

Other beaches have met similar fates. The Philippine island of Boracay was named the world's best island by *Travel + Leisure* magazine in 2012. By 2018 the government shut the beach down for six months, in part to stop the dumping of raw sewage into the ocean. Success on that front has reportedly been limited, due to cost-cutting and corruption. However, Boracay has recently achieved a reputation as the most Bitcoin-friendly destination outside of El Salvador.

Overtourism became a major issue in the twenty-first century. Crowds besiege popular beaches, destinations and monuments, clutching dog-eared copies of *1,000 Places to See Before You Die* as they race the clock. Perhaps if Leonardo da Vinci were alive he could devise an ingenious method of getting more than fifteen seconds to look at the *Mona Lisa*.

The problem of overtourism led Fodor's Travel to create a "No List" for besieged spots tourists should avoid, for their own good and more importantly for the health of the destinations themselves. The "No List" published in November 2019 included Bali. "In 2017 a 'garbage emergency' was declared over the amount of plastic on beaches and in waters," Fodor's said. "The Bali Environmental Agency recorded that the island produced 3,800 tons of waste every day, with only 60% ending up in landfills—an obvious observation to anyone visiting the island."

Fast forward to 2021. From January to October, Bali recorded forty-five international tourist arrivals. Forty-five people. That's a single tour bus. Who knew Fodor's possessed such power?

It was of course not Fodor's but COVID-19 that caused Bali tourism to stop like Wile E. Coyote smacking into a painted tunnel. And Fodor's had not been warning of a pandemic when they advised people to stay away. Still, the arrival of coronavirus and its global spread could stand in for a host of issues. It serves as a reminder that if travel problems are not fixed, they may fix themselves in uncontrollable ways.

Anyway, no need to concern yourself about the potential issues that might face a tourist-free world. According to the United Nations World Tourism Organization, international arrivals were up by 172 percent for the period of January to July 2022 when compared to the same period in 2021, with positive numbers from every global region. Revenge travel, they called it. Just who is the victim of this vengeance is a matter of opinion.

Various destinations have been struggling to find solutions for crowd management. Among the most unexpected twenty-first-century crowd magnets was Iceland.

The recent history of Icelandic tourism is a rather bizarre tale—a cascade of lucky catastrophes no marketing strategy could ever devise. Per Unheim, head of Icelandic public affairs and trade in Canada, says the country's tourist boom was largely fuelled by a natural disaster. "The major Grímsvötn volcanic eruption in May 2011 really put Iceland on the map," he says. "People started seeing these brilliant images and dramatic landscapes and wanted to come. It was a twist on the historical record of eruptions causing out-migration." (A similar phenomenon did take place in Pompeii, although the process took a little longer.)

But it wasn't the island's first beneficial crisis. Iceland's ambassador to Canada, Hlynur Guðjónsson, says the 2008 financial crisis also played a role. As the global banking system reeled, Iceland was hit hardest—all three of the country's major banks defaulted and the Icelandic króna collapsed in value. Suddenly Iceland was in every newspaper. "Over seven weeks in October and November 2008 we had over 660 articles on the Icelandic economy in top-tier US media outlets," Guðjónsson says. "I was in New York at the time. You'd take a taxi, the cabbie would ask where you're from and then say, 'Aren't you bankrupt or something?' So we got an enormous amount of attention. It started out a little negative. And then it turned into a much more positive review of Iceland, how the government was responding to the crisis.

"At the same time the devaluation of the króna made Iceland a value destination. We sent out a press release in September 2008 and told the story of the McDonald's hamburger. It had cost twelve dollars [in Reykjavík]. Now it was six dollars. Icelandair saw a huge jump year-over-year for September. We realized that the US consumer was OK maybe with paying $150 or $200 a night for a hotel, $300 for airfare—but it was out of the question to pay twelve dollars for a McDonald's hamburger."

Apparently there is no such thing as bad publicity. But there is such a thing as too much success. "Their marketing was great," says Claire Newell of Travel Best Bets. "But they were nowhere near ready in terms of infrastructure. Iceland is a place that has three hundred thousand people and they see more than a million tourists a year."

"We reached a peak in 2018, around 2.2 million travellers coming through Iceland," Unheim says. "And yeah, initially Iceland did not really have all the infrastructure in place to manage those numbers appropriately. Sites were being damaged. There weren't sufficient gates and guidance infrastructure, washrooms, campsites, hotels, to meet that volume.

"But over the last decade, that's improved drastically. The pandemic allowed us to catch up. The pandemic also was a welcome breather for Icelanders who finally were able to really, after many years, kind of enjoy the country for themselves. Demand has now come back, and we're again projecting 2.2 million visitors for 2024."

No destination has faced more crowd control issues than Venice, the international capital of travel glut. Venice is in danger of becoming the first major world city eaten alive by tourism, its dwindling population replaced by throngs of cruise ship day trippers until it reaches a critical level, below which it no longer functions as a community. The designated mayor of Venice will be whoever disembarks first on a given day.

"One of the things Venice did [that] I thought was interesting was put up turnstiles to charge visitors coming in," says Greg Oates of travel consultants MMGY. "And that didn't work out so well."

In fact it was locals who objected, tearing down the turnstiles as an offence to their dignity. "There was the idea that if you put up turnstiles you are turning it into a Disneyland," Oates says. "But it already is a Disneyland."

"I think that sort of thing is going to happen around the world," says Newell. "When I was a little girl I was allowed to touch Stonehenge. You can't even get close anymore. At Machu Picchu I was able to walk on it with my family. But people will not be allowed to do that."

Venice eventually opted for subtler alternatives to turnstiles, charging day trippers a fee that changes according to the expected traffic, and a sliding scale of smaller fees for hotel stays.

My own two-day stay in Venice, back in 2002, was disillusioning. From canal to table, my companions and I faced price gouging and thinly veiled hostility. Yet when I saw what service staff had to put up with, I couldn't really blame them. I watched one tourist barge into a man setting tables, knocking him sideways and then walking away without a backward glance. I caught the waiter's eye and he merely shrugged. For him, clearly, it was just another day in Venice. (I confess to some cruel enjoyment as I walked past a shell game being operated on the Ponte dell'Accademia just as an American woman plaintively asked, "But do I get my fifty euros back?")

"The most toxic word in the global tourism industry is *capacity*," says Oates. "Nobody wants to talk about capacity limits. Tourism is a business. Tourism businesses hire a lot of people and bring in a lot of taxes that provide a lot of community services."

Part of the issue is seasonal. "A responsibility of anyone working in the travel and tourism industry is to try to get people travelling in off-peak times," Newell says. "If you don't have kids that are pigeon-holed to summer vacation or winter break, why not go to, say, Europe in April, May or early June, or late September, early October? Those are my favourite times to go anyway. Of course it will be different times of year for different destinations. But going in those off-peak times is a way to make the impact not so brutal on the residents."

"Maybe you want to shift volumes across the week rather than just the weekend," Oates says. "So you would bring in reservation systems like they have done in Banff. Banff has done a nice job of introducing reservation systems for buses—you have to buy a ticket so they can manage the flow. It's not to say that there are fewer people in a week. It's just about not having three-hour lineups."

"Set quotas, raise entrance·fees and use the additional funds raised to create new jobs for locals and pay for carbon offsets," says Bangkok University's Edward Koh. "These are all good things to do."

I love Rome and on every visit I am reminded that I share that love with millions. It's why I try to steer clear of spots like the Trevi Fountain. Featured in a number of movies—1953's classic *Roman Holiday*, 1954's *Three Coins in the Fountain* and, most memorably, the 1960 movie *La Dolce Vita* when Anita Ekberg and Marcello Mastroianni waded in its waters—the Trevi is mobbed all day, every day. It's unlikely many members of those throngs have ever seen Federico Fellini's classic film but the fountain's fame has become self-sustaining. It's a guidebook must-see. Trevi is beautiful. But Rome has a wealth of beauty and history, arguably the most of any city. The mobs around Trevi have a dispiriting feel, the mindless quality that goes with compulsory tourism. Trevi functions like a bug light.

La Dolce Vita's fountain scene was filmed on a series of cold nights in March 1959, which allowed Ekberg and Mastroianni to wade in peace. But there weren't as many crowds around anyway—tourist numbers in Rome approximately sixty-five years ago were a fraction of current totals. Cheap airfare has been a boon for tourism. It has made international travel afford-able to people who in another era could never have dreamed of a grand tour. It has also been, environmentalists say, a disaster for the planet.

Earlier I reported Professor William Rees's drastic solution of a com-plete ban on air travel. After giving the idea some thought I contacted Rees again, suggesting that such a ban, even if possible, would unavoidably fall upon economy-class passengers and exclude the very wealthy, the govern-ment and the military, none of whom could ever feasibly be denied access to air travel.

"Probably correct," he replied. "In other words, things will be pretty much the same for climate provisions as everything else. The wealthy already get away with all sorts of things beyond the capacity of mere mortals—tax breaks, if not outright tax evasion, come to mind. Inequality has always been a fact of human life, at least in so-called 'organized' or 'civilized' societies. I'm not condoning these sorry realities, merely pointing them out as a fact of human social organization. Humans in groups are a hierarchical species. We establish pecking orders, just like chickens and horses.

"On the other hand, the coming energy shortage could shut down airlines. If governments get sensible about climate change yet recognize that there are as yet no quantitative substitutes for fossil fuels, then we should see the remaining fossil fuel budget allocated to essential uses only."

Travel agent Shalene Dudley takes strong issue with that argument. "I have my own bone to pick with sustainability," Dudley says. "Supporting tourism for countries that base their economy on tourism is sustainable. If a country's GDP is based on tourism and we stop going there, what happens? Let's worry about people who can't even get to their families when they are bereft of resources. People can't even eat and you're worried about the carbon footprint? Sustainability is important. But you can't have all these other things without the human element. If you want people to be able to work together to conquer these problems we need to support each other. If people aren't eating every day they're not worried about their carbon footprint. That's not on their hierarchy of needs."

Professor Rees counters that climate change will hit the lower economic classes hardest. "Bottom line," he says, "poorly handled, climate change is likely to exacerbate the divisions between rich and poor within countries and between wealthy and developing nations. That said, the key word is *potential*—if people are sufficiently enraged, we could have an equitable situation from below."

When discussing overtourism, issues of class are hard to avoid. In *Overbooked*, Elizabeth Becker contrasts two cruises she took with her husband—one on Royal Caribbean's *Navigator of the Seas*, and one on the much smaller *National Geographic*–sponsored ship *Sea Lion*. Becker points out that the *Sea Lion* paid its staff a living wage (whereas Royal Caribbean staff were dependent upon tips to augment appallingly meagre salaries), had a much smaller passenger load and offered a more intimate and illuminating exploration of natural wonders as opposed to relentless flogging of deals on handbags and bracelets. The *Sea Lion* experience, Becker says, was vastly more enjoyable. It was also significantly more expensive—$4,800 for an eight-day cruise in 2011. Doing things the right way and paying people fairly for their labour costs money. If a cheaper alternative is right there for the taking, well—there's a reason Royal Caribbean ships can hold six to seven thousand passengers.

"You have your hard-core conservationists at one end of the spectrum and at the other you have your business owners that have no respect for anything but the bottom line," says Oates. "We need to do a better job of understanding, at what point are we doing a disservice to the environment, to the community and potentially harming a destination permanently through overuse? But the definition of that is so fluid. We have to be cognizant of the impact of travel on the community. That's the three pillars: people, planet, profit."

It isn't only popular destinations like Venice and Bali that are trying to walk the line of sustainability. Small towns, some struggling to survive, are balancing those issues as well. My journey to one such place involved two commuter trains and a languorous bus journey into the heart of Honshu, Japan, there to find a sleepy village recently anointed by the United Nations as an exemplar of wise tourist philosophy.

CHAPTER TWENTY-THREE

Miyama

There are times when Waka Takamido feels like the village villain. "I some-times feel I am doing bad," she says with a laugh.

Takamido is no evildoer. As head of the Miyama Tourism Association (total staff: two) she is engaged in an ongoing effort to revive and preserve her tiny Japanese hometown, about fifty-five kilometres north of Kyoto. It involves a bit of coaxing—in effect, a quiet attempt to encourage a bit of greed. In collaboration with locals, Takamido must find ways to generate the tourist income that will enable its dwindling population to remain in place, while not disturbing the character of a town so quiet it restricts the number of vending machines. The fine line she must walk is illustrative of challenges faced by the travel industry in places far beyond this remote Japanese village.

The United Nations World Tourism Organization, showcasing small towns taking smart and sustainable approaches to tourism, recently rec-ognized Miyama as one of its "Best Tourism Villages." The town has also been acknowledged as an important preservation district by the Japanese government thanks to its many thatched-roof cottages, known as *kayabuki*.

Before COVID-19 hit, Miyama averaged around nine hundred thousand tourist visits per year, most arriving on bus tours from Osaka, Kyoto and Amanohashidate.

On this January morning in 2023 there are about five of us wandering around. No tour buses, no charter jets—we all got here via two trains and a public bus, taking just over two hours to travel the fifty-odd kilometres deep into the countryside. Our reward is a timeless rural vista of thatched roofs, fields dotted with spooky conical haystacks, and low fog over the mountains. The only sound comes from the two local goats. Tokyo this ain't.

It is a beautiful winter morning and on either side of the Yura River the fields stretch away, brown with patches of green. No white anywhere. This is not a good thing—the annual snow lantern festival is coming. "That's a problem," Takamido says ruefully. "This is the first time we have had absolutely no snow. In January we usually have at least one snowfall so this is quite rare. Global warming."

The locals, ever ready, have a backup plan. "I just talked with the villagers before coming here," she says. "A few years ago we had very little snow, so we made balloon lanterns."

Takamido and I are sitting in front of the grandly named Café Milan, in reality a little wooden shop not much bigger than a bus shelter. It is privately owned but the town's other café is community-owned, as is the souvenir shop, folklore museum and a couple of the town's overnight accommodations. Community ownership is part of the Miyama philosophy that has helped the town retain its charm. But there is more to it than that. The residents of Miyama have an attitude to profiteering that the modern traveller rarely encounters, and it is this very attitude that Takamido must discreetly push back on.

"One project I tried to do was make the volunteer guides into professional guides," she says. "We have about ten volunteer guides in this village. We need to make them professional guides in order to get an economic benefit from the tourists. But they don't want to accept the money. If you accept the money you have to be professional, which means you have to study harder than before. They don't want that."

"Taking money is considered a bad thing in the countryside," Takamido says. "While I am working in the office I don't say the word *money*."

Refreshing as that may sound to anyone who has had to run the gantlet of trash-hawking hucksters at virtually any popular destination, the village could probably use a bit more avarice. Like many similar centres it is leaking citizens. "Every year our population drops by about one hundred," Takamido says. "We have 3,400 people now but maybe next year that will be 3,300. We have a beautiful place but unless we earn enough money to support our families we can't do what we want to do."

Takamido herself is a rare bird—a local who came back. "When I was in elementary school I had seven classmates," she recalls. "Only I have come back to Miyama." Not long before our conversation the Japanese government had offered cash to people who follow her example—over ten thousand Canadian dollars per child for families who agree to leave Tokyo for the sticks. Takamido, though, did not need the bribe. She was determined to find some way to combine her personal and professional worlds.

Takamido attended university in Kobe and spent a year in Sheffield, England. But her village called to her. More specifically, it was her dad. "After university most of my classmates went to Tokyo to get a job," she says. "I felt like, is that the only way to live or survive in this world? I want to find a career in the countryside. I didn't start job hunting, because I thought I can start a business in my hometown. Then I got a call from my father." Her father issued an invitation to join the Miyama Tourism Association, which was then being formed. Now her career and her town are one.

Despite the local reluctance to cash in, Takamido says Miyama residents' enthusiasm and ideas are key to what has made the town a model for thoughtful tourism. Initiatives include a January snow lantern festival and a May rice-planting festival. "All the tourism projects came from local people's ideas," she says. "Local governments support the ideas of locals. Local stakeholders all co-operate."

She believes the pandemic pause in tourism had some positive aspects for the town—it reinforced the benefits of tourism. "For more than thirty years people from Miyama have tried to energize the town by welcoming people from the city," she says.

But while local people in Miyama understand how important tourism is in the village, the problem is implementation. "We have ideas but few human resources," she says. "That's a huge problem in Miyama. The local villagers are quite positive about the tourism industry. They have lots of ideas. I regret I can't make everything happen. My staff, we have only two people, including me."

Gazing around at peaceful Miyama with its *kayabuki* on a terraced hillside, I am reminded of a different time and place—yet another Japanese scene introduced to me by my expert tour guide, Kyoko.

In the mountainous, central Japanese prefectures of Gifu and Toyama are several villages that have existed for centuries, built by a defeated clan whose warriors fled into the mountains to hide and, gradually, begin a new life. Now recognized as UNESCO World Heritage sites, they are the Gassho houses of the Shirakawa-gō and Gokayama regions.

Kyoko took me there on a day trip from Kanazawa, down the Hokuriku Expressway that led into the Japanese heartland. Turning off to head into the hills, the route took us through a remarkable ten-kilometre-long tunnel that ran straight through a mountain.

Japanese road trips are oddly familiar but with jarring little twists, like the roadside sign with the silhouette of a samurai herding cattle (I looked everywhere but I didn't see any), rice paddies in place of wheat fields, odd roadside shrines featuring small statues of children, attendants who guide you out of gas stations, and the narrow little cars that make you think you're looking at a widescreen film that's been squeezed onto a small TV. There was even the requisite country music on the car radio—in this case a Japanese genre known as *enka*. Kyoko informed me the plaintive little tune translated roughly to "Treat Me Like a Hooker." Kyoko also helped me identify which hotels on the outskirts of the towns we pass were "love hotels," the colourful accommodations designed for clandestine trysts or young lovers still living with their parents.

Searching for the Gassho houses meant following the trail of the Heike. In twelfth-century Japan, the Genji and Heike clans met in the epic battle of Kurikara. The Genji were victorious, and the surviving Heike were forced to flee for their lives into harsh mountainous terrain where their enemies might not follow. Over the succeeding centuries the Heike evolved into a very different sort of people—silk farmers and ingenious architects whose tall, steeply pitched thatched huts were constructed without nails. Today the Gassho houses are considered marvels of their kind, containing multiple floors that provide indoor habitats for silkworms and space for paper production. The houses are much taller and more steeply pitched than the thatched homes of Miyama. No other structures in Japan are quite the same.

The name *Gassho* translates to "praying hands," a description of the perilously sloped, gabled straw roofs that must be rebuilt on a regular basis (renovations that, Amish-like, involve the entire community). Large windows give needed light and ventilation for the silkworms, but the resulting structural weakness required the invention of a system of internal trusses unique to the Gassho style. It's a design that is thought to have been perfected in the sixteenth century. Declining silk demand led to a sharp decline in Gassho houses, from a pre-war level of around 1,800 to about 150 today. The three remaining Gassho villages on the shores of the Shō River—Ainokura, Ogimachi and Suganuma—look remarkably unspoiled. Except for the tour buses.

Escaping into the mountains worked for about a millennium or so, but eventually the fugitive Heike were found. Not by their ancient enemies, but by a German architect named Bruno Taut who described the Gassho houses in his 1939 book *Rediscovering Japanese Beauty*. Being designated a UNESCO World Heritage site in 1994 was something of a mixed blessing for the villagers. True, it meant a huge boost to the tourist trade, which had long supplanted silk production as an income producer, after nylon supplanted silk in the world market. But it also meant that their cozy homes were now bona fide world treasures and as such were not to be messed with or altered in any way. And it also brought those tour buses.

Kyoko took me to Ogimachi village, where we wandered amongst the tall houses and sampled local treats like grilled mochi on a stick with miso. I couldn't help but notice the souvenir stands allowing visitors to commemorate their visit to the Gassho houses with various Hello Kitty trinkets.

It is this aspect of the tourist trail that Miyama seems determined to avoid. As Takamido tells me, Miyama residents came up with their own set of rules to govern their approach. "After this village was designated as an important preservation area by the national government, they created their own charter," Takamido says. "Keep gardens clean, try not to start new businesses, try not to put vending machines in the road, no new souvenir shops, not to make the village like Disneyland."

Still, Miyama's viability depends on some degree of commercial activity. Although the pre-pandemic tourist numbers were impressive, the visitors don't exactly pave the streets with gold. "They spend less than one thousand yen [about ten Canadian dollars] per day," Takamido says. "If you visit Kyoto the average cost will be twenty thousand yen [about two hundred Canadian dollars] per day."

Miyama does offer many accommodations, including cozy thatched-roof cottage B & Bs. But, Takamido says, "They don't usually stay overnight. They just spend one hour in the village.

"That's why our association is needed in Miyama. We are in the middle between the tourists and the villagers and we create the product. We need the balance."

Overtourism is a scourge. But as Takamido understands, a sensible approach to tourism can be the difference between life or death in an isolated community. "The UN 'Best Tourism Village' definition mentions society, environment and economics," she says, "and this balance is quite important. We have great environment, great culture and society. Our weak point is economics. Without benefits perhaps the town can't survive."

CHAPTER TWENTY-FOUR

Kyoko in Kyoto

Peter MacIntosh and I have an acquaintance in common. A little surprising, since he has lived in Kyoto for thirty years and this is our first meeting. But as we sit at the 2ème Maison café beside the Kamo River in January 2023, I mention a name he recognizes. "Teruhina," he says, nodding. "I saw something about her recently. We met a few times."

I met Teruhina just once, but the occasion was memorable. It was twenty-two years earlier at the Ichiriki Teahouse, the oldest and most venerable geisha establishment in Kyoto's fabled Gion district, a venue so exclusive that even Arthur Golden, the author who set much of his best-seller *Memoirs of a Geisha* within its walls, had never been inside. That I was allowed in was, of course, all because of Kyoko. Once again she had made use of her remarkable connections so that we could spend an evening in the company of Japan's most emblematic entertainers.

MacIntosh, a large man with a greying goatee and receding blond hair, did some scouting and advising for the 2005 movie version of Golden's book. He is in the geisha business, albeit in an indirect way. He does not run a geisha venue, an *ochaya*, much less an *okiya*, the houses where geisha are trained and lodged. Instead MacIntosh arranges geisha outings with foreign clients. Although his well-heeled customers lack the pull to gain entrance to geisha houses (mere money is not enough), MacIntosh himself is a regular and respected client, and thus able to hire geisha for private dinners and parties with his own clientele. I have arranged to meet with him on my return to Kyoto to discuss the current state of the industry.

It is clearly a challenging time for geisha establishments. It has been a disastrous period for Japanese tourism in general. Few countries mounted as drastic a response to COVID-19. Back in February 2020 it was the *Diamond Princess* cruise ship that provided the stage for the coronavirus coming-out party in Yokohama, and Japan subsequently closed its borders to visitors. Even the expensive, much-hyped Tokyo Summer Olympics were sacrificed, postponed for a year and eventually staged largely without spectators while COVID-19 cases spiked across the country.

For the geisha industry the recovery from COVID-19 has not been total. "They're still not coming back as much," MacIntosh says, "because old people are still afraid of corona, and most of the clientele is older. I talked to a geisha I know well, she says it's 60 percent back since COVID. I lost close to a million dollars in possible income. I just about lost my shirt."

Geisha society is largely closed off from the outside world. Established geisha, especially the older ones who entered the industry years ago, often live in an insular environment. "I hired an older geisha about ten years ago and a customer said to me, 'Ask her if she's ever had foreign food.' She said 'Does deep-fried shrimp on rice count?' No, that doesn't count. She said, 'I guess I haven't, then. But once I saw on the television, someone opened a box and there was this gooey, cheesy thing that came out.'"

"It was pizza," MacIntosh says. "She didn't know it was pizza."

The genesis of geisha culture is usually dated to the mid-eighteenth century, and the first geisha were men. Originally assistants to prominent courtesans, geisha gradually became the main attraction, in the process becoming exclusively female. *Okiya* would educate young women in the arts of music, dance, hospitality and presentation. After about four years of training, teenage girls debut as *maiko*, the colourfully garbed novices of the trade. After paying her dues the young *maiko* reaches the day of her *erikae*, or collar-turning, when she becomes a full-fledged geisha.

Early-twentieth-century geisha culture flourished in Kyoto, Kanazawa and Tokyo but World War II dealt a serious blow to the industry. The postwar era too was difficult, partly because Japanese sex workers often wore geisha garb to appeal to American GIs. This led to a blurring of the lines between the geisha and sex industries, at least in the Western mind.

Today the profession continues to grapple with the modern world. MacIntosh feels that in order for geisha culture to survive, certain traditions need to be adjusted—or perhaps acknowledged as already dead. "They are still spreading these little white lies," he complains. "Like '*Maiko* don't have cellphones.' Come on, they do. I can call one right now and she'll answer. You see a taxi go by with a *maiko* in it and her face is blue from the cellphone screen. It's OK to change. What fifteen-year-old is going to enter this profession if she can never have a cellphone?"

Just a few months before my meeting with MacIntosh, the geisha world had been shaken by scandal. A former *maiko* named Kiritaka Kiyoha had sent out a tweet in Japanese that translated to: "This is the reality of being a *maiko*. When I was sixteen, I was made to drink so much alcohol, you could take a shower in it. I was then coerced into mixed bathing—another name for taking a bath with a customer. (Although I tried with all my might to run away.) I would like you to consider if this is truly what one would call traditional culture."

More tweets followed: "I had clients slip their hands through the side openings of my kimono to fondle my breasts, and when in private rooms they'd opened the hems of my kimono so as to touch my crotch. *Maiko* don't generally wear underwear, you see. When I told the house mother about these incidents, she directed her anger at me, saying I was at fault."

"I was close to having my virginity sold ... for ¥50,000,000 [around $370,000 US]. And that money doesn't go to the *maiko* herself ... If no one speaks up, nothing will change. I didn't want to continue in silence when confronted with the annual suicide attempts of my junior *maiko* or their mental anguish ... I don't want the geisha occupation to disappear. The industry should rebuild, aligned in a better direction. I want it to hone the art of those who love the arts, passing down our traditional culture. Until now, it's been a closed occupation. I think it's time for it to open."

Kiritaka's tweets got international coverage. MacIntosh says the impact was almost immediate, and evident at an event he had organized just the previous night. "Now even though the *maiko* was nineteen—they used to get hammered, they'd be walking down the street sloshed—she's not allowed to drink," he says. "Not until they're twenty. So we said 'We'll turn off all the cameras,' and the older *geiko* said 'Top secret.' Even the eighteen-year-old *maiko* aren't allowed to work past ten o'clock now because of the official labour laws."

MacIntosh does feel there have been some positive changes in the industry in recent years. "I think what's going to be the saviour of geisha culture is the number of female customers and couples hiring them," he says. "Back in the days before the bubble burst, you either had money or you didn't. If you had money you hired geisha. And in the days when wives stayed at home only the males hired. Women took care of the house. Japan started getting a little wealthier and couples started going out. Why shouldn't women have fun with geisha? Geisha are charming to everyone, male or female.

"Thirty years ago in Japan, if you weren't married when you were twenty-five years old you were called 'Christmas cake' [a derogatory term for something that has passed its best-before date—no longer wanted after December 25]. That's changed a lot now. Women are getting married in their thirties if they get married at all. So they've got money. That's a big change in geisha culture, the clientele."

The profession may be changing, but through it all the Ichiriki Teahouse has persevered. MacIntosh has not done a lot of business with the Ichiriki—it is a particularly expensive locale. "I'm not a customer there," he says. "I have another teahouse I use. I don't need that extravagance."

Kyoto's tourism approach is somewhat complicated. Geisha culture is intrinsic to Kyoto's identity. Its beautiful and alluring imagery features in much of the city's promotional material, and yet its inner sanctums are off limits to casual visitors. As MacIntosh puts it, "It's a tourist draw, but it isn't."

So it was in Kyoto, more than any other destination, that Kyoko was able to give me a rarefied Japanese experience in that spring of 2001. Before I ever landed in Japan to begin our shared voyage, she had been making arrangements.

Our stay in Kanazawa had come to an end and Kyoko and I were riding the Thunderbird train to Kyoto. As I admired the passing scenery her cellphone began playing "Waltz of the Flowers." Out from the blizzard of unintelligible chatter I caught a word: *Ichiriki*. I knew what it meant. Kyoko was speaking with her good friend Mr. Nakamura. He was telling her that tomorrow night he will escort Kyoko and me through the gates of the most famous geisha house in all of Japan.

Kyoko had also arranged for us to stay at another hallowed Kyoto institution, the Hiiragiya *ryokan*. It has hosted Japanese prime ministers, authors, dignitaries and visiting royalty like Charlie Chaplin. Expensive as our own quarters seemed to me—about five hundred US dollars per night—the real celebrity digs can cost three times as much.

I don't know what the Little Tramp's accommodations were like but our room was typically Japanese—spartan, covered in tatami mats and almost devoid of furniture. The room was windowless except for glass doors on one side that faced onto a small interior courtyard. Two futon beds lay in the centre of the room. They were taken away in the morning and not returned until after supper, except by request. Meals were included and went a long way toward justifying the price; they were magnificent, served in your room by your own personal attendant. Ours was the calm, quietly smiling Keiko, who knocked gently before arriving with fresh courses. "*Ohkini*," I said, showing off my brand new word, regional Kyoto slang for "thank you." In Japanese, Kyoko instructed Keiko to acknowledge my greeting. With a nod and a smile, she did. And it seemed to me utterly sincere.

It was a seasonable early May evening as Kyoko and I set out to meet Mr. Nakamura. As with all Japanese taxis, the back door swung open unaided, and soon the cab was crawling through the narrow streets of Gion. The sight of two women in kimonos excited me, but I am a raw rookie— they were just bar hostesses. The shops looked modern and the street like any Japanese nightclub district, until we crossed Shijō-dōri and the architectural styles receded centuries in an instant.

The Ichiriki is no samurai Studio 54. Greasing the bouncer's palm or being Gisele Bündchen will not get you past the lineup. There is no lineup. The right to patronize the four-hundred-year-old Ichiriki is, like the right to Japanese citizenship, a very tough nut to crack, sometimes involving generations of history. It's also jaw-droppingly expensive, but that's just an afterthought—the real trick is to establish a relationship.

"You know why that is?" MacIntosh would explain to me twenty-two years later. "It's not snobbish. Think about it—you're a geisha, wearing sixty grand worth of clothing. The belts they wear are usually worth twenty thousand dollars. The little brooch they wear, anywhere from five to thirty thousand. A kimono might be ten to fifteen thousand, the obi [knotted belt at the back of the kimono] is maybe another ten to fifteen. And maybe some drunk asshole is spilling wine on them. If he says 'I'm not paying for that,' who's going to take responsibility? But if I spill wine on somebody, and I don't want to pay for it, they're going to call the person who gave me the introduction to the *ochaya*. It will be his responsibility. Someone has to put their reputation on the line for you. It's an insurance policy."

So we would be Mr. Nakamura's responsibility. He is the president of a company that has patronized the Ichiriki since long before the war, which gives him the right to invite guests for an evening's entertainment. That, and perhaps about five grand US. I didn't know for certain how much the evening would cost—our genial host never disclosed the total. Mr. Nakamura would have been offered a variety of options for our evening's entertainment, including traditional games that *geiko* sometimes play with their guests. Kyoko tells me he has selected for our benefit a sort of introductory primer—some dance, some conversation; some *geiko*, some *maiko*. He will be billed accordingly.

Mr. Nakamura is a very successful businessman. That he is also a believer in tradition shows not only in his enthusiastic support of Japan's vanishing geisha tradition, but also in his relationship with Kyoko—Mr. Nakamura is her Go master. Teaching the intricacies of this ancient board game to a select few students is both a hobby and a calling for Mr. Nakamura, himself a champion-level Go player. Hearing that his student's *gaijin* friend was accompanying her to Kyoto, Mr. Nakamura felt honour bound to showcase for us the ultimate in Japanese culture. Naturally, I reciprocated with a nice box of chocolates.

Confusion about the *geiko* world is not limited to foreigners; Japanese citizens too are more likely to be familiar with baseball's Ichiro than Gion's Ichiriki. Throughout *Memoirs of a Geisha* and in guidebooks, places like the Ichiriki are referred to as "teahouses." But Kyoko shook her head emphatically at this. The word *ochaya*, she admitted, can also be translated as "teahouse." But the Japanese language has many words that carry double meanings. *Kumo* can mean spider or cloud; *hashi* can mean bridge or chopsticks. And, Kyoko told me, the Ichiriki is no more a teahouse than the Rainbow Bridge can pluck sashimi out of Tokyo Bay. It is a place for geisha, not for tea.

The Ichiriki's Japanese eminence has little to do with *Memoirs of a Geisha*. Nor does its reputation come merely from age. The Ichiriki's esteemed position comes largely from its role in one of Japan's favourite historical tales—the legend of the forty-seven *rōnin*.

Sometimes called the Akō vendetta, the epic of the forty-seven *rōnin* is so well known that tales and legends surrounding it constitute an entire genre of Japanese storytelling, known as *Chūshingura*. (The postwar American administration even saw fit to ban such performances for several years, considering them unhealthy throwbacks to the feudal age.) The story begins in 1701, during Japan's Edo period (named for the capital city which has since become Tokyo). It begins with a regional warlord (daimyo) who lived in Harima Province. Asano Naganori was young, headstrong and hon-est to a fault, the kind of master who inspired devotion in the samurai who served him. Those samurai, numbering more than three hundred, were led by Ōishi Kuranosuke. His roguish reputation contrasted with that of his respected young master. But Ōishi too was fiercely loyal to his boss.

Regional potentates like Lord Asano served at the pleasure of Japan's overlord—the Shōgun Tsunayoshi, whose Edo palace was then the seat of national power. One day at the shōgun's palace, disaster struck young Asano. Goaded into anger by a treacherous old don named Kira Yoshinaka, Lord Asano lashed out with his sword, wounding his enemy.

Despite the water-cooler consensus that the old bastard deserved far worse, the shōgun was outraged—Asano had tarnished the dignity of the palace with his attack. The disgraced young master was forced to commit seppuku, or ritual suicide. Kira had outmanoeuvred his naive young adver-sary in a fatal game of court politics.

Instantly, Ōishi Kuranosuke and the other samurai were adrift. They had become *rōnin*—in effect, freelance samurai. Their beloved Lord Asano was dead, they were rootless, and Kira Yoshinaka was to blame. Everyone waited for Ōishi Kuranosuke's inevitable revenge.

And Ōishi Kuranosuke said, "Don't hold your breath." Telling anyone who'd listen that he had no interest in anything but the good life, Ōishi holed up at the Ichiriki, partying like it was 1799. While the Ichiriki's exclu-sivity kept Ōishi safely out of sight from any of Kira's mercenaries looking to mop up opposition, the unemployed warrior proceeded to carouse with a string of Gion's loveliest. So effective was Ōishi's endless bender that many of his own followers abandoned him, disgusted at his truly un-samurai-like live-and-let-live attitude. Eventually, only fifty-nine faithful *rōnin* remained. And when almost two years had passed and his enemies had long since relaxed, Ōishi Kuranosuke put down the sake cup and gathered those war-riors around him. He sent thirteen warriors home to their families, leaving forty-six plus himself. On a winter morning in December 1702, these forty-seven *rōnin* attacked the castle of Kira Yoshinaka and overwhelmed the defenders without losing a man. They found their hated rival hiding in an outhouse. Soon Kira's severed head adorned the grave of Lord Asano.

The public acclaimed the forty-seven *rōnin* as heroes, and the shōgun was impressed at their loyalty. A year later they received their reward. Rather than ignominious execution, the general allowed them to commit seppuku as honoured warriors (sparing only the youngest). A truly Japanese happy ending. The forty-seven *rōnin* passed into legend—and with them, the Ichiriki.

Our taxi stopped on the street. A man in traditional dress greeted us and led the way through the gate into an outer courtyard. There was scarcely time to pause for a moment's disbelief at the ease with which we had penetrated an invisible barrier—the one separating modern-guidebook Japan from an ancient world that still carries on alongside, like Brigadoon made visible. We were inside the Ichiriki.

CHAPTER TWENTY-FIVE

Kyoko in the Ichiriki

Peter MacIntosh arrived in Kyoto from his hometown of Halifax in 1993. The Japanese bubble had just burst, commencing a long period of economic stagnation. "I could still smell the remnants of the bubble," he says, "and see people in denial."

His introduction to geisha culture came when he acquired a patron. "I had a sugar daddy who took me around," he recalls. "That's how I got my start. He needed a drinking buddy so he took me under his wing, sort of a surrogate son. He just didn't want to drink by himself anymore. He was born and raised in Kyoto, made his money manufacturing train signals. He hired geisha for dinners and karaoke."

Eventually MacIntosh became a respected client himself. Part of it was immersing himself in geisha culture. "I study professional singing," he says. "I know these geisha songs."

But he says that is increasingly rare these days. "Their clientele is literally dying out. How will they get new customers? Their new customers are these real estate agents. They don't study singing, they don't have a fucking clue about geisha culture. The client with knowledge and sophistication is unfortunately disappearing. There's a responsibility to teach them.

There's one geisha in Tokyo who has seminars for her Japanese customers. They come for group lectures and actually learn the songs. You can learn."

MacIntosh decries the shallowness of online fact-finding. "YouTube sensei," he says, laughing. "Wikipedia sensei. People get instant answers but they have no depth because they didn't learn it. That's what geisha culture has to do—teach. Even the *maiko* don't always know what they're singing. The older ones know. That's why it's an apprentice system. The longer you're in it the more you know. If you don't know where it came from, you can't change the lyrics and have some fun with it. That's where the real entertainment comes."

Needless to say, I was not the ideal audience for a traditional geisha performance with my dozen-or-so-word Japanese vocabulary and clumsy Western ways. Yet here I was at the legendary Ichiriki. What would the geisha make of me?

Smiling and bowing in the entrance, an older woman in a kimono bid us trade our shoes for sandals and, eyeing my six-foot-two frame, pointed to the archway by way of warning. Down red-panelled halls we went until we were shown into a spare Japanese room lined with tatami and furnished only by a low central table with a red lacquer surface. Mr. Nakamura stood to greet us.

He was a small, balding figure in a well-tailored blue suit, a fit-looking sixty-something with an ever-present smile and an intent gaze that suggested your every reaction would be instructive for him. (Kyoko suggested he looked like a Japanese Danny DeVito.) We sat with our legs in the well beneath the skirted table, and Kyoko translated my profuse thanks to Mr. Nakamura for the opportunity he has given us. We had brought *omiyage*, the gifts of greeting and/or gratitude that Japanese friends exchange at every opportunity. There were chocolates from Vancouver and a large bottle of Kanazawa-style sake. But before we could present them the door opened. Our first *geiko* had arrived.

No matter how many photos and documentaries you see, it's impossible to be prepared for this moment. Or perhaps it is precisely the many photos, books and documentaries you have absorbed that increase the sense of wonder and import, yet still leave you unready for the magnificent presence that joins you. She backed into the room, turned and smiled, a red lipstick slash on a shocking white background topped by an elaborate coif of jet-black hair. Finally she knelt to bow and bid *"Okoshiyasu,"* a welcome peculiar to Kyoto.

Her name was Yuiko. She had graduated from the ranks of *maiko* only a year before; her white collar indicated that she was now a *geiko*. Green and pink flowers decorated her kimono of bright-yellow silk, secured by an obi of burgundy with a white bamboo design. When she turned, pink flesh was visible at the back of her neck where the white makeup suddenly stopped. I had heard of this sly technique, intended as an alluring hint of the naked skin beneath the careful makeup. The effect was exactly as advertised—a reminder that beneath this awesome finery is a young woman.

Yuiko was followed shortly by two new arrivals. Like a tiger and its keeper, they presented a striking contrast—Komomo, a modest-looking young *geiko* without makeup or elaborate hair, dressed in a subtle pink kimono and black obi; and Teruhina, as brilliant as her companion was discreet, clad in a kimono of shimmering green and white, with purple and gold flowers, her red-and-white obi, and an elaborate hairpiece of long white flowers and dangling silver bars swaying as she turned and laughed.

Teruhina was a *maiko*. Her gorgeous plumage was not a case of the bridesmaid upstaging the bride—young novices traditionally dress with more flash and colour than older, established *geiko*. Teruhina had joined her okiya two years previous, fulfilling a dream first inspired when a *maiko* visited her classroom at school. As an apprentice, she spent her days studying dance, flower arranging, Japanese drums and shamisen, the three-stringed lute that all *geiko* are expected to master. "It's more fun than I thought it would be," she insisted to me in unsteady English.

The presence of a *maiko* represented no bargain for Mr. Nakamura. In fact, one Japanese friend suggests to me later that *ochaya* guests must pay more for a *maiko*, despite her comparative lack of training and experience. More popular *geiko* and *maiko* can charge higher fees. That may seem only natural but, as Kyoko pointed out to me, it represented a contrast with traditional Japanese corporate culture. Too often Japanese companies are gerontocracies where seniority, regardless of ability, inevitably means prominence. By contrast, Gion is a ruthless meritocracy. Charm or die.

Teruhina's dazzling costume, so soon to be put away forever, may well be intended to mimic the first, passing blush of virginal beauty. And while a refined *ochaya* patron might prefer the company of a mature *geiko*, it would not surprise me to discover that Teruhina's more perishable charms bring a higher price. The disturbing stories later told by Kiritaka Kiyoha offer a potentially unsettling undercurrent to the *maiko*'s appeal.

Now an unexpected honour—the mistress of the Ichiriki arrived to pay her respects in person. Kyoko Sugiura was a lovely woman in a trim hairdo and white and grey kimono. She joined the Ichiriki nineteen years ago via marriage to the owner's son. As Kyoko translated for me, Ms. Sugiura reminded us that the Ichiriki is no drop-in centre. Wads of money are sometimes offered by casual would-be visitors, but to no avail. We were here solely by the grace of Mr. Nakamura—his money would be gratefully accepted on our behalf. Ms. Sugiura explained these things with a pleasant smile; her manner indicated that we were nonetheless honoured guests. For now, at least.

Mr. Nakamura nodded in acknowledgement of his honoured position. He knows Gion well and proclaimed the Ichiriki to be the best *ochaya* of all. Which is a lucky thing, he added with a roar of laughter, because even if the Ichiriki were the lowliest of *geiko* houses he would have no choice—he must spend his money here or stay home. For *ochaya* are not merely hard to enter—once entered, they are difficult to leave. The anonymous barfly is free to flit from speakeasy to roadhouse, but those whose custom is accepted by an *ochaya* are locked into a relationship that tradition expects to be monogamous. Mr. Nakamura's company patronized the Ichiriki long before his time. When he joined the firm, he joined the Ichiriki—for life.

I had brought along my copy of *Memoirs of a Geisha*, wondering what the habitués of modern Gion might think. The mistress of the Ichiriki was familiar with the book and also with former *geiko* Mineko Iwasaki. Iwasaki had recently brought suit against Golden, alleging breach of privacy.

Ms. Sugiura thought the suit was misguided. "Mineko's career came after the war," Ms. Sugiura said, "and most of the book takes place before the war. No one would think the book is about Mineko."

As filtered through Kyoko, Ms. Sugiura's attitude toward *Memoirs* seemed dismissive. She pointed out that to the best of her knowledge the author has never been inside the Ichiriki, agreeing with Kyoko that this is not a teahouse and should not be called one. Nobody in Gion cares about the book, she claimed.

Maybe not, but Komomo had certainly read it. "I'm Komomo, not Hatsumomo," she said, laughing, making reference to *Memoirs'* nasty *geiko* villain. "She's cruel!"

Komomo, visually the least prepossessing of the trio, made up for her relatively straightforward appearance (she wore no evident makeup) with skill and accomplishment. Her presence tonight probably had something to do with her English, which though limited was by far the best of the three women. More talents soon became evident.

Komomo, Yuiko and Teruhina left the room briefly. Komomo soon returned with a shamisen. Taking it to the far side of the room, she knelt and waited. Now Yuiko and Teruhina re-entered, each carrying a cone-shaped platter covered with pink flowers. As Komomo began to pluck the shamisen and sing a quavering melody, they danced. Their song was called "Flower Umbrella," and they performed without expression. Emotion was conveyed through movement, not mugging.

The next song caused Kyoko to sigh—her mother sang it to her long ago. As Yuiko and Teruhina glided through a wistful pas de deux, Komomo sang of life in Gion—pain and grief unseen beneath white makeup. "*Gion, kanashiiya darari-no-obi-yo* ..." Gion, like a sad, drooping obi, trailing behind a *maiko* as she walks.

Loud applause from our small group, and the performers returned to their social roles at the table. Mr. Nakamura was well past his first sake and looking quite at home. I was striving to converse with my exotic table-mates but frequently required translation by Kyoko and Komomo, and in the general hubbub the system often broke down—I'd ask a question about Go and get an answer about golf. Most of what was being discussed flowed by me like dinner conversation past the family dog. In fact, I later learned that entire parallel evenings were going on without my knowledge; for example, Kyoko's valiant efforts to parry constant paternal questioning from Mr. Nakamura about the exact nature of our relationship.

Sake and conversation are central to the *geiko*'s art. It has been said that a superb *geiko* will entertain through wit and charm while a lesser talent, if she's wise, will pour sake down a customer's throat until wit and charm become irrelevant. All of which made me sorry for my new friends, since I represented a *geiko*'s worst nightmare—I spoke almost no Japanese and didn't drink. This could prove to be the Japanese equivalent of a sober St. Patrick's.

Still, we all struggled for common ground. I spoke of my wonder at the breathtaking speed and energy of Tokyo, pointing out that the metropolitan area of the Japanese capital has a population equal to that of my entire nation. And since that nation is Canada, my *geiko* companions assured me of their sincere intention to visit Niagara Falls someday.

"I like the music of Alanis Morissette," Komomo informed me, displaying her ready knowledge of Canadian pop stars. "I once neglected my studies for an important exam so that I could see Bryan Adams in concert."

Yuiko and Teruhina also expressed their admiration for the Vancouver-based rocker. And to my horrified amazement, I found myself talking about the night he sat at the table beside mine in an all-night restaurant. Well, damn it, I wasn't faced with a lot of conversational options here.

But this nattering about celebrities was oddly fitting. In a way, the world of the Ichiriki is like the world of *Entertainment Tonight*. The modern worship of fame has created an entire population that would swoon over the merest brush with Brad Pitt. And the aura and spectacle of this *geiko* world had left me eager to make any contact, forge any bond, with these women. Their job was to entertain and yet, conditioned by decades of desperate party chatter, I was incongruously worried that they'd get bored with me.

The conversation hiccupped along carefully, through a combination of simple, direct statements and relayed translations. But so focused was

I on bridging the linguistic divide, I soon realized I had failed to consider another gulf—these young women and I were born seven US presidents apart. Add Yuiko and Teruhina's ages together and I still came away with an extra four years' worth of pension contributions. Beneath its mesmerizing exterior, this encounter with living embodiments of Japanese history was basically a flirtation with a teenager and a couple of twentysomething young women. One underscored by centuries of tradition and the weight of a nation's disappearing heritage, but nonetheless.

Teruhina had moved to sit beside me now, poking through my reporter's notebook. Flipping to a back page, she drew a little heart. Then, touching her finger to her bright red lips, she transferred the scarlet smudge to redden the little ink heart on the page. "Secret," she told me.

I impressed Teruhina with the special Bruce Lee watch I bought in Tokyo—his nunchucks moved in time with the second hand. She responded by laying out her own personal treasures. Teruhina was in fact bedecked with an emperor's ransom of finery—the collar of her kimono alone probably cost five thousand dollars, and she wore a jewelled belt with a diamond and ruby buckle that was among the most valuable possessions of her *okiya*, worth perhaps fifty thousand dollars. But these were not the things she showed me—my Bruce Lee timepiece required a different response. Proudly she produced her own Hello Kitty watch and a Tintin keychain. Soon she was admiring my new Astro Boy wallet, purchased in the Ginza district of Tokyo. We were thick as thieves.

Five or ten grand to trade pleasantries about Bryan Adams and Niagara Falls? It had a surreal quality best appreciated when the cash was coming out of someone else's shoe. But at last, God help me, I was beginning to get a glimpse of what really pays the bills in Gion. And it's not sex—that's not even on the table, though it may be lurking under it, down in that foot well somewhere or peeking out of that little pink gap in the makeup. No, it's the chance to be flirted with by a sort of costumed superhero whose powers are of fascination—Captain Coquette, Sultana of Spark, had eyes only for me tonight.

But it was a sign of Teruhina's bright career prospects that she kept an eye on Kyoko, too. Unaware of our relationship when she entered the room (Kyoko and I had been seated at opposite ends of the table all evening) Teruhina clearly figured it out pretty quickly and took pains to put Kyoko at ease. When Kyoko innocently asked what Teruhina wrote in my notebook, the *maiko* happily displayed her artwork with a friendly laugh. So much for our little secret.

Ms. Sugiura did not find Kyoko's presence unusual. Women, she explained, have been guests at the Ichiriki for over a century. And as Kyoko assured me later, the evening held considerable interest for her. "I enjoyed watching you, too," she told me, with a look that mixed equal parts amusement and threat. Apparently I was not the only one taking notes.

By now Yuiko had excused herself to attend another engagement. Ms. Sugiura offered to show us around the Ichiriki. Down the hall we entered a large central room, used for hosting the largest parties. Traditional Japanese paintings on the wall dated back centuries. Ms. Sugiura led me over to a shelf holding a model, a tiny theatre holding rows of miniature samurai. These were the forty-seven *rōnin*. Their shrine had been here for 150 years.

I was curious about the story's ending—why did the *rōnin* not seek vengeance against the shōgun, who forced their master's suicide? And was their mass suicide really a happy ending? But Mr. Nakamura and Ms. Sugiura agreed that the shōgun found the proper solution. The loyalty of the *rōnin* had to be rewarded, and yet their defiance could not go unanswered.

Teruhina took me over to the glass patio doors to show me the garden. Above us, the moon was nearly full. Teruhina howled. I joined in and we burst into giggles. With Komomo translating, I told her of the coyotes that howl at the moon near the town where I grew up. What is the word for *wolf*, I asked? "*Oukami*," Komomo replied. Suddenly Teruhina began to sing to me dancing lyrics that ended with a repeated word—"*oukami, oukami, oukami.*" Then I recognized the melody. Teruhina was serenading me, in Japanese, with "Who's Afraid of the Big Bad Wolf?"

Pictures were posed for and small gifts of Canada left behind—chocolates for Ms. Sugiura, maple syrup for our *geiko* and *maiko* entertainers. I promised to return tomorrow to drop off personal cards for Yuiko, Komomo and Teruhina. As we stood at the front archway waiting for our shoes, Teruhina stood close and looked up at me. "I hope to see you again," she said, pronouncing the English words carefully. Her serious tone may have reflected the caution of someone repeating a memorized foreign phrase, or perhaps the formal presentation of a ritual farewell. Or perhaps her unlikely wish was sincere.

Back on the street again, Mr. Nakamura decided that our night should not yet end. He led us around a corner and into a narrow alley lined by solid wooden fences, stopping at a small door cut into the high wooden wall. We stepped through, and it was a rabbit hole into Wonderland—in a beautiful floodlit garden, a path led past the long, tall windows of a secluded bar. This was the Fukushima *ochaya*. Like many of its competitors, Fukushima had been forced to find new revenue streams, and a drop-in bar (albeit an exclusive and hidden one) helped augment the more traditional *geiko* party business.

We entered and took a small table. Once again we were joined by the proprietor—Mr. Nakamura was a treasured customer wherever he went. A *maiko* sitting at the bar was drawn to our table and posed for pictures. Kyoko noted details that escaped me—this *maiko*'s bright-yellow kimono, she told me, was not in the same league as Teruhina's. (Later, as we examined the photographs from Kyoko's digital camera, she noted disapprovingly that this *maiko* leaned against me provocatively. In my photos with Komomo and Teruhina, Kyoko pointed out their sweet discretion—they sat upright beside me, and yet their sleeves were gently touching mine.)

The young bartender dropped by our table to chat, and I showed her the digital photos we took at the Ichiriki. Kyoko tapped my arm urgently and gave me a warning look—if I wasn't careful I would get Mr. Nakamura into trouble. The proprietor of the Fukushima, sitting close by, must not know where we had come from. Likewise, the mistress of the Ichiriki would not be pleased to discover our presence at the Fukushima. Mr. Nakamura was, in effect, cheating on her.

Mr. Nakamura was now certifiably squiffy. Draped over the upholstered bench, jacket undone, tie hanging loose, he asked for my impressions of Japan, then began to tell me his thoughts about the state of the nation. He did this by directing a stream of spirited Japanese at Kyoko, concluding each speech with a triumphant wave of his arms from Kyoko to me, indicating that she should let fly with the same lively rhetoric, only in English.

Kyoko's first translation: "He's very drunk." Clearly she was concerned about her friend and patron, and I would not be getting the unadulterated goods. But the version that I eventually coaxed out would be familiar to any bar stool occupant from Wenatchee, Washington, to Bangor, Maine—Mr. Nakamura believed Japanese government policies had been sending his beloved country straight down the toilet. Five years, he figured, and then disaster. The dire details did not survive the journey into English.

At last we bade him goodnight with effusive thanks and returned to our cozy futons at the Hiiragiya.

The years that followed our visit were sometimes difficult ones in Gion. The Ichiriki itself even spent some time in receivership, owned by a bank, though MacIntosh says that as of 2023, the Ichiriki is once again thriving, still run by the Sugiura family.

"The geisha haven't really changed that much," MacIntosh says, adding, "I don't think any of them are joining as a lifelong career anymore. Things change. I'm not against change. It's just how far do you go? Do you sell your soul?"

MacIntosh seems to know everyone working in the Kyoto sector of what the Japanese sometimes call the floating world. And the women who entertained us that night? "I haven't seen Komomo for a while," MacIntosh tells me.

But who knows? She may still be translating idle chatter from dazzled foreigners. "The oldest *geiko* in Kyoto is ninety years old," MacIntosh says. "She was a geisha in Osaka and quit because most of the geisha districts there disappeared. She got head-hunted to come to Kyoto when she was eighty-two, because there weren't enough shamisen players. I hire her quite a bit. She's great."

Then there is Teruhina. On one of my return visits to Kyoto Ms. Sugiura was kind enough to emerge from the Ichiriki to greet me and provide an update. After becoming a *geiko*, she told me, Teruhina had left the profession and gone to New York to study English.

Following tips provided by MacIntosh, I search for her online. And at last, there she is. If she ever left Japan, Teruhina has indeed returned. Her real name, her blog reveals, is Akane Imai. She now teaches classes on the art of choosing, donning and wearing a kimono. She responds politely to my Instagram message and says she has not heard about Kiritaka Kiyoha or her tweets about the abuses suffered by *maiko*. "I don't use Twitter," she tells me.

You can however follow her on Instagram and sign up for her courses. The geisha world may face difficulties, but there are still many who want to know how best to wear a kimono.

CHAPTER TWENTY-SIX

Ice and Plastic

When I email Claire Newell, she apologizes that she is not currently available for an interview. "I'm in Antarctica," she explains.

Oh lord, not that lame excuse again.

Once back in Vancouver, Newell, travel consultant, is only too happy to chat. "It's not for the faint of heart," she says of her recent voyage. The trip involves a crossing of the Drake Passage, where the Atlantic and the Pacific converge. "It's a thousand-kilometre stretch," Newell says, "and it can either be the 'Drake Lake' or the 'Drake Shake.'"

Her ship got the latter. "Someone broke a wrist," she says. "Someone had stitches."

All the same, her ship seems to have gotten off easy. The same month Newell travelled, a woman was killed when a rogue wave struck a Viking cruise ship en route to the frozen continent, shattering windows and spraying glass. Also that month, two elderly cruise passengers drowned off Elephant Island when the Zodiac boat they were on capsized. As Newell says, not for the faint of heart.

Antarctic tourism is among the more extreme examples of ecotourism, a phenomenon heralded as a saviour of the industry. The United Nations

World Tourism Organization declared 2002 the International Year of Ecotourism (perhaps you missed it). Their definition: "All forms of tourism in which the main motivation of tourists is the observation and appreciation of nature, which contributes to its conservation, and which minimizes negative impacts on the natural and socio-cultural environment where it takes place."

A noble concept. Is it wishful thinking?

Although the term was coined in the twentieth century—and has been succeeded in the twenty-first by the more frequently used "sustainable tourism"—ecotourism is certainly not a new concept. It's the idea that gave birth to the national park system. In 1864 President Lincoln signed a bill allowing the state of California to set aside Yosemite as a protected area, and the first true national park, Yellowstone, was established in 1872. In Canada, Banff National Park was created in 1885, only eighteen years after the nation itself.

National parks have been a tremendous boon to both tourism and conservation. But the two are often at odds. Yellowstone and Banff have long since become as pristine as Walmarts on Black Friday. Social scientist George H. Stankey coined the phrase "recreational succession" to describe the process by which a particular area is discovered by adventurous travellers, who are then followed by increasing numbers of tourists until the characteristics that originally attracted visitors are lost. Call it the Yogi Berra effect—as the legendary New York Yankees catcher once said, "Nobody goes there anymore, it's too crowded."

"Ecotourism was originally based on the idea of scarcity rent," says Professor C. Michael Hall of the Department of Management, Marketing, and Tourism at New Zealand's University of Canterbury. "Charge people more to see nature and reduce numbers, but maintain or increase income to communities. Unfortunately, that got lost along the way, and ecotourism has now become more of a catch-all phrase."

In 2007, New Zealand researchers James Higham of the University of Otago and Michael Lück of the Auckland University of Technology wrote, "Paradoxically, whatever the intentions, ecotourism offers great potential to destroy the very resource upon which it depends … The search for 'pristine' environments (if such a thing exists at all) is doomed to be futile as the very presence of tourists, and the demands they place on environments in terms of transport, accommodation, service, and entertainment, are brought to bear upon the environments in which they seek to achieve the ecotourism experience. The more successful an ecotourism destination … the more it threatens its own future sustainability."

Among the most cynical views of the ecotourist was that offered up in 2004 by the University of Edinburgh's George Hughes. Hughes used the term *ego-tourism* (a term that seems to have been independently coined by more than one writer), which he described as, essentially, a show-and-tell performance driven not by a genuine concern about the environment but rather the desire to pose as an enlightened traveller.

Ecotourism can be dangerous too, on land or sea. Every year hikers, snowmobilers and heli-skiers in the British Columbia backcountry fall victim to avalanches. Spring 2023 was particularly deadly in BC, with over a dozen fatalities and more injuries. As a Las Vegas tiger is never truly tamed, nature will always hold peril for those who venture beyond the guardrails.

Ecotourism has offered real promise as a way of preserving wildlife habitat, particularly in Africa where programs to promote a tourism industry have aimed to curtail poaching and slash-and-burn subsistence agriculture. But the Maasai people of Tanzania are among the local populations that have raised objections to the prioritization of tourism over their own rights. (A June 2022 Maasai protest resulted in the deaths of a Maasai man and a Tanzanian police officer.) And even one of the architects of the conservation strategy, conservationist Richard Leakey, has expressed doubts. "Ecotourism is an oxymoron," Leakey told *Overbooked* author Elizabeth Becker. "Tourism is a short-term benefit but in the long term humans and wildlife don't mix."

Even if the label has been abused and cheapened, Hall does believe the ecotourism concept is possible. "To me, sustainable tourism is tourism within environmental and social limits," he says. "The sustainability of tourism needs to be understood in a wider context of sustainability of communities and regions, not just in a narrow sense of what is good for tourism, since ultimately tourism depends on that wider environment."

Newell believes the Antarctic tours are getting it right. "The Antarctic is an inspiration for anyone who promotes sustainable and even regenerative travel," she believes. "No ships go down there that don't have naturalists and a discovery team on board. You're only allowed to go on land in a certain group size—no more than one hundred people at a time, and the first and last people to go are always part of that naturalist team. You only go between posted flags. You can't be closer than five metres to any of the animals, which will come right up to you."

Hall agrees that thus far, Antarctic tours have been responsibly handled. "They are reasonably well supervised, and it is sometimes argued that such visitors become Antarctic ambassadors," he says. "However, the emissions costs of such trips are not considered enough, and the likelihood of introduced species always remains. Unfortunately, the more tourists go to Antarctica or similar locations the harder it is to prevent their negative impacts."

It was perhaps an unfortunate omen that the first ship to engage in Antarctic cruising, Sweden's MS *Explorer*, was also the first such ship to end up at the bottom of the Antarctic Ocean. Launched in 1969 as the *Lindblad Explorer*, it was the first vessel ever to circumnavigate Antarctica's James Ross Island. On a November 2007 cruise intended to retrace the doomed 1914 voyage of explorer Ernest Shackleton, the *Explorer* struck ice and capsized. All aboard—ninety-one passengers, nine guides and fifty-four crew—were rescued, but the ship left behind a slick of marine fuel and, reportedly, barrels of gasoline and lubricant that went with it to the bottom of the sea.

The fate of the MS *Explorer* has not discouraged its many successors. Today, Argentinian and Chilean ports fight for predominance in a booming Antarctic cruise industry, with a parade of ships departing from Ushuaia in Argentina and Punta Arenas in Chile. Long gone are the days when a single plucky boat sailed to the seventh continent—over 150 ships typically make the trip each season. Some are giant ocean liners that simply cruise around, but more common are smaller expedition ships that allow passengers to disembark. Tourist numbers have risen exponentially from the MS *Explorer* days. Figures vary—the International Association of Antarctic Tour Operators combined cruise-only visitors, landed visitors, and "deep field" visitors who fly into the interior, to come up with a 2022 to 2023 summer season total of 105,331 non-penguin bipeds.

Some of those bipeds are behaving badly. In April 2023 UK marine biologist Emily Cunningham reported finding plastic left by tourists in penguin colonies. "Every single sample we took in Antarctica as part of our microplastic research contained plastic microfibres," she said. "We even found a big piece of plastic on the seabed."

A 2021 report published in the *Marine Pollution Bulletin* said each passenger on a seven-day Antarctic cruise can produce an amount of carbon dioxide emissions equal to what the average European produces in an entire year.

As the only land mass on Earth never truly settled by humans, Antarctica has long been considered pristine. No longer, it seems. "Definitely not," says Pablo Tejedo Sanz of the Department of Ecology, Autonomous University of Madrid. Sanz, lead author of a 2022 *Journal of Environmental Management* study on the current state of Antarctica, says the changes have not been gradual. "I have visited Antarctica on several occasions since 2009, and even in that short time have directly witnessed very evident changes. It is certainly very worrying."

The damage is not necessarily connected to tourism. "Numerous global pollutants reach Antarctica, even from the northern hemisphere," Sanz says. "Multiple studies indicate local wildlife and flora are affected by microplastics, heavy metals, or endocrine disruptors, among other chemicals."

And tourism? Sanz has mixed feelings. "I do not feel morally qualified to say, 'I have the right to be there because I am a scientist and you do not because you are a tourist.' I have been working in protected areas for more than 20 years, and I believe prohibiting access to the public is only justifiable in very specific cases in which the resource is at risk of suffering an irreparable damage. It is almost impossible to differentiate the impact of tourism from the negative effects produced by other human activities, such as industry."

Sanz does believe that most tour operators act responsibly, and that the increased awareness fostered by first-hand experience of the Antarctic could offer benefits. "Whether this environmental sensitivity translates into pro-environmental changes once they return home is something that has not yet been studied in depth," he says. "I would like to think that the Antarctic experience of tourists contributes to reinforcing the protection of the planet."

Meanwhile the problem is growing—or more accurately, shrinking. NASA estimates the Antarctic is losing 150 billion tons of ice per year, and in July 2023, sea ice data from Japan's National Institute of Polar Research indicated a "six sigma event," meaning levels six standard deviations below the previous daily mean average. Is that unusual? If you accept that *Homo sapiens* appeared roughly three hundred thousand years ago, a naturally occurring climatic event like this might be expected once in every twenty-five spans of human history. The fact that it's happening now and we have a front-row seat would not appear to be a coincidence.

There are other destinations that have cast themselves as ecotourism meccas. Belize, located on the east coast of Central America, actively markets itself as an ecotourism paradise. One high-profile Belize project involves, ominously, the man who inadvertently did so much to destroy Thailand's Maya Bay—Leonardo DiCaprio. In 2015 the star of *The Beach* announced plans to open an island eco-resort at Blackadore Caye, a long, slender interruption of the Caribbean Sea. DiCaprio claimed it would "change the world" and become a showcase for just how eco-friendly tourism can be. Villas that would sell for up to fifteen million dollars would sit on pylons over the sea, with protected marine habitat and artificial reefs below. A

Deepak Chopra anti-aging and wellness centre was just one of the amenities planned for visitors.

The UK paper *The Sun* gleefully chronicled the troubles that followed. Locals protested that the project would in fact interfere with the thriving fly-fishing industry and harm the environment in general. Dr. Aaron Adams, a Miamian conservationist, said, "It will be a disaster—habitat destruction that is an assault on the fishery."

A "Defend Blackadore Caye" Facebook page showed DiCaprio hanging in effigy. One resident said, "They got really bent out of shape by the notion that he was going to 'heal' us by building an over-the-top resort for rich people."

As of 2023 Leo's Belizean dream appears to be, to put it optimistically, on hold. His pet project once again raises the paradox of ecotourism: Can you really help the environment by piling lots of tourists onto it?

Greg Oates of travel consultants MMGY points to New Zealand as a destination that shifted its priorities in recent years. "New Zealand used to have the same strategic goals as everywhere else," he says. "You know—raise volumes, raise spending, raise time on site, increase air access, all these drivers to get more money and more people into the destination. They've completely changed that now. Their four strategic goals are aligned with the pillars of sustainability. Any decision, any development idea or strategy has to be put through the lens of those four. They have something called visitor sustainability. You focus on the sustainability of culture, environment and economics but you also have to make sure that you're still getting lots of visitors and looking after the stakeholders. They say OK, if we're thinking about this hotel or this experience, how does it line up against all four of these?"

Professor Hall says sustainable tourism is about more than just the environment. "In terms of sustainability it needs to pay the real costs of its environmental and social impacts," he says.

Social impacts are often economic. The United Nations World Tourism Organization's description of ecotourism emphasizes local partners, small businesses that will gain economic benefits and income opportunities. Are communities and residents truly benefiting from tourism?

Icelandic ambassador Hlynur Guðjónsson says that country's tourist boom has done a lot to spread the wealth. "What it has done is put economic pillars in place in many smaller communities. So you're seeing hotels, restaurants, coffee houses, all kinds of tourism-related businesses popping up outside of the capital area. It's not just Reykjavík that is benefiting."

"The missing 'eco' in ecotourism is economics," says Dan Fraser of Thailand's Smiling Albino Tours. "People really overlook the tangible economic benefits of doing ethical ecotourism. I think that's what Smiling Albino is, an ethical luxury travel company. We don't squeeze suppliers for their cheapest possible price."

The company caters to a high-end clientele with tours that start at around two to three hundred US dollars for day trips, multiday trips ranging up to five thousand US dollars per person per day, and big-time luxury adventures, some involving helicopters and security details, running well into the mid–five figures per day. One of the keys, Fraser believes, is making sure the benefits trickle down.

"The way the supply chain is typically viewed in luxury travel, or any kind of mass tourism–oriented travel," Fraser says, "is to contract for the best possible pricing to extract the best possible benefit."

It's a destructive strategy, Fraser believes. "Not enough people working in tourism were making enough money. But we're nothing without our great partners and suppliers. So we say what's a fair price, within reason? OK great, we'll do that price. We don't spend hours negotiating.

"Our guides are another example. One of the ills of the developing world's tourism industry—Egypt is infamous for it—is you're always on some sort of kickback conveyor belt. We have a zero-tolerance policy for that. We pay our guides a fair and reasonable wage. We give them opportunities for training and development so they get more skills and ideally more tips, which is a great incentive. We don't base our business on third-party alliances of convenience.

"It's the economics of treating vendors and suppliers and guides and drivers fairly," Fraser says. "That was a bedrock philosophy of ours from day one. Do you really want a driver who's disgruntled and underpaid driving your family around the city?"

Hidden Japan is a small tour company based in Yamagata Prefecture in northern Honshu. Creative director Derek Yamashita agrees sustainable tourism means local tourism. "We focus on small group tours, local experiences," Yamashita says. "We do factory tours where you get to meet the artisans, temples where you meet the monks, cooking workshops. So it's not sightseeing, it's getting to meet local people. We give back to the local economy."

When it comes to Antarctica the noble goal of benefiting locals does not apply—penguins do not need funds to rent those tuxedos. Antarctic cruises are the prime example of tourism targeted at uninhabited destinations that lack the infrastructure to deal effectively with hordes of visitors. There are, however, tourist boats that come and go from more populated areas, where infrastructure is already in place. They too are carrying camera-toting passengers, seeking encounters with tuxedo-clad residents of the wild. These creatures, though, have three-inch teeth.

CHAPTER TWENTY-SEVEN

Stalking the Killers

It is approaching six p.m. on a warm June day, and the catamaran *Salish Sea Dream* has been on the water since 2:30. After easing out of its Granville Island dock, the boat, with a full load of ninety-five passengers and five crew, has wandered between the mainland and Vancouver Island, tiptoeing among the Gulf Islands and bouncing over light chop in the Strait of Georgia, searching for its quarry. So far it has encountered a community of placid harbour seals clustered around a small reef, a lone bald eagle awaiting its mate beside a massive nest on an otherwise uninhabited island, a few stately BC Ferries ships, small lighthouses, the idyllic homes and cottages on the waterfront of Gabriola and other Gulf Islands. Little more. The catamaran is crossing open water now, pointed back toward its Vancouver base. Passengers gaze at the horizon or their phones. There is an air, if not of disappointment, at least of resignation. People are not scanning the waves with the same eagerness as at 3:30.

Abruptly, the *Salish Sea Dream* makes a sharp turn to port. People look up, stand, move to the railings. This sudden swerve is surely significant. Marine biologist and tour guide Lucas Crosby confirms it—the course correction has been ordered by first mate Sandy Quinn, stationed on the bridge above us with binoculars. "Sandy spotted blows," Crosby says. At last we are on the track of whales.

The *Salish Sea Dream* is owned by Prince of Whales, one of many whale-watching tour operators in BC. (The company got an unexpected plug in 2019 when President Trump tweeted about meeting the "Queen of England and the Prince of Whales," but it is anyone's guess whether any bookings or cancellations resulted.) Prince of Whales has another base on Telegraph Cove on Vancouver Island, but their Granville Island dock is a fairly short bicycle ride from my apartment. After over thirty-five years in Vancouver, 2023 is when I take my first whale-watching tour. It is often said that many New Yorkers have never visited the Statue of Liberty; here I would seem to be the Vancouver equivalent. But it is the local tourism angle that has drawn me here today. I am a guest of the company, invited on board by Claudia Milia, head of marketing and communications.

In a 2007 essay, "Ecotourism: Pondering the Paradoxes," James Higham and Michael Lück made two related points—one, that ecotourism was ideally experienced without a long, emissions-heavy journey. "Perhaps the definitive paradox associated with this phenomenon," they wrote, "is that the ultimate eco-tourist is the one who stays at home, or close to home. The ultimate eco-tourist may seek out nature-based experiences that can be achieved in the absence of fast, long-haul travel."

Secondly, the appeal of unspoiled wilderness aside, Higham and Lück wrote that ecotourism is best done in places where no intrusive infrastructure must be built. The traveller who seeks a wilderness experience ought to depart, ironically, from a place where wilderness is mostly a distant memory. "Urban ecotourism can combat many of the problems associated with ecotourism and urban development," they wrote. "Environmental impacts can be kept to a minimum. There is no need to travel and penetrate remote, relatively untouched natural areas. Cities offer well-developed transport and service infrastructures for locals and tourists alike."

Vancouver might be the poster city for Higham and Lück's argument. I live steps away from magnificent Stanley Park and can easily bike to areas where signs warn hikers to watch for bears. And whale-watching fits the urban ecotourism bill precisely, departing from the city centre into the wild. Higham himself collaborated on a 2014 book on the industry, *Whale-Watching: Sustainable Tourism and Ecological Management*.

There are limits to one's commitment to local tourism though. My whale-watching trip was initially booked for Easter Sunday. Gale-force winds and heavy rains were predicted. Is it an environmental crime to vomit in endangered whale habitat? Happily for all the mammals involved, the tour was cancelled.

Prince of Whales is confident in its ability to deliver the goods—they boast a 95 percent success rate in finding whales and offer a free return trip to any customer who doesn't see one. That 5 percent can be pesky. On this trip I meet three Lithuanian tourists who are on their second trip in three days, having seen no whales the previous Sunday. (There is no promise you will see any particular kind, or colour, of whale, so if Captain Ahab wants a refund he can go pound sand.)

Lithuania is perhaps the most distant country to contribute passengers to this run, but my informal survey also finds travellers from Tampa and Islamorada, Florida; Austin and Houston, Texas; Chattanooga, Tennessee; Toronto, Ontario; Las Vegas, Nevada; and Bavaria. Aside from staff, I appear to be the only local aboard. On this voyage at least, that particular ecotourism box remains unchecked.

But Milia points out that an urban base does offer advantages. "We have all of our staff in Victoria and Vancouver, we don't have to relocate them," she says. "We don't have to pay for transportation or have them move around. It's a lot more convenient than remote places in which employees have to find accommodation, or if there is no accommodation and they have to transit there, which is not great for the environment."

The Strait of Georgia holds large humpbacks and greys, but the most commonly seen cetaceans here are orcas, a.k.a. killer whales. They are not actually whales but members of the dolphin family. Big, fast and relentless, they are like happy little Flippers that have been bitten by radioactive great white sharks to become apex predators. The transient variety are also known as Bigg's orcas, after the late Michael Bigg, a Canadian marine biologist whose research in these very waters provided breakthroughs in understanding their behaviour, identification and the vulnerability of the relatively small population. The name fits—Bigg's orcas are indeed large, preying on seals, sea lions and harbour porpoises, and sometimes striking their prey with such force that the stunned target will fly metres into the air.

It was Michael Bigg who discovered that a smaller local group, called the southern resident killer whales, were a distinct population. Unlike the transients, the residents eat only salmon, and the decline of salmon stocks has put that population in such danger that whale-watching boats like ours are not permitted to pursue or observe them. They are to be left alone. The marine biologists on board can easily distinguish between the smaller residents and the relatively supersize transients.

In 2018 the plight of the endangered southern residents gained world-wide attention via the heartbreaking spectacle of orca J35, a.k.a. Tahlequah, carrying her dead newborn calf, Tali, for seventeen days before finally letting her go. Two years earlier, J34, a southern resident named Doublestuff, washed up near Sechelt, BC, the victim of a ship strike.

Dr. Ruth Joy lectures at Simon Fraser University and is a member of the Sea Mammal Research Unit. She has studied the effects of shipping on whale populations. While ship strikes are an obvious problem, the issue of underwater noise is more complex. "It can make it difficult to communicate," Joy says. "The whale is in constant vocal communication with its pod. If you listen through the hydrophone the whales are chattering like a flock of chickadees, with constant knowledge of where each of them is. They may be hunting together and communicating about the hunt.

"When there's a lot of noise, at first whales will raise their voices just like we would in a noisy bar. Then at some point we stop talking because we can't hear. Killer whales do the same thing. They raise the energy that they put into their vocalizations up to a point, and then they go quiet. That has to affect their hunting as well as their ability to keep track of one another."

Whale-watching boats in Canada and the United States have adopted strict policies to minimize their impact. They are not allowed to approach closer than two hundred metres to orcas. If the orcas or whales approach the boat themselves, the vessel will cut its engines and drift. (Crosby tells me of a humpback named Nike who loves whale-watching boats. "He'll see us and come right over," he says. Is it sexual? There's no judgment.)

Lauren Laturnus, a field assistant to the Boundary Pass whale project organized by the Saturna Island Marine Research and Education Society and Simon Fraser University, spent the summer of 2022 looking at the whale-watching industry and other boats in this area. "Whale-watching companies that are part of the Pacific Whale Watch Association [Prince of Whales among them] often have experienced and educated crew members or researchers that are able to collect data on whale identification, movement and behaviours," Laturnus says. "The PWWA also collaborates with many conservation groups that are dedicated to researching and restoring marine environments.

"Marine mammal regulations and interim orders have been put in place to limit the disturbance that vessels can have on whales. The problem is the whale-watching industry does not always comply. I conducted five months of land-based research on Saturna Island in the summer of 2022 and regularly saw whale-watching boats getting too close to whales, following them for longer than the regulated time limit, leap-frogging—where the boats would position themselves to be directly in the whales' path before turning their engine off—as well as entering the interim sanctuary zone, put in place to provide a safe area for southern resident whales. Currently, there is very little enforcement on the water and until companies are held accountable, there will continue to be players who break the rules and keep the industry open to justified criticism."

Prince of Whales boats respect the rules. But the small deck crew of the *Salish Sea Dream*—Crosby and fellow staffers Petra Catsi and Róisín O'Sullivan—are not without qualms. "We are educating people on these tours," Catsi says, "and we hope the education outweighs any harm we might do. We are out here burning fuel, after all."

Crosby knows something about the environmental downside of the tourism industry. He spends the off-season in Bimini in the Bahamas, where he participates in shark research. From the Bimini Biological Field Station he has seen the Resorts World Bimini development on North Bimini, with its casino, cruise ship terminal and Hilton hotel, reshape the island landscape. Huge swathes of mangroves that provide ideal habitat for lemon sharks have been clawed out, and coral has been dredged away to create a shipping channel for resort supplies.

On the positive side, hammerhead shark diving has offered Bimini locals a lucrative alternative to hammerhead shark hunting. The tourism–preservation calculus is at work in Bimini, as it is in the Strait of Georgia.

Not every whale-watching jurisdiction is as regulated as the West Coast of Canada and the US. Writing in *Hakai Magazine*, Egill Bjarnason described the Wild West attitude that prevails in some whale-watching zones. "In the Azores, off Portugal … the number of whale-watching boats allowed at sea is strictly limited by a licence system," he wrote. "In Iceland, as in Norway, all you need is a licensed seaworthy ship and skipper, preferably sober, to join the crowd."

Bjarnason cited a disturbing photo posted on Facebook in 2021 that showed over one hundred tourists, some of them snorkellers, mobbing seventy to eighty orcas and a single humpback in Norway's Kaldfjorden. "But no one was officially chastised that day," he wrote.

"There has always been an uneasy relationship between this industry and science," Dr. Joy says. "Many of the whale-watching staff are trained scientists that love whales, but their industry is dependent on paying guests who want to be up close and personal with whales, and these same staff want to deliver this on their trips."

That dual identity is clear aboard the *Salish Sea Dream*. Catsi may have spent years studying whales and ocean-going mammals, but today she is also tasked with dispensing coffee, hot chocolate and Twix bars. (The canteen task rotates among the staff—next voyage it will be Lucas or Róisín handing out refreshments.)

Still, Catsi has the satisfaction of knowing that she played a key role in a recent whale rescue. The previous year a Prince of Whales catamaran spotted a young humpback named Scuba. For marine biologists, the Strait of Georgia is like a small town—they know all the regulars, drunk and sober. And Scuba was acting weird. "He was breaching [lunging out of the water] over and over," Crosby says. "That's great for whale-watchers, but it's not normal."

It was Catsi who spotted the reason. "There's a rope in there," she said. Like many humpbacks who swim these waters, Scuba had become entangled in fishing gear. A call was made to the Department of Fisheries and Oceans and a team dispatched to try to free Scuba. The operation was a success, though recent sightings of Scuba have shown the resulting scars.

An old adage claims, "A son is a son till he takes a wife, but a daughter's a daughter all her life." Debatable, but when it comes to orcas, the reverse is true. Orca pods are matriarchal and a male will stay in its mother's pod as long as the matriarch lives, while a female with calves of her own will depart to start a new pod (though they don't usually go very far from the matriarch). Older males who outlive their matriarchs must drift here and there in search of companions. One roaming male named Harbeson is known to be over sixty. He's not even the senior cetacean in the strait—a female named Esperanza has been around since at least 1955.

As in any community, there is gossip. Orca pods will sometimes congregate into superpods where hookups can occur. Meanwhile in the humpback clan, Scuba likes to hang out with another whale named Schooner. They are in fact brothers, offspring of a female named Zig Zag, but do they know this? Do they have the same father? No one can say for sure. Our catamaran is cruising through a marine soap opera.

Three and a half hours into our tour the *Salish Sea Dream* is at last tracking whale activity. Crosby points to a bright stretch of water ahead, near Gabriola Island. "See the blows?" he says.

Honestly, I don't. It all looks like whitecaps to me. But Crosby is confident. A small prize is offered to any passenger who is the first to see a whale but the crew have been to this rodeo before. "It's hard to beat Sandy," Crosby says.

Tracking whales is a pursuit that unites commercial operators, casual boaters and marine biologists. "We can track what they're doing, their behaviour, how they're moving," says Milia. "And this is of great importance to researchers."

A website called Happywhale gives whale watchers amateur and professional around the world a chance to report sightings and create a map of whale movements and habitats. "Whether Prince of Whales and other companies are actually in harmony with whales is open to interpretation," says Dr. Joy, "especially if you're a whale. But the data they collect is making its way more and more into the local community as citizen scientists play a more active role in data collection and analyses, as federal governments struggle to afford field programs."

"Realistically," Milia says, "they [researchers] spend less time in the water than we do."

The boat slows when we reach the stretch of water where the spouts were seen. A scan of the surface reveals nothing but waves. We drift awhile, then turn and head back where we came. "There's a lot of water out here," Crosby says, "and these guys can disappear pretty fast. At top speed, they are faster than our boat."

Nor is an orca a creature to be trifled with. At the time of our voyage reports from Spain had been all over the news, telling of orcas striking, damaging and even sinking small vessels in coordinated attacks like those usually launched against prey. Still, even putting aside the still-extant professional whaling industry, whales have suffered more damage from us than they could ever hope to repay.

We pass a BC Ferries vessel, a majestic white castle headed the other way. Ferry passengers could easily see whales by chance, which seems unfair. They only paid to get somewhere. Our passengers forked out for a show.

It takes a while, with the boat executing a search pattern near the last sighting. But at last, showtime. As Captain Anthony Kaulfuss eases the catamaran into position, the passengers crowd to the starboard railing, phones aloft. A couple hundred metres away the surface is broken by shiny black forms, emerging from and plunging back beneath the waves. There appear to be four, one significantly larger than the rest. This, Crosby tells us, is pod T123. The matriarch is Sidney, orca T123, from whom the pod gets its designation. The larger whale is Stanley, a twenty-three-year-old, seven-and-a-half-metre-long male. Stanley got his name because in 2011, the last year the Vancouver Canucks made the Stanley Cup Final, he appeared in Vancouver Harbour like a magical talisman.

One of the young females is named Lucky. Sidney was pregnant with her when she somehow got stranded by an ebb tide in Prince Rupert. Locals kept Sidney and another whale hydrated until high tide allowed them to swim free, hence her calf's subsequent nickname.

The pod was seen hunting earlier today but now they are simply travelling, moving easily and steadily to the northwest. Captain Kaulfuss cuts the engine a couple of times to let them get farther ahead, and then we sneak up again.

It's Stanley who is the real showstopper here. He's huge, his dorsal fin rising like a glossy black sail over the water. Everybody is recording but the resulting videos will likely make little impact on anyone who wasn't on board. We are not really seeing a lot of whale skin. Yet the effect is no less awe-inspiring. I find myself gasping whenever Stanley surges back into view. No one is chattering. We can hear the whales breathing as they surface. Except for the phones, it's like being in church.

After about twenty-five minutes we bid adieu to the pod and turn for home. It has been a longer-than-normal outing, lasting five and a half hours and covering 108 nautical miles. Everyone on board appears pleased. It seems no whales were interfered with on this day, though as Dr. Joy points out, you'd have to be a whale to know for sure.

It's certainly not the worst reason humans take to the sea to pursue whales. These shores were once home to brutally efficient whale killers. In Nanaimo on Vancouver Island, a whaling centre that opened in 1907 had to close after two years because it had slaughtered all of the region's ninety-five humpbacks. Vancouver's scenic Coal Harbour, where today pedestrians and cyclists crowd the waterfront and kayakers ply the waters, was home to a busy whaling facility as recently as 1967.

As for orcas, until 1975 it was legal in BC to capture them and send them to aquariums. (Iceland did not ban the practice until 1989.) Vancouver Aquarium, once home to as many as five performing whales, held an orca named Bjossa until 2001. I recall a Vancouver International Film Festival gala held at the aquarium where one could wander down poolside, drink in hand, and watch Bjossa drifting about. The effect was somewhat surreal, like attending a Bond supervillain's cocktail party. It certainly did not resemble the experience of seeing whales in the wild, rhythmically cleaving the ocean surface.

The whale-watching industry boasts a lot of satisfied customers. A 2015 survey by Raincoast Conservation Foundation estimated whale-watching generated between $16.8 and $24.5 million Canadian in annual revenue for BC, creating up to 359 jobs in high season. Globally, according to a 2017 survey conducted by whale researcher Erich Hoyt, whale-watching brings in over two billion US dollars and employs over thirteen thousand people.

Marine biologist Petra Catsi is one of them. And she enjoys it. She cares about whales, studies them, watches them on almost every voyage. But she wonders, too, about the ethics of chasing wild creatures, like paparazzi after a princess. "Does education and awareness balance the equation?" asks Catsi. "That's the question."

CHAPTER TWENTY-EIGHT

Selfies and Serendipity

Wandering is heaven. Searching is hell.

Serendipity is my guiding principle on the road. It has taken me to unforgettable places, sometimes as the result of intentional aimlessness and sometimes through simple idiocy. I once got a lengthy bus tour of London that ended in the charming village of Crouch End. I had been trying to get to Trafalgar Square but boarded the double-decker going the wrong direction. Another time I rented a cheap bike in Luang Prabang, Laos, and set off to find a little village where they make paper lanterns. Sixteen kilometres later it seemed clear I had missed the turnoff. And I had, by fifteen kilometres. But on that ride I met two tree-climbing children who gave me some tamarind seeds. Later I came upon a sad-looking monkey in a small cage and fed him the tamarind seeds. On the way back, hot and parched, I stopped at a riverside spot for a cold can of Birdy coffee that tasted like the elixir of heaven. I remember that ride far better than I remember the paper lantern village.

"A good traveller has no fixed plans and is not intent on arriving," said ancient Chinese philosopher Lao Tzu.

Works for me. Getting lost is almost the only way I ever get anywhere.

Serendipity goes with pedalling, and especially with walking. When I travel, I walk, rambling down city streets and alleys. My favourite walking shoes are a pair of Campers, purchased on my first visit to Rome. This year they are marking their twentieth anniversary. Over two decades I have spent several times their initial cost on repairs, and despite all that work they currently look like prop shoes for a movie hobo. For a while they changed colour, the result of an unfortunate street shoeshine in Delhi. I wish they came equipped with an odometer—I would truly love to know how many miles they have logged. I will never throw them out. When at last they lose all viability they will be retired to a little closet farm to live out their days.

My wandering strategy is the antithesis of that popular buzz phrase, the bucket list.

A bucket list (i.e. a list of things one must do before kicking the bucket) is not inherently bad. You can put anything on a bucket list, including getting a PhD in microbial ecology or reforming the US prison system. But buckets can be nasty. People do vile things in buckets. As it is commonly applied to tourism, the bucket list approach (a.k.a. *1,000 Places to See Before You Die*) encourages the shallowest form of travel—get off the bus, take the selfie, check the box, move on.

Serendipity is the bucket with a hole in it. Wandering is the empty blueprint. There is no bucket, no basket, no navigational app, no discernible strategy. Yet, although the rambling is largely unplanned there is still a search going on—a search for the surprising, the entrancing, the sublime. Sublimery is what you're after. Don't let spell-check tell you that's not a word.

I have frequently been reminded of the power of serendipity on recent travels and how it can even coexist with scheduling. In Japan I travelled to Miyama to interview the tourism official Waka Takamido. After she returned to her office down the road, I wandered the village, eventually climbing to the Shinto shrine that overlooks the town. Tucked into a wooded grove, it was deserted—well-maintained yet appearing to be in the process of reclamation by the forest. I sat down on a wooden bench and pulled out some packaged sushi I had brought along. The countryside was quiet as a temple. Eating department store sushi at a deserted shrine deep in the Japanese countryside—what kind of bucket list would that be on? One that I lack the imagination to make.

Serendipity has its limits of course. I prize spontaneity so much that I frequently miss out on seeing the most exalted wonders and tour book attractions, simply because I cannot bear the thought of climbing onto a packed shuttle bus and then shuffling shoulder-to-shoulder, or worse, past the Thing to Be Seen.

The Taj Mahal, Angkor Wat and the Palace of Versailles are just a few of the global wonders I have avoided. At Mount Rushmore I drove past the parking lot, looked to my left, confirmed that it looked very much like the postage stamp, and headed back to the highway, having never stopped the car. It took me five or six trips to Paris before I visited the Louvre (whereupon I realized I had been a stubborn fool).

On the other hand I did go see the pyramids of Giza (that visit is not really optional if one is in the area). While I am not sorry to have seen them, the experience as a whole was one to be endured rather than enjoyed. At one point I broke into a run, chased by a man on a camel who seemed unable to accept my decision not to hire his noble beast.

Another limit to serendipity: sometimes you actually have to find something. That's when the hell begins. Maps usually present to me like Egyptian tomb inscriptions, and I combine that cartographic illiteracy with the navigational skills of a three-wheeled shopping cart. My phone is so old, any navigational apps would likely direct me to the nearest zeppelin terminal. If I swear by serendipity, perhaps it's because it's all I am capable of.

Searching for a specific location—my next hotel, a meeting place or a recommended restaurant—can leave me screaming, literally. Once, in Edinburgh, I was in a rental car trying to find a particular neighbourhood. For an hour I had been driving up one street and down another like a diligent street sweeper. Then I passed a lovely neon sign that offered up the J.R.R. Tolkien quote *Not all who wander are lost.*

"Well I sure as fuck am!" I yelled, apparently to the sign. I never did find the neighbourhood.

Full disclosure: I don't make it easy on myself. On my most recent journeys I have carried no phone. Most people I mention this to blink at me as though I just told them I have gills. A man I admitted this to on a Singapore subway said simply, "You are a very special person." I am pretty certain he was using *special* euphemistically.

In Rome at Hotel Orlanda, Marco was bemused. "No phone?" he said. "You are like a terrorist. You are like Pablo Escobar. The satellites cannot find you."

But there are solid reasons for what might appear on the surface to be mystifying self-sabotage. For one, Canadian roaming charges are brutal. For another, my phone (an iPhone 4, introduced about four months before the debut of Instagram) is so ancient it does not support any useful navigational apps anyway. It would be a pointless hole in my pocket. And I have a laptop, so I'm not entirely reduced to sundials and star navigation.

But people do have phones for a reason. I acknowledge that. And my phonelessness has been the cause of some of that hell I mentioned earlier. Serendipity doesn't work when you actually have to get somewhere. Phones do.

Serendipity can be a fickle force. It is first cousin to chaos. Serendipity is a bitey cat that purrs until the very second you feel claws raking your hand. I try to avoid the claws; before a journey I generally plan transport and accommodation carefully. Unless you are on a random road trip there is no fun to be had scrambling for a last-minute bed. The serendipity kicks in after the basic necessities have been taken care of. French novelist Gustave Flaubert said, "Be regular and orderly in your life, so that you may be violent and original in your work." Travel is like that too. First get your ducks in a row so that later you can take wing.

How common is my approach? Hard to know. But my own unscientific observations suggest the current trend in travel does not favour serendipity. Rather it appears to take its cue from Instagram. Social media influencers have become a major force in the travel industry. Instagram and TikTok are inundated with their carefully chosen pictures and video. While some tourists are merely sharing images from their travels (I do it myself), many others monetize their social media accounts to become professional travellers. The old invite-your-friends-to-watch-a-travel-slideshow routine has morphed into a viable career path.

Dr. Ulrike Gretzel is a senior research fellow at the University of Southern California's Center for Public Relations. She says modern social media influencers represent more of an evolution than an innovation.

"Word of mouth has always been super important in travel," Gretzel says. "Even before the rise of social media, bulletin boards and forums like Thorntree forum, VirtualTourist and Tripadvisor emerged, in which members contributed content, moderated discussions and answered questions.

"The real revolution started when blogs became widely available. The tourism industry had a lot of experience working with traditional influence agents like travel journalists, writers and travel agents. Thus when travel bloggers started amassing audiences, tourism marketers were quick to recognize their value and offer them free travel in return for exposure.

"With the launch of the iPhone and the first self-facing camera, as well as the GoPro, travel vlogging emerged. This meant that the main focus on text and scenic still imagery shifted to selfies and video. When Instagram started, many bloggers immediately took advantage of the visual display and curation affordances it offered. Again, the travel industry was quite quick to recognize the advantages of having attractive content produced for a fast-growing audience."

In 2012, Hamilton Island, Australia, held one of the first-ever "Instameet" events, designed specifically to attract Instagram influencers to a particular destination. They are now common in destinations around the world.

"As far as the industry is concerned, influencers constitute a new stakeholder," Gretzel says. "They have added a new marketing channel that allows for more precise targeting. Influencers are also critical for translating messages for audiences the industry doesn't know how to communicate with, and they help tourism marketers enter platforms like TikTok and live streaming. During COVID, influencers were very important for communicating about travel restrictions and requirements."

A 2022 Kicksta.co blog post by Sam Hackett declared that Instagram influencers must carefully curate their content to find the proper niche and attract the right eyeballs. I checked out some of the travel accounts recommended in the post. The first one featured a series of magazine-type photos starring a beautiful young woman posing in exotic locales, as well as a video (marked as a paid partnership) promoting a "Crypto Treasure Hunt." It seemed less about travel and more about lifestyles of the rich and sketchy.

"There is a lot of overlap between fashion and travel influencers," Gretzel points out. "They try to diversify their income streams, so there is a lot of modelling of outfits happening."

Gretzel doesn't feel all social media influencers deserve to be lumped together. "It really depends on the type of influencer," she says. "There are plenty of sustainable and responsible travel influencers out there who try to change the way people travel in positive ways. There's one for every type of travel, from digital nomads and vanlifers, to cruise travel, sustainable travel, travelling with kids, gluten-free travel, yoga travel, female solo travel, luxury travel and so on."

When I suggest to Dr. Gretzel that Instagram and TikTok might encourage the sort of take-a-selfie-and-get-out travel I dislike, she demurs. "I don't think shallow travel is the problem," she says. "It's the stupid challenges and culturally insensitive, environmentally questionable, ethically problematic or simply dangerous things that influencers do and promote that I am concerned about."

An example would be Tizi, the vlogger fined by Chinese authorities in 2023 after posting a video of herself cooking and eating an endangered great white shark in the Sichuan city of Nanchong. (Two fishermen were subsequently arrested for catching and selling the shark.) Another couple, Sabina Dolezalova and Zdenek Slouka from the Czech Republic, treated their tens of thousands of followers to a video of Slouka splashing holy water on his partner's ass at a Hindu temple in Bali in 2019. It did not go over well locally. But these examples pale before the case of Logan Paul, who in 2018 entertained his sizable YouTube following with video of a suicide victim hanging from a tree in Japan's Aokigahara forest, near Mount Fuji. "Yo, are you alive?" Paul yelled at the dangling corpse. "Are you fucking with us?"

Paul's forest video got 6.3 million views within twenty-four hours. That's influence.

But Gretzel sees many positives to the social media influencer movement. "They have helped inspire people who might not think they can travel, or travel in a certain way," she points out. "They often call out unacceptable industry practices. They help show sides of destinations that travel agents might not advertise because there is no money to be made. They sometimes organize trips—such as solo female trips or yoga retreats—that are very tailored to their audiences. They also provide information for niche markets that the industry doesn't serve or doesn't serve well enough, like LGBTQ+, disability, neurodiversity, Black travellers, people with dietary needs, etc.

"Like travel reviewers, influencers have also added a lot of transparency to the industry, for example revealing tricks to get cheaper tickets or upgrades. They also create travel trends. Vanlife, for instance, is very much linked to Instagrammers. In China, one of the early travel bloggers created a huge backpacking trend.

"Influencers have affected where people go. For example Morocco is suddenly a big destination for millennial North Americans, largely because of influencers."

It's true that on my ride to Miyama, the other five bus passengers were all from Taiwan. As Waka Takamido explained to me later, a Taiwanese blogger had helped popularize her town for Taiwanese tourists.

Downsides, as Gretzel sees them, include fostering travel envy, painting an unrealistically problem-free picture of travel, and irresponsibility. "Not all of them are responsible," she says. "Many travelled during the pandemic despite restrictions. Some travel on private jets. Most frequently travel long distances and therefore are a sustainability issue. Some advertise places, trips or events without vetting them, as we saw with the Fyre Festival." (Fyre was a heavily hyped 2017 Bahamas musical event that turned out to be a poorly organized disaster.)

Then there are the ethical compromises of sponsorship. "If they take brand deals," Gretzel says, "they are less likely to provide authentic representations because their contract might prevent them from saying negative things."

That, to be fair, is an issue by no means limited to social media influencers. Much of the travel writing industry, even the kind of pieces that have typically filled newspaper travel sections, is little more than glorified advertising written by people whose expenses have been paid by the various destinations and resorts they are writing about. If your faithful correspondent got food poisoning in the hotel dining room and battled scorpions in bed every night, you would never find out about it. Five stars!

The trips I take are somewhat unusual—they often fall into a grey area between leisure and professional. My journeys are almost always self-funded—generally, I don't enjoy going where I am told and gushing about an assigned destination, and that means I pay my own way. But after planning my itinerary I often seek to defray my costs by selling stories to magazines and newspapers. On several occasions I have benefited from perks offered to journalists. My whale-watching trip with Prince of Whales, for example, was comped. And I did once take an all-expenses-paid trip to the Florida Keys to write a Canadian magazine article. Happily I was free to say whatever I wanted about Florida itself. (It was Election Day 2012, and while the nation was in the process of returning Barack Obama to the White House, I was struck by the roadside campaign signs for mosquito-control officers. Are there really partisan positions about mosquito control?) However, the trip was being underwritten by Cadillac, so I was required to mention at some point the sweet ride in which I was cruising the Overseas Highway. It seemed like a minor concession. But as the old anecdote says, once the transactional nature of the relationship has been established, it is just a question of haggling over the price.

Gretzel sees other potentially negative aspects to the influencer phenomenon. "They can create a hype around a destination that can lead to capacity problems or other issues," she says. "For instance, the Schlegeis [suspension] bridge near the Olpererhütte in the Tyrolean Zillertal [in Austria] was frequently portrayed by influencers and is now completely overrun, causing huge traffic problems in the area, environmental degradation, plus accidents because Instagram tourists don't realize how challenging the climb is."

As social influencers become ever more influential their demands are ramping up, Gretzel says. "Influencers are becoming more expensive and want to be paid per post. I think this trend will continue."

They can be an entitled lot. Kimron Corion, communications manager of Grenada Tourism Authority, recently told CNN, "One of our executives had an encounter with an influencer who said he 'doesn't fucking pay for anything, ever' after she informed him that some of his meals weren't going to be covered."

A backlash would appear to be underway. After one too many freebie requests, Los Angeles ice cream truck owner Joe Nicchi made the news in 2019 with a sign reading *Influencers pay double*. CNN also reported on Gianluca Casaccia, manager and co-owner of the White Banana Beach Club on the Philippine island of Siargao, ripping into freeloaders posing as influencers. "We would like to suggest to try another way to eat, drink or sleep for free," Casaccia posted on Facebook. "Or try to actually work." Casaccia later clarified that he did not include all influencers in this category. "A real influencer is called as such by the rest, he does not address him/herself as an influencer," he wrote. "They are bloggers. We have actually collaborated with a few of them, and we support them."

"Some embrace them, some absolutely hate them," Gretzel says. "Some just don't know what to do with them. Many establishments had to put influencer policies in place to deal with the inquiries they get. Smaller players don't usually have the resources for strategic influencer marketing."

If the social media influence game is frequently about constructing and projecting an image, there are those who at least have fun with it. Some have taken up the "plane window challenge," in which beautiful views apparently seen through the window of an airborne jet are actually revealed to be video clips shot through the rim of a toilet seat. (Insert your own metaphor here.)

Gretzel feels the ranks of legitimate influencers could soon thin out. "I think there will be a bit of a shake-out, with many travel influencers quitting. We already saw a bit of that during the pandemic when some were quick to look for other income streams or other topics. Influencers are increasingly dealing with mental health issues because the job is super tough and it is hard to keep up with the demands."

As someone who has written about travel, and on occasion gained financial assistance from a sponsor or tourism board, I have little moral standing to criticize professional influencers. Yet I still fear the travel culture some influencers promote. Their growing impact seems to me reminiscent of the upsurge in online sports betting, where an onslaught of advertising has often served to transform pro sports from a primarily fan-based culture to a more predatory gambling industry. The profit motive tends to consume wonder and simple enthusiasm.

Influencers have their place. I know there is a lot to be said for a solid travel tip. I might never have gone to Bangkok had my friend Martin not insisted. Even my initial trip to Japan was inspired, before I ever met Kyoko, by stories from my friends who had lived there. They were my personal influencers, and were paid in Ultraman trinkets and tasty Japanese snacks.

I understand that serendipity can only go so far. One must make plans, get recommendations, buy tickets, make reservations. But I feel the prominence of influencers, bucket lists and online recommendations serves to distort an essential truth of travel—that it is, to some degree, unquantifiable. Travel is not a package one opens to consume the expected contents and then rate thumbs up or thumbs down.

For me the random quality of travel extends even to my return home. There is an involuntary serendipity that takes hold after the journey ends—the serendipity of memory. I can never predict which moments will resurface after the fact, which experiences will retroactively reveal themselves to have been the most powerful. It is almost never some particular attraction, or anything that could be posted online. Recollections are often of random occurrences or unexpected bursts of emotion—my espresso-fuelled moment in that Palermo alley, for one. Other experiences rise to the surface when the white noise of consciousness fades. Perhaps you were distracted at the time but looking back you marvel at a fleeting moment of wonder.

On my most recent Asian trip, in 2023, I had to get to Bangkok's Don Mueang International Airport at an ungodly hour, and spent many a moment calculating the best way to get there on my dwindling cash reserves. Come flight day I was humping a heavy gym bag up the steps at the BTS station at 5:15 a.m., then making connections one after another. The stress did not abate until I was safely on board my flight. So it was only in hindsight I recalled the moment I disembarked from the train at Mo Chit Station and dragged my bag down the stairs to the bus stop to find a group of morning commuters being serenaded by a DJ working a light show and spinning an electro version of "Achy Breaky Heart." Only in Bangkok.

That's typical of these random memories—they often pertain to the travel itself, in particular the necessity of getting to the airport. Many people dream about high school tests they didn't study for, but my most common stress dream is battling bizarre complications as I struggle to catch a flight.

Years ago when I visited Lyon, France, I spent the week worrying about catching another brutally early flight to Rome. Ultimately I decided to stay awake and catch a shuttle bus before dawn. As my ride rumbled toward the Lyon airport I sighed with relief and looked forward to returning to my favourite city. The sun began to rise—a novelty for a late sleeper like me—and the Grateful Dead's "Touch of Grey," with its line about dawn breaking everywhere, started to play in my head. That moment is more indelibly stamped in my hippocampus than anything else I experienced in Lyon. There was no Instagram at the time, and just as well. It wasn't something you could photograph.

CHAPTER TWENTY-NINE

Freedom

There's a café on Via dell'Esquilino in Rome, beside the church of Santa Maria Maggiore. It's a hangout for street vendors who peddle hats and umbrellas and wooden crafts to tourists. They like it because the café is located at a tour bus stop, allowing them to throng each bus in turn, holding up their wares. I like the tour buses too. I like to watch them drive away. Sitting there sipping my espresso, I feel like a truant on a sunny day, watching the other unfortunate kids trudge off to school.

Travel can impart a sense of freedom. My own sense of travel freedom takes the form of solo wandering, free of itineraries or competing agendas, the freedom to linger when interesting photo opportunities present themselves. But for me, travelling alone is not just about escaping the company of others—it's about escaping my own. When I'm alone, I don't have to hear myself talk. In company, it's almost inevitable that I will be babbling on about irrelevant nonsense or getting cranky about something. I'm not always sure how my companions feel about it, but I know I get tired of listening to that guy. I prefer my stream of consciousness and roving attention to my own sometimes inane prattle. Freedom, to me, means the freedom to go my own way alone. How much of that freedom do I take for granted?

In December 2020 Maria Ressa—who would win the Nobel Peace Prize in 2021—wanted to travel from her home in the Philippines to Florida to visit her mother, who was scheduled for cancer surgery. Her request was denied by the government of Rodrigo Duterte. It was a bad travel year for a lot of people, but in Ressa's case the issue was not COVID-related. As a critic of the Filipino government, Ressa has been a target for prosecutions, including a spurious cyber-libel charge. In her book *How to Stand Up to a Dictator*, Ressa wrote, "The Court of Appeals handling the cyber-libel case ... labelled me a flight risk."

Appearing on *The Late Show with Stephen Colbert* on November 29, 2022, Ressa said, "You don't really know what freedom means until you're about to lose it. When I began losing my freedom, like the right to travel, then I realized I was taking it for granted."

Freedom. At its most basic, it means freedom of movement. Attempts to restrict travel would therefore seem to be prima facie evidence of tyranny. Authoritarian and totalitarian governments have always restricted the movement of citizens. That was certainly the argument made in Ottawa in the first months of 2022, an argument made primarily via truck horns. The so-called Freedom Convoy, consisting of fleets of semi-trucks and other vehicles, rolled into Canada's capital city and blockaded the streets to protest federal restrictions imposed to limit the spread of the COVID-19 virus. There they stayed for several weeks, blaring their horns and blocking traffic.

Frequently referred to on social media as the "free-dumb convoy," it was disparaged by critics as an eighteen-wheeled tantrum, an orgy of self-centred whining by people unwilling to shoulder the collective responsibility demanded by a major public health crisis. At least four Canadian polls released in early February showed similar national opposition to the protest. In the Leger survey, 65 percent of respondents agreed the convoy crowd consisted of "a small minority of Canadians who are thinking only about themselves." Fifty-seven percent thought the convoy was not really about vaccine mandates at all, but "an opportunity for right-wing supremacist groups to rally and voice their frustrations about society" (although, hedging their bets in typically Canadian fashion, 44 percent in the same poll also said they sympathized with the frustration).

The 2020 pandemic resulted in a near-cessation of global leisure travel. Like the bans imposed by authoritarian governments, the restrictions came from the top and in some cases carried legal force, making them easy to characterize as government overreach. But the restrictions often had broad public support. They were widely seen as a necessary response to a frightening new reality.

Freedom—like acceptable pizza toppings, it's a flexible concept. When you talk about freedom, do you mean freedom to, or freedom *from*? Freedom of action, or freedom from responsibility? Freedom to do what you want, or freedom from having things done to you? Freedom of speech, or freedom from consequences?

Freedom is one of the key promises offered by the travel industry. Dr. Hazel Andrews's study of British tourists in Magaluf found the idea took a number of forms. "There was a sense of freedom," she says. "You're sold this idea that you are going to be more free, regardless of whether it's about Britishness, or sexism, or exposure of the body, or whatever. Some women felt more liberated, some parents felt more comfortable allowing their children a greater amount of freedom because it felt like a safer environment."

It was also paradoxically a place where UK tourists seemed to feel freer to express xenophobia and complaints about immigration levels. "What I found was that this was an expression of British identity that they couldn't express when they were at home," Andrews says. "I don't think many tourists are travelling to engage with another culture, regardless of what kind of holiday they go on. It's usually about the self. How do we understand who we are? It's usually by a contrast with a kind of 'Other.'"

My own identity as a very white—perhaps even slightly luminescent—male surely plays a role in my preferred travel style. How much of my cherished freedom to wander comes from who I am? Would I be left to my own devices if I looked different?

"I was speaking at my college about travel writing," says Dallas journalist Alex Temblador. "One female student asked me, 'Is it safe for you as a woman travelling around?' And I said, it's one thing as a woman and another as a woman of colour. Both can be tricky. I am always, always on. I don't get to not be on when I'm travelling. I have written so many stories about women getting harassed, being pushed into hotel rooms by other guests or workers."

She describes her experience on a trip to Spain. "I love walking around. I love to walk ten to fifteen miles a day in a city. But I'm getting followed around and harassed and have dudes right next to me saying things in Spanish, some I can pick up, some I can't. That's not comfortable."

Temblador's Texas roots go back to the nineteenth century, but as a woman whose ethnic mix includes English, German, Norwegian and Mexican, she must sometimes deal with the "Where are you from?" question from people she meets. "If I say Texas, they'll say, 'Where are your parents from?' Texas. They'll literally go down my line until I get to what they're looking for."

Temblador's eclectic heritage has also led to a weird chameleon-like phenomenon when she travels. "I have a look where, whatever area I'm in, people think I'm whatever they are. I've been in Bali where people don't necessarily know I'm not Balinese. I was getting yelled at and cussed out in Balinese because I had short sleeves and wasn't covered up. They didn't know I was American."

People of colour must frequently battle assumptions about just where they fit in. "I don't know how many stories I've seen about a person of colour standing in line to board first and it's like, 'Ma'am, please move aside,'" Temblador says. "That happens to us a lot."

"I've had it happen myself," says travel agent Shalene Dudley. "You know, lining up for a business class seat and hearing 'Sorry, you're in the wrong lane.' I'm not. It happens. And not all of it is deep-seated racism. It's prejudice, right? As in, we pre-judge."

Temblador sometimes wonders about the thought process behind the assumptions. "If someone is clearly a tourist, and if they have enough money to get to another part of the country or overseas, then yes, they clearly have money to be here," she points out. "I don't know how they assumed I got over there."

The effects of 9/11 lingered for many air passengers of colour. I recall returning to Vancouver in the late aughts, chatting with my seatmate, a Pakistani Canadian who owned a plumbing business in Surrey, a city just north of the Canada–US border. As we disembarked we agreed it was good to be home. Then security officers stepped into his path. I still recall the look on his face, a mix of surprise, consternation and fear. They escorted him away for extra screening. I was free to go my way.

Freedom is often framed as a personal issue. The Ottawa truck convoy was a collective protest against what were perceived to be infringements on personal freedom during the pandemic. Those opposed to the protests cited the need for collective responsibility. A similar dialectic has emerged around travel and climate change—freedom to travel versus collective responsibility to the planet.

COVID-19 had the motivational advantage of being a clear and present danger, not a vague future threat. And although we are increasingly seeing undeniable effects of climate change, for many it still remains a distant prospect. As with vaccine and mask mandates, there are loud voices claiming (without credible evidence) that the dire climate science is wrong. At the very least, these deniers give people a banner to rally around if they want to conduct business as usual.

How, then, do we balance those opposing ideas when it comes to travel and climate? For many, travel represents freedom (which may or may not be connected to the adoption of alternative COVID therapies, such as the sauna-and-vodka treatment recommended by Belarussian president Alexander Lukashenko or the protective amulets favoured by Mexican president Andrés Manuel López Obrador).

Governments that forbid citizens from travelling are generally authoritarian or worse. Yet battling the climate crisis, like fighting a pandemic, would seem to demand collective action and sacrifice. As people on both sides of the political spectrum are fond of saying, facts don't care about your feelings.

"The problem is not that there are so many trips," says Professor C. Michael Hall, "but that they are so far away and so brief. Reduce the distance and change the mode of travel and you would have an industry that is a lot more sustainable. However, that requires a rethink from both industry and consumers."

Hall could have been referring to our old friend, Leo DiCaprio. Testifying for the prosecution at a Washington, DC, fraud trial in April 2023, DiCaprio described how fugitive Malaysian financier Jho Low once flew him and a party of guests to Australia to celebrate New Year's Eve, and then whisked them to Las Vegas to celebrate the same event again in a different time zone. "Did you make it back in time to celebrate?" a lawyer asked.

"It depends on how you look at it," DiCaprio replied to laughter from the gallery.

Whirlwind trips are often pitched as glamorous (see the *New York Times'* regular feature, 36 Hours). And then there's the long-running CBS reality series *The Amazing Race*, which took the concept of Jules Verne's 1873 novel *Around the World in Eighty Days* and turned it into a televised competition. Teams of two fly from country to country—frequently countries that have paid to showcase themselves to potential travellers—and compete in various tasks, seeking to be the first to cross a finish line and claim a million bucks. It is designed to be fun to watch. It certainly isn't designed to be an ideal vacation. Get off the plane, drive to an empty field where you must shoot a watermelon at a target with a sling shot, drive to a warehouse where you string a bunch of stinking fish heads together and load them into a wheelbarrow, go to a barn and eat four pounds of cow udders, etc. "It's like an anti-travel approach to travel," says Concordia University's Seth Wynes.

The show debuted on North American television September 5, 2001, six days before hijacked airliners would fly into the towers of the World Trade Center, the Pentagon and a Pennsylvania field. Early ratings suffered as international travel endured its greatest setback since World War II. Yet somehow the series survived (just as it survived the temporary production shutdown of season thirty-three due to COVID-19), going on to become an Emmy-winning TV staple.

Whatever else it might do, *The Amazing Race* glorifies a world in which international air travel is as ubiquitous and convenient as a civic streetcar grid. "This is celebrating a lifestyle of fast travel and cheap vacations and not actually getting to know a culture when you show up to visit a country," says Wynes.

TU Dortmund University's Giulio Mattioli has suggested that cheap air travel might even be reshaping the world, just as cars reshaped twentieth-century cities. "If you grow up getting used to high levels of long-distance travel and holidays abroad, you will end up taking that for granted," he says. "We had a sample of students at Dortmund University, and found that students who had a lot of holidays abroad as kids tended to take more holidays abroad as adults.

"I had a student in the UK who was doing a master's thesis on climbers. They tend to be very environmentally minded, very green people. But they fly a lot, for various reasons depending on the way that they climb. There's a certain style of climbing they can do in the UK but there is another sort they can only do in the French Alps. Another issue is the weather. If you go to southern Europe you can be sure that in certain weeks you will not get rain. So a lot of air travel became embedded into the practice of climbing. Even these people who were very environmentally minded found it very difficult not to do that."

Mattioli says we are not yet at the stage where cheap flights are considered a basic right. "With the car it's almost too late," he says. "It's been locked in already. We would have to rebuild our cities to make substantial reductions in car use possible, especially in places like the US. Whereas for air travel I think we're still in that process of locking in."

Those who would prioritize air travel should be aware of the stakes. "Assuming for the sake of argument that the goal is mass international air travel, with much higher levels of participation than we have now, then we probably have a trade-off between that and keeping climate change within certain temperatures," Mattioli says. "It's societies and politics that should decide which of the two goals gets priority, not scientists like me."

Wynes can even picture a popular anti-travel sentiment coming from the grassroots, a Greta Thunberg–style social revolution. "You might imagine a social movement from the masses that says, disasters are unfolding," Wynes suggests, "aviation is an unfair source of emissions, we need to cut it drastically, and governments becoming terrified of this movement and cutting it."

One recent study from Icelandic and Polish researchers suggests Wynes is being optimistic. The 2023 study, published in the *Journal of Sustainable Tourism* and titled "I Am Not a Typical Flyer," suggests environmentally conscious travellers are more likely to rationalize their behaviour than change it. "Travellers deal with tensions between the benefits of flying and its environmental impact by applying various strategies to reduce cognitive dissonance instead of changing behaviour," the authors write.

People who care about the environment will recycle, turn out the lights, turn down the thermostat, ride a bicycle or buy an electric car. But when it comes to air travel they are more likely to cite other responsible behaviours as mitigating and thus excusing their flight emissions. "Some pro-environmental actions may serve as an excuse for not performing others," the study says. "Study participants use local pro-environmental behaviour as a surrogate response to air travel reduction."

It's the "I jogged five miles, so I can have a glazed doughnut" approach to climate action. The study's co-author, sociologist Dr. Filip Schmidt of Adam Mickiewicz University in Poznań, Poland, expands on my analogy. "Many of the mechanisms described in this paper are also about this: My doughnut is more justified than yours. Because it's more sophisticated or because I use it for better purposes than others. If, for example, travelling abroad has given you a great education, or you now have a family living in another country or countries, or half of your friends are scattered around the globe, or colleagues or co-authors are on different continents, this gives you a stronger moral justification for travelling. And you can justify it by pointing to others who eat their doughnuts for less legitimate reasons, like flying just to get some sun."

It's not hard to see why people seek to justify their international journeys. Long-distance air travel is fundamentally irreplaceable. At Starbucks, you can feel good about reducing waste by bringing your own mug. But with long distance flight, your options are do it or don't. If the only way to feel environmentally responsible at Starbucks was to drink coffee no more than once a year, how many of us would?

Freedom is a powerful concept. Blue-faced Mel Gibson did not yell "Collective responsibility!" to his warriors in *Braveheart*. Threats to freedom are something everyone can understand. And, unfortunately, some of what we consider freedom is really privilege.

Will climate change spur real action in the travel industry? It seems to me far more likely that the world will wait for technological solutions to solve emissions issues. The question is: What will the world look like when those solutions are finally available?

Home Port

I live in Vancouver, about a block from Lost Lagoon. It's a relatively short walk to the beloved seawall that encircles the 405-hectare Stanley Park (bigger than any park you'll find in Manhattan). Spending a warm spring Saturday sitting on a bench on the seawall is instructive. You learn about the remarkable variety of languages spoken daily in Vancouver. You are reminded that the wheel was a far more important invention than the internal combustion engine, as examples roll past in an ever-growing set of configurations and power sources. You learn that bike lanes are too narrow, especially given the increasing popularity of high-powered e-bikes and scooters. You learn things about music and its purposes—not employed merely for personal enjoyment but as a statement of identity, a fact made clear by the riders who eschew the privacy of earbuds to blast their chosen tunes to the world through portable speakers. You learn that Helen definitely did not appreciate Shelley's passive-aggressive remark at Sandra's bachelorette party last weekend. And you learn that, in Vancouver at least, tourism can indeed be local.

Most of the people whizzing or strolling past my bench give every impression of being residents. Vancouverites love the seawall. As do I. Getting here used to take me days. Now it is a matter of minutes.

But herein lies another indictment. If I have moved to a city that was once a travel destination and made a life there, why isn't that enough? If I solved the ecotourism emissions problem by moving to a favoured spot and making it my own, what am I doing flying to Rome and Tokyo and Bangkok?

My first visit to Vancouver came at age fourteen. I was the guest of my friend Al's family. A yokel from the Prairies, I was in awe of the West Coast, a feeling hidden at the time behind a wall of resentment. "These people think they are so damn cool," I muttered. I was a pickerel out of water, a long way from my usual vacation spot of Clear Lake, Manitoba. Yet the city and surroundings were imprinting on me in ways I would only later understand.

It seems likely that at least one powerful theme of my later travel aspirations was set by that early Vancouver visit. Beneath the insecurity I felt, there must have been a secret desire to fit in, to be a part of it, to be accepted. Subsequent events bore that out, as I would later make Vancouver my home. In my other travels I have struggled, often quixotically, to achieve a similar sense of belonging. That desire has helped shape my preference for longer stays rather than short whirlwind visits. According to my unofficial prosecutor Giulio Mattioli, that preference aligns with good environmental practice.

But what if, by staying longer, I develop closer ties to a destination, thereby motivating more long-distance travel? "I never thought about that," Mattioli says. "If you look at research on sustainable tourism, they argue that we need a different kind of tourism, not just a weekend getaway in a city but to stay for a couple of weeks. But as you say, the longer you stay, the more likely you are to develop some social networks and bond with people who live there, and that might lead you to travel more to maintain these social relationships. That's an interesting hypothesis. A pessimistic one."

I am digging myself in deeper here—if I had a lawyer he'd be keeping me off the witness stand.

There is also the question of whether a tourist can truly understand and appreciate a faraway place, as I have sought to do. In Vancouver I have played both roles, visitor and resident. That has given me a chance to compare my first touristic impressions of the city with my current reality. Is it true that no traveller can ever truly see and experience the places they briefly and superficially experience?

Obviously visiting Vancouver did not offer severe cultural challenges to be overcome, aside from my painful lack of hipness. There were no linguistic barriers and I didn't even need a passport. Still, Vancouver was a large city over two thousand kilometres away from my relatively little town, a distance few ever covered before the advent of train travel, and the city offered a very different geography and vision of daily life.

While my current picture of Vancouver is deeper and necessarily more practical, my lived experience has not exposed that initial view as some sort of lie. My first impressions still hold, and remain as guideposts for me today. I often seek to remind myself of early visits as a way of tearing away the grey veil of the everyday and experiencing once again the beauty of my chosen home.

So that question again: Why do I travel, if I live in a paradise? There is one force that exerts an inexorable pull: novelty. Beautiful as it is here, I often find myself paralyzed by familiarity, unable to muster the energy for a bike ride to places I have visited hundreds of times before. Like many, I travel for novelty.

It may even be true in a neurological sense. Research by Alex Kafkas and Daniela Montaldi of the University of Manchester suggests that things we know and recognize are processed in different parts of the brain than things new to us. So a journey from the familiar to the novel may involve a trip across our cerebral geography.

But I have run myself into a contradiction here. If I travel for novelty, what about this cherished goal of fitting into faraway places? If I succeed in fitting in wherever I go, doesn't that subvert the entire point of the enterprise? If one truly becomes part of the landscape, part of the crowd, one's relationship to the destination changes. It is a destination no longer. I travelled to Vancouver as a dazzled teenager—now it is home, the place I do laundry, the place I leave behind when searching for excitement. You can only sustain the sense of wonder for so long. I do not stroll down the street with a debonair swagger that says, *Look at me, on my way to save seventy cents on a can of minestrone.*

So why do I want to destroy the novelty of travel by becoming a regular? Do I even know what I want? Possess the cake! Consume the cake! Am I a hypocrite or just pitifully confused? "The tourist remains mystified as to his true motives," author Dean MacCannell wrote. You could illustrate a PowerPoint presentation on that theme with my passport photo.

Yet perhaps those contributions are not completely irreconcilable. Novelty is not simply about geography. It is about ways of thinking and ways of living. "Becoming a truly skilled traveler, a tourist-plus, if you will, can transform you in the same way as learning carpentry, studying painting or gaining a facility for gardening," wrote *New York Times* columnist Ross Douthat, "not with a sudden mystical rush, but as a slow-motion acquisition of capacities you didn't have before."

My travels have introduced me to much more than a set of new landscapes. Travelling has meant encountering different styles and attitudes, from Japan to India to Italy. It was probably Italy that hit me hardest. Visiting the country opened my eyes to the importance of fashion, something I had previously disdained. For a guy inclined to shop for clothes at Canadian Tire, visiting Rome was like biting the apple and knowing shame. After observing local style I started shopping with new role models in view. It's not so much that I reshaped my personal style—I finally developed one.

But with the zeal of the new convert, I may have overdone it. My new Euro look featured striped linen pants and bright-citrus-coloured slacks, two-tone shoes and summer jackets that might have come from a *Great Gatsby* remake. It was a bit much. While it's admirable to confidently own your style, eventually I had to admit to myself I wasn't entirely comfortable playing the role of Euro fashion standout on the streets of.Vancouver. I wanted to look good without being stared at. So I dialed it back a little. Not all the way, though—Italy had opened my eyes to the idea that dressing well need not be a frivolous pursuit.

New places inevitably leave their mark. There are people who journey thousands of miles only to eat at faraway McDonald's, but even if you never step off the tour bus you are going to see different ways of doing things.

Almost any traveller in Europe will encounter public spaces that are alive in ways that would make North American city planners sigh with envy. My travels in Japan have left me with entirely new visions of community, from architecture and urban planning to concepts of shared responsibility. The lessons offered by Bangkok could take a lifetime to untangle—and are certainly a very mixed bag—but experiencing this cityscape of slapdash functionality, full of wonder and enterprise and the best street food you will find anywhere in the world, must certainly change your conception of the possibilities offered by urban life.

My time in Vancouver has also taught me that there is another stage to be reached in your relationship with a city. The death of novelty, the onset of dull familiarity, need not be the end point. Living in Vancouver has shown me that the gulf of initial disenchantment can be bridged; one can emerge on the other side with an appreciation based on more than just initial fascination and discovery—a love based on more intimate knowledge. (I suspect marriage is also like that, but I really wouldn't know.)

It's also a bonus that time spent away lends freshness to our perceptions of home. As T.S. Eliot put it,

> We shall not cease from exploration
> And the end of all our exploring
> Will be to arrive where we started
> And know the place for the first time.

Kyoko arrived in Vancouver in 2001, about a month after the end of our Japanese tour. Her plan was to study English with the ultimate goal of entering Columbia University in New York. Our roles were now reversed. Kyoko was the one on unfamiliar turf. Perhaps that helped me relax a bit—cruelly, since the extra burden of cultural stress was now squarely on Kyoko.

Vancouver held some particular attractions for her. For one thing, Kyoko was crazy about raccoons. Not just aren't-they-cute crazy—she felt a bond. In Philip Pullman's *His Dark Materials* trilogy, people have animal companions called dæmons that represent a sort of external soul. There is no doubt what shape Kyoko's dæmon would take. Yet she had never seen a raccoon; she'd seen only photographs and two plush versions I bought for her in a Vancouver gift shop, which she promptly named Stevie and Stephanie.

One day not long after her arrival I took Kyoko to Prospect Point in Stanley Park, the promontory overlooking the Lions Gate Bridge. Sure enough, there they were, along a wire fence at the edge of the public area— her dæmons. There were people at the fenceline feeding the raccoons with french fries. This behaviour was officially frowned upon by park authorities, and besides, Kyoko felt it would not be necessary in her case. The raccoons would come to her out of kinship. They would recognize her. Kyoko went to the fence and began calling to them.

Prospect Point raccoons, it turned out, have eyes for nothing but french fries. Poor Kyoko was forced to admit defeat and soon returned from the concession stand with a tray of deep-fried snacks. With this inducement, the scavengers finally recognized their spiritual cousin and came ambling over. Kyoko, a bit crestfallen at their transactional attitude, was pleased nonetheless.

It was fun being a Vancouver tourist with Kyoko. Lighthouse Park, the summer fireworks festival, cafés, shopping for cheese at La Grotta del Formaggio on Commercial Drive, a ferry to Bowen Island, a side trip to Whistler—it all took me back to my first visit at fourteen, bathing my surroundings in the pleasant glow of novelty once again. Tourism is a matter of perspective. Kyoko's appreciation for the city was not only infectious, it was a powerful reminder of how my own Vancouver history began.

September 10 was Kyoko's birthday. That evening we had a lovely dinner at CinCin and talked about her plans for New York. Next morning my apartment buzzer rang at eight a.m. I was a late sleeper, but shuffled over to the receiver to mumble hello. Kyoko's frightened voice came through the line. "Can I come in and watch your TV?" she said. "World War III is starting and my parents want me to come home."

Watching the devastation in New York on September 11 carried an extra weight of dread for Kyoko. Vancouver had been challenge enough. Did she really want to study at Ground Zero? As it turned out she did not go home—not quite so soon.

Kyoko got a particular kick out of Halloween which, despite the Japanese love of cosplay, was not a traditional celebration back home. She donned a Viking helmet and fur cape, while I posed as a conquered warrior on the end of a chain leash. It's about as kinky as I got.

Our day of decision was approaching fast. Kyoko's visa was up in early November. Her pursuit of a place at Columbia University would now continue from Japan. "When I go back to Japan," Kyoko told me, "I want us to stay together."

I wished I felt the same way. I didn't. Why? It's the question every teary, roseless contestant is asking as they ride away in a limousine at the close of each episode of *The Bachelor* or *The Bachelorette*. Why? Why? And the scientific answer is: I dunno, whaddya gonna do? It's never fair. One person reviews every conversation, obsessively analyzes every shared moment, while the other just shrugs. I know from repeated and painful experience how infuriating that shrug can be. It covers for the uncomfortable truth few want to face—that most of us don't truly understand our own romantic reactions, much as we pretend to. "He makes me laugh," they say. Well, so do three martinis. It's possible the jokes aren't really that funny.

Then Kyoko had to leave. My secret shame was that my growing comfort level with our relationship may well have stemmed from the knowledge that it came with a natural expiry date. The awful truth was I had been waiting for this. Yet over the course of our time together in Vancouver I had also realized the many ways I had been unfair to Kyoko. I worried that her first real relationship would be difficult to let go of. But in my anxiety I had underestimated her. Kyoko was an adult. Had I been infantilizing her with my concern that she would not be able to accept disappointment? "I am strong," she would tell me.

She did, however, have a little backup plan for us. It was something she often mentioned during her Vancouver stay, perhaps an indication that the writing had been on the wall. "If we part," she said, "we should plan to meet again."

Kyoko had chosen a date and time—two p.m., August 25 (the day before my birthday, so I would remember), in eight years' time. At that hour, she instructed, we should meet at the Caffè Artigiano location on the corner of Pender and Thurlow in Vancouver. She made me promise, and I did.

Then we were at Vancouver International Airport for a tearful farewell. "It's OK," she said. "I am a lone wolf."

Life resumed. Our Japanese experience receded in memory, as such things tend to do in the persistent current of daily life. And then one day it struck me like a cattle prod.

Back in the InterContinental Tokyo Bay during that first week with Kyoko, there was only one English-language channel to be had: BBC World Service. Lacking any commercial content, the news channel would lead up to the top of the hour with spacey theme music for three minutes at a stretch while I, desperate for a connection to the familiar, sat staring at the swirling graphics, waiting patiently for content, something I could understand.

One Vancouver day long after Kyoko's departure, I was sitting in an office. A nearby TV was tuned to the BBC. The spacey theme music began. The effect was like some hypnotic cue, the kind that professional showmen employ to make hapless audience dupes become boneless or start clucking like chickens. The whole Japanese experience returned in a heartbeat, distilled into an emotional cocktail of stress, uncertainty, foreboding and a sense of disconnection, shaken together with wonder and filtered through altered perception. It flooded my system like a general anaesthetic, leaving me momentarily frozen.

And yet there was still an irresistible process at work in me—the inevitable reshaping of experience and recasting of memory. The recollection of emotional states ebbs, leaving behind a more prosaic mental record of events. Sometimes I would start waxing sentimental about Kyoko and our epic trip. This disgusted my friend Martin. He would pointedly remind me of my desperate, ranting phone call from a pay phone in Kanazawa, screaming about my need for a little breathing space. He was right, of course. But it was also true, I reflected, that at the time I was being neurotic. I had underestimated Kyoko, and, in hindsight, I had been much more anxious than I needed to be.

At any rate, it would be good to hear from Kyoko again. Where was she now?

I once had the thoroughly discombobulating experience of going to the movies and seeing a former flame suddenly pop up onscreen, semiclothed. Could Kyoko perhaps have seen me pop up (fully clothed, thank goodness) as she watched the Japanese TV show *vs Arashi*?

I had heard nothing. Attempts to reach out had been futile. Kyoko had disappeared from my world entirely.

Departures

Travel companies have trotted out hundreds of slogans over the years: "It matters who you travel with." "The holiday makers." "Get up and go." "A world of experience." "Low fares made easy."

I propose a new slogan, tailored for veteran travellers: "That place you loved isn't there anymore."

My post-pandemic trips have had the hopeful theme of reconnection, of rediscovering fondly remembered places. And how has that been going? Frequently, not well. Familiar shops in Rome are closed. My favourite old hotel in Tokyo has disappeared. A plaza in a Ueno neighbourhood, a corner in an Osaka laneway, a modest locale beside an underground staircase near the Umeda Hanshin Department Store, now missing the elements that once made them special—a charming café, a *takoyaki* stall, a down-and-dirty *kushikatsu* joint, all vanished. Bangkok, that city I love, is an ongoing lesson on impermanence. You get the impression that nothing is safe from development there. If the right palms are greased, Grandma and the orphans are out on the pavement and a shiny new shopping complex is on the way.

In the spring of 2023 I arrive in Palermo for the first time in four years. High on my agenda is a sentimental return to the hole-in-the-wall coffee bar where once I sat at a plastic table sipping espresso while Al Stewart sang in my head. In light of the many disappearances I have recently encountered, I feel, if not exactly a premonition, at least some trepidation as I pop open my umbrella and enter the narrow Via Sant Agostino on a drizzly Sicilian morning. The streets are nearly empty at this early hour and many shops shuttered. Yet when I reach the spot, I know. It is not just the closed and locked shutter—the Bar Genovese sign is gone. It's hard to imagine an absence of tourists killing a place like that—if they ever got any, surely I was the only one to make that mistake twice. But something did.

Next door a man stands smoking under an awning. "How long since Bar Genovese closed?" I ask. He shrugs. "A long time ago," he says, betraying neither sadness or concern. Apparently not everyone misses having their daily shot served by a woman who glares at you as though certain you are about to stamp your name on her shit list for good. It seems I alone will grieve this loss.

I have often wondered about my desire to return to familiar yet far-off places. While it is true that I seek connection abroad, I have come to realize there is more at work. My return trips to favourite locations like Rome, Siena and Tokyo have not simply been driven by a desire to belong. When standing in a distant city that I love, I find the possibility that I might never visit again unsettling. And what would prevent me? A lack of financial resources, certainly, or a lack of opportunity. Ultimately, though, there will be the more decisive impediment. Someday I will be unable to travel due to the lack of a pulse and an inability to fog up a mirror. Part of my desire to return to familiar spots, I have come to understand, is to deny the prospect of death.

It's a motive that has been cited by others. After the June 2023 *Titan* submersible disaster that took five lives, writer Danielle Crittenden suggested that such high-end adventures are driven by a similar impulse. "It's a desire to conquer mortality itself," she wrote. "Proving you can survive again and again performing extreme feats of daring reassures the survivor of his own invincibility."

Thankfully I have not been tempted to risk death in order to deny it. My methods have been more mundane. I simply want to return. To say definitively that I will never be back to a beloved spot carries frightening implications. I reject those implications. I return, therefore I (still) am. Perhaps it is a variation on the Instagram ethos. Instagrammers travel to showcase their fabulous lives—I travel to forestall my inevitable death. Tomayto, tomahto.

There is a bit of this feeling in every journey. A long trip is like a brief life, and its ending, a little death. I have said that when I arrive at the airport the domestic man goes to sleep and another awakens, the one who travels. For that man the end of a voyage looms as a return to oblivion. Upon my return home, Jekyll murders Hyde.

Is it true that I travel to escape the spectre of death, to reaffirm the endurance of life? If so, I'm foolish. It's futile. Death comes in instalments. Our personal landscapes are relentlessly plowed under. Your favourite haunt is now a ghost.

It has been said that stasis is death, while change brings life. Don't be fooled. Change, bringer of life, is also a double agent—Death's emissary. "All things must pass," it says, looking you square in the eyes.

When your relationship with a destination is intermittent, the changes seem more drastic. You return for the first time in years and what may have been a gradual process of alteration and decay for locals hits you all at once. It works that way for people too. "You haven't changed a bit," they tell you, the shameless liars.

But change is coming. It's not just local, not just personal, not just here and there, plucking out the odd familiar place. Change is coming on a global scale. Death's emissaries are marching on an ever-widening front, coming for fragile ecosystems—forests, mangroves, coral reefs, rivers, glaciers and wetlands endangered around the planet, threatening dependent species, ours among them.

The recently installed retractable floodgates intended to protect Venice from rising waters are already being raised more frequently than planners either expected or intended. In the Maldives, the lowest nation on Earth, the city of Malé is ringed by seawalls to hold back the encroaching Indian Ocean. But the Intergovernmental Panel on Climate Change warns that rising seas could make the Maldives uninhabitable by 2100.

Environmentalists ask us to consider planetary peril when we make travel decisions. But it is difficult to convince us with abstract notions. The sad truth is that real awareness probably depends on climate disasters becoming a reality for wider swaths of the population.

Loss is personal. That's the level on which we experience and understand it. While we stand in danger of losing the experience of the world as we have known it, we deal every day with losses that feel more tangible and immediate. And change is not always gradual.

When I return to Hotel Orlanda in 2023, four years and a pandemic after my last visit to Rome, I expect some change. Marco has already told me familiar faces like Simone had been let go. But Marco hasn't told me everything.

The morning after my arrival, I find Marco leaning on a cane. He shows me a long red scar on his scalp. A couple of months after I began making joyful arrangements for my return to Orlanda, Marco had found himself with an unexpected reservation of his own—a month-long stay in a Roman hospital.

One January morning Marco had been riding his scooter to work. Stopping at an intersection, he proceeded on a green light. A woman in a white Fiat ran the red and smashed into Marco's scooter. Waiting for the ambulance, Marco was convinced he was not badly hurt—maybe a little problem with his leg. He called his wife. "Tell Paolo to come in to the hotel," he said. "I can't make it."

Shortly afterward Marco's wife drove past the accident site, roped off and attended by police and paramedics. She paid it little mind. That couldn't be Marco's accident, she thought—he had sounded too calm.

It was January 15—the Ides of January. "You are like Julius Caesar," I tell him.

"I don't want to be Caesar," Marco says. "Being Caesar—it's good for the poets. It's good for the writers. It's not good for Caesar."

Now three months later, there are lingering issues. He has a tingling sensation in several fingers, ligament damage in his shoulder and leg, and not much stamina. "I am lucky," he says. "People die all the time, for nothing."

He has a renewed gratitude for routine things. "The first time I get up out of the hospital bed to go to the bathroom by myself," Marco says, "I am king of the world. Money, power, awards—they are nothing compared to this."

Rome has not completely recovered either. The little snack bar in front of Orlanda is gone, the hotel across the street, closed. One April day I walk out of Orlanda, down Via Panisperna to Piazza Venezia and then set out across the Tiber to visit a favourite spot, a *gastronomia* some blocks away from the Vatican that has been a Roman fixture for decades. But when I arrive, that sign is gone too, the metal shutters down. I go into the shop next door and ask the manager: "What happened?" "Last year," he says, "they closed."

"The pandemic?" I ask. He shakes his head. "No, no. The owner's son. He is not too bright. For ten years he has been mismanaging that place until finally it was destroyed."

Well. There's no vaccine for that.

Generally, though, Rome appears to have rebounded well. Even in a rainy April week, there are plenty of tourists thronging Via del Corso. Along Via dei Fori Imperiali, which leads from Piazza Venezia past the Roman Forum to the Colosseum, there are so many talented buskers playing for appreciative crowds that walking it is like sliding along a radio dial: a combo playing a jazzy "Girl from Ipanema," a band doing a bluesy take on Amy Winehouse's "Back to Black," a Liberace-style "Für Elise," "Despacito" on the violin.

Hotel Orlanda is full too. I can't even get my beloved room 505, as the fifth floor is jammed with Milanese students on a school trip. I see them at breakfast, preparing for a day of immersion in history and culture,

Juliet stealing a glance at the nearby table where Romeo sits munching granola. If any place can be said to be a bulwark against change, it is the Eternal City.

My reconnection tour then takes me north, three hours by train to Siena. My return comes months before the cherished day of days when the horses will once again career around the Campo in pursuit of the Palio, but it is a holiday—April 25, Liberation Day in Italy. When I arrive Siena is awash in a tourist wave that could make the *Mona Lisa* jealous. I make my way across the Campo to Via Duprè and the shores of that other noble wave, the Contrada Capitana dell'Onda. Once again I find that dreaded change has preceded me. Bar L'Onda, once run by the friendly and welcoming Onda resident I knew only as Gianni, appears to have closed for good. A couple of doors down, a woman is sweeping the patio of her small restaurant. I ask about Gianni. "He is still here," she tells me. "But his brother left and he couldn't keep the bar open on his own anymore—it is difficult to find help now. But he is around. He works at Santa Maria Della Scala Café, near the duomo."

From Via Duprè to the duomo is uphill all the way, and as I climb through the narrow, sloping streets I am wondering—not for the first time—about the futility of my efforts. Much as I loved it, the late lamented Bar Genovese was fairly representative of my various attempts at connection, in that the affection was all on one side. My love for that Palermo café was definitely unrequited. Is that enough? Is it necessary that a place love you back? Or is it sufficient to find the places you love, love them, take them as they are and ask for nothing in return but toleration of your presence?

Siena's magnificent banded-stone duomo comes into view, and there to my left, Santa Maria Della Scala Café. I ask for Gianni but he sees me first as he comes in from wiping down tables. He breaks into a wide grin and grips me in a warm hug. It has been at least fourteen years and, frankly, I am stunned. Gianni remembers me. My Italian is hardly worthy of the name, and Gianni's English is sketchy. But we reminisce on Palios past. We sing the Onda hymn together—happily, I have brushed up on the words for the occasion. "*L'Onda ha colore del cielo and la forza dei mare*," we sing in the café, "*la piu bella de la citta.*"

I exit the café with a grateful sense that perhaps some connections can endure. And a reminder that not everything will go. The Palio, at least, is forever.

My trip to Italy is not the only return voyage for me this year. I have also returned to Japan. I started in Tokyo, where Kyoko and I spent our first eventful week exploring together and crying consecutively. Next I moved on to Kyoto where I walked in Gion once more. And twenty-two years after we first travelled to Kanazawa, I am going back. I have not been to Kyoko's former hometown since then. I want to find her old house by the river where we once ate luxurious breakfasts and watched termite parades.

The train trip north from Kyoto is more beautiful than I remember; I suppose I had other things on my mind back then. I watch the sun rising through hazy cloud over Lake Biwa as we roll past fallow winter fields. (The Thunderbird train also passes near a town called Obama, definitely not something I would have made a note of in 2001.) The Kanazawa train station is new—large, modern and impressive. I drop my bags at the hotel and strike off in search of Kazue-machi, the riverside village where Kyoko's old house sat. I find the street, looking just as it did—the wooden foot bridge, the little park, the row of narrow, tightly packed traditional houses fronted by a stone wall. But I can't find Kyoko's house. There are several possible candidates. But to my embarrassment, I am just not sure. None of them seem exactly right.

A number of the old homes are now modest retail businesses. One of them, a possible candidate, is a little coffee bar run by an old gentleman who welcomes me in. I try to explain my mission in English but to no avail. The proprietor pulls out his phone, brings up the audio translation app, and hands it to me. I say, "How long have you been here?" The phone takes in my words, and the screen displays the results as "Bow wow."

I have never been so insulted by a device in all my life.

I go a couple of doors down to another possible site that now houses a restaurant. I try my English with an employee but get only a blank stare. Kanazawa is not cosmopolitan Tokyo.

Next day I visit Kanazawa Castle. It's an impressive complex, a massive traditional Japanese structure situated in a beautiful landscaped park. But historical? Like the train station, the castle was not around in 2001, when it was still being worked on. Much of what stands now essentially dates from the twenty-first century, built according to old plans to augment a few surviving historical remnants. Kanazawa Castle stretches the definition of preservation. Separating old from new can be hard here, as I am discovering.

I decide to make another run at finding Kyoko's house. Naturally I get badly lost in the process. By the time I hit the Asano River and begin following it downstream toward Kazue-machi, Kyoko might have been calling the police—if she were expecting my arrival. But at last the old town comes in view. And today I have a plan.

Near Kyoko's old street there is a little museum dedicated to author Izumi Kyōka, whose 1894 story "The Righteous and the Chivalrous" was later made into a silent film called *The Water Magician*. Its central character was apparently based on Izumi's neighbour, the famous geisha Michiyyako. Michiyyako's house later became Kyoko's house, the cozy little termite-ridden pile where we spent a spring week together. I will go to the museum and ask where it is. Perhaps their translation apps are superior.

The museum is—I should have guessed—closed. Perhaps they saw me coming. I cross the street to the local Shinto shrine where Kyoko once parked her car. The old man at the shrine pulls out his phone but in this case we don't even get to the insult stage—he can't make the translation app work. Anyway, I understand his words. He just wants to tell me politely he doesn't know what I'm babbling about.

I go back down to the stone walkway one last time. Two young women in kimonos are posing for pictures. One of them, Hannah, is of British descent and speaks perfect English. She mentions a 2007 earthquake that shook the area. Might that have finished off Kyoko's house? The street looks unharmed, but there is at least one house in the row that looks suspiciously new. Could Kyoko's home have finally fallen prey to termites and neglect?

I tell Hannah and her companion, Kana, that I was here twenty-two years ago. "Kana and I are both twenty-two," she says.

Strange as it may sound, it is only during my return that I am truly realizing twenty-two years is a very long time.

The street is familiar and well-preserved. It is a pleasure to be standing here once again. Still, I feel like a fool. I have crossed the ocean and the island of Honshu to visit a part of my past I have often recalled. The house may well be here, somewhere right in front of me. And I can't see it. A veil has been drawn across my vision. This phantom haunt has eluded me.

And Kyoko herself? She vanished too. I have made attempts to reach out without success. I even sent a letter to her mother once. No reply. Perhaps it was a language issue. Perhaps not.

But there was a date marked on our calendar long ago. Once upon a time Kyoko extracted from me a promise. Determined to ensure that the veil of years and distance would not fall between us for good, she had planned a rendezvous, a reunion set for a specific date, time and place. On that date I did my best to keep the promised rendezvous. Did she?

CHAPTER THIRTY-TWO

This Year's Hottest Destinations

Ten flights scheduled for 2023—ten flights duly taken. Endless zigzag lineups that ideally should have led to Space Mountain; involuntary participation in sociological experiments on the effects of crowding and stress; boarding passes identifying your boarding group with three digits; the Darwinian struggle for overhead bin space and the silent battle of wills for control of the middle-seat armrests; some flight attendants who, despite endless provocation, remain as cheerful as the San Diego Chicken, and others who clearly missed their calling as dungeon masters; a seat-back superhero movie if you're lucky, a screenless seat reclined almost into your lap if you're not; your laptop open at a forty-degree angle behind a snoring passenger; and hours spent marvelling at how Einstein somehow understood the accordion-like variability of time despite never having been wedged into seat 36H on a seven-and-a-half-hour budget flight where they charge you for a swallow of water.

And somewhere just below me as all this was going on, over one million tonnes of soot being expelled into the high atmosphere. This environmental offence is part of the indictment I face. Millions stand in the dock beside me.

A damning coincidence occurred in July 2023. July 3, 4 and 5 were each identified in turn as the hottest days on record since global records have been kept. The next day, July 6, was the busiest day in commercial aviation history. According to Flightradar24, there were 134,386 planes in the air. Correlation is not causation. But it has to look bad to a jury.

For years climate scientists have predicted dire consequences, even as they wondered what it would take to bring the impact of climate change home to lay people. Receding ice caps, rising seas, more powerful storms— all compelling evidence, yet experienced first-hand by relatively few. Who would have guessed that the Pale Horse of climate change would be heralded by our most valued friends and allies?

Trees are the answer, we have been told. Trees are our bulwark, our panacea, our magic solution—more trees to eat up more carbon dioxide, and we're golden. But in the summer of 2023 New Yorkers awoke to find that our allies had turned. Huge swaths of Canadian forest were aflame and the skies were thick with wildfire smoke funnelling down from the north. By mid-July, air quality warnings were also in place in Chicago, Detroit, St. Louis and Cleveland. A nation obsessed with border security was discovering just how porous international boundaries truly are.

Recent Vancouver summers and falls reliably feature spells when the sun is a glowing red ball still high in the sky. Noonday light colours walls and floors with the orange tint of sunset. Your living room smells like a recently doused campfire. Now New York and other major US cities were discovering what people in my hometown had long since learned—in a warming world, summer becomes smoke season.

But 2023 had worse in store. That August, the climate front lines swept over a tourist destination long held up as emblematic of earthly paradise. Lahaina, on the island of Maui, was partly razed by wildfires aided by the winds of a passing hurricane. As the death toll climbed steadily to rank as Hawaii's worst-ever natural disaster, and newly homeless residents waited for relief supplies, charter boats of snorkellers continued to unload nearby. Paris Hilton was in the area, and not to hand out water and sandwiches. "They don't give a shit about us," local Alika Peneku told CNN. Canada's Global News found an evacuee, Jacqueline Mayuga, who had won a trip to Maui on *Wheel of Fortune*. Did she know the fateful wheel would follow her to Hawaii? And that it always turns?

Even as devastated Lahaina locals contemplated the flip side of tourist crowds, I made an unsettling discovery close to home. One day that week I stopped by a favourite spot in Stanley Park. It's a secret place—or so I would like to think—with a big stump that offers a sublime cliff-front view of Burrard Inlet and the North Shore. On this day though, I found my secret had been discovered. Party evidence was littered on the ground—plastic lids, bottle tops, a beach towel, scraps of trash. Two items were of particular interest. One was a plastic card issued by the Disney Cruise Line. The cardholder—his name was Tim—was a passenger on the *Disney Wonder* and certified as a silver member of the Castaway Club, a Disney Cruise loyalty program. And stuck into the side of the stump was a makeshift torch. Fashioned from sticks, duct tape and a roll of charred brown paper, Tim and friends had apparently used it to create a charming holiday mood.

A few hundred metres downhill I found a parked fire truck dealing with a spot fire in the park. There had been many that week, one of the summer's hottest. I showed the charred torch to a fireman, who just shook his head and shrugged. He'd seen some shit.

As we spoke, news reports were taking on an increasingly apocalyptic cast. That same day an evacuation order would be issued for Yellowknife as fire closed in. A good friend of mine was preparing to pack up his cat and join the line of traffic crawling south from the capital of the Northwest Territories toward the Alberta border. A province-wide state of emergency was about to be declared in BC. Homes in the city of West Kelowna would soon be in flames. Thousands were evacuated and tourists were warned not to travel to the Okanagan, a popular wine-and-fruit destination. It felt as though we were collectively turning a corner into an oft-predicted yet ultimately unpredictable new reality.

And Tim? If his party torch had started something serious in Stanley Park, perhaps he would be off to Alaska by the time this weary fireman was called in to help deal with it. But watch yourself, Timmy. They won't dig your act up there either.

At the beginning of this book I quote Seneca: "Though you may cross vast spaces of sea ... your faults will follow you whithersoever you travel." The Roman philosopher was referring to whatever demons are inside you, but millennia later his words apply equally well to the world we have created. Stay home, go abroad, no matter. You can't escape the new environmental reality.

There are many contributors to climate change. But air travel is one. International flights create emissions, and longer flights are far and away the biggest offenders. How do we deal with the issue? Are we, the tourist class, guilty of crimes against the Earth?

"If we are hoping to not have aviation swallow up a bigger and bigger chunk of our carbon footprint," says Concordia University's Seth Wynes, "it would be helpful to reduce demand. Instead we are seeing demand increasing."

UBC Professor Emeritus William Rees advocates for a complete shutdown of air travel. He is an outlier, and to be fair he does not consider himself a politician or policy-maker. "I'm a scientist," he says. Rees presents data and scenarios, makes recommendations (then pronounces, to use one of his favourite phrases, "It ain't gonna happen").

But even Rees admits that you could never stop everyone from flying. Air travel, overused and abused though it may be, is an irreplaceable service. It is this reality that enables bad-faith attacks on any environmental activists who travel. "But you flew here!" the critic crows. "Gotcha!"

"I don't know about getting rid of aviation altogether," Wynes says, "when there are good policies that can target people that fly the most. You want to level it off for wealthy countries so that up-and-coming countries can use some of that carbon budget that the wealthy nations have been hoarding. Whether that be through taxes or preventing more airport expansion, people who are serious about aviation and climate change are trying to figure it out."

"I don't think anyone in the environmental movement is actually proposing to introduce restrictions to international travel per se," says Giulio Mattioli. "It's more about taxing rather than incentivizing travel by a particular mode—air—which happens to be particularly climate-damaging."

"If there is only a limited amount of carbon that we can emit," Mattioli says, "then we have to allocate our remaining carbon budget between different countries and sectors of economic activity. Those who participate in international air travel tend to be affluent global north citizens and their main travel purpose is holidays and leisure. From a justice perspective, it is hard to argue that we should prioritize those activities over more basic needs like domestic electricity and even daily car travel."

Reducing consumption is the goal. The question comes down to priorities.

In April 2023 Gabriel J.X. Dance reported in the *New York Times* on the energy use of Bitcoin-mining operations—one located in Rockdale, Texas, used as much power as the nearest three hundred thousand homes. Thirty-four of these kinds of operations identified by the *Times* used the same amount of electricity as three million households. According to the Cambridge Bitcoin Electricity Consumption Index, worldwide Bitcoin mining is estimated to consume more energy annually than the Netherlands or the Philippines. This Bitcoin "mining" does not involve digging, but instead running massive computer networks to reveal mathematical codes. As energy uses go, it's hard to imagine anything less essential.

But Mattioli says my citing of Bitcoin is an example of whataboutism, the finger-pointing exercises that dog so many public debates, particularly on climate. Small countries point the finger at larger ones, and the largest emitters point fingers at each other, just as I, air traveller, point the finger at a different industry.

"If we were to rank energy uses depending on how useful and necessary they are, we would probably have Bitcoin farming at one end," Mattioli says, "and heating our homes to avoid freezing to death at the other end. The question is, Where does air travel fit along this continuum? I suppose it depends on the purpose of air travel. Air travel to distant destinations for holiday purposes would probably be closer to Bitcoin than to home heating. But these are discussions that we would need to have collectively, to decide which forms of energy use have to be guaranteed and which discouraged, through taxation and other means. Air travel is incredibly unequally distributed. Saying 'It just contributes 3 percent to global warming, we shouldn't worry too much about it' is a bit like saying, 'I know peeing in the swimming pool is bad, but as most people except me and my mates don't do it, urine will not be more than 3 percent of the pool, what's the big deal?'"

Travellers like me hope that technology will ride to the rescue. Will it?

Eventually, says Wynes. "We're going to get some sort of technology, assuming society keeps growing and developing and we are not derailed by an even worse pandemic or nuclear war."

"There are two questions," says Paul Chiambaretto of Montpelier Business School. "There's the question of whether we will develop new technologies and there's the adoption of these technologies. It's a challenge about innovation but it's also a challenge about replacing the entire fleet with the most efficient planes. We tend to overlook the second part. Today we have the new technology but nothing will happen in the next fifteen years because it will take time to replace these twenty to thirty thousand aircraft.

"The same thing is true with the SAF [sustainable aviation fuels]. The technology exists. What we don't know is how the air transport industry can scale up production. The challenge is not about inventing the technology, it is about ensuring it is easily available to the actors in the industry.

"Taxing airlines or airports, you reduce their ability to invest in your efforts. By contrast an intelligent government would say, instead of taxing all airlines let's create differential taxes depending on the type of aircraft you have in your fleet, so that you create bonuses for the most virtuous airlines and taxes for the ones who do not make the effort."

Everyone I spoke to agrees that waiting for technological solutions is not enough. "In a lot of ways, it's a waste not to take actions now," Wynes says. "You just have so much low-hanging fruit—so many flights that don't need to be taking place, either because they could be replaced by Zoom or because there are wealthy people taking private jets to faraway places for frivolous reasons."

Emissions aside, what about tourism itself? Its pleasures are undeniable, its problems and consequences real and multiplying. People want to travel. Destinations want tourist revenue. But can a win-win situation lead to catastrophic losses? Can leisure travel ultimately be justified?

"I don't think we're ever going to be able to stop travel," says travel consultant Claire Newell. "It has become such a privilege, to be able to go into another country, to learn their culture and to step into that world. It's a gateway to peace and tolerance and learning."

The question of whether tourism is a positive or negative global force is contentious. In a 2015 postscript to *Overbooked*, Elizabeth Becker said governments play a key role. "What is clear is that travel is neither good or bad," Becker wrote. "The travel industry, however, is having good and bad impacts, and governments, as never before, are central to determining what that outcome is. Tourists aren't neutral either. Individually they make profound choices and when travelling in hordes can do tremendous damage."

Rees believes the main responsibility lies with government. "We've been talking a lot about what you can do as an individual," he says. "And what individuals do is important. But it's relatively marginal. A couple of studies have shown that if individuals did everything they could as individuals to reduce their carbon footprints it might make a difference of between 2 and 10 percent. You as an individual cannot impose the appropriate carbon tax to make sure that fuel consumption doesn't increase as we get more efficient. You as an individual cannot fund rapid transit. The heavy lifting has to be done by governments."

Dr. Hazel Andrews agrees that putting the blame on individual travellers is the wrong approach. "I don't think that's really fair," she says. "It's bigger than that. It's structural inequalities, it's capitalism, it's business, and how we're channelled through that and how we can be exploited. For me the bottom line is the role of business. The travel industry represents an exploitation of our desire to move, because we have this need we can't explain."

Still, as Becker says, we make choices, and our choices matter. And even if it's true that governments bear the main responsibility, we in democracies put them in power.

International travel is not going away. But the ways we travel must change. "It doesn't have to be worse," Wynes says. "Just different."

Even Nobel Peace Prize winners can disagree on the net effects of tourism. "I remember a long time ago hearing the Dalai Lama speak and addressing the question of whether people ought to visit Tibet, because it's occupied by China," Andrews says. "And his view was, 'Yes,' because it helped keep the idea of Tibet and Tibetan culture alive. And you can compare that to Aung San Suu Kyi who said, when she was under house arrest years ago, that tourists shouldn't come to Myanmar because that would be funding the regime. And once the people were free the country would still be there, the cultural things people wanted to see would still be there. There are different ways of looking at it. It can be seen as a force for good or the other way."

In a rather surreal moment, I once stood on a stage about fifteen feet away from Aung San Suu Kyi. It was early 2013 and the Burmese politician and activist was addressing a crowd gathered at Yangon's Inya Lake Hotel for a new event called the Irrawaddy Literary Festival. The fact that I, a man with no credentials, was able to grab my camera and follow a group of photographers onto the stage to take shots has rather disturbing security implications. But more to the point, there I was in Myanmar, during what appeared to be a new era for the nation. President Obama had visited the country months earlier, and the woman many locals simply called the Lady had been freed from house arrest. "She is like my mother," one young woman told me.

"She has won three Oscars," said a man I met. "No, Nobels. Three Nobel Prizes. No one has ever done this before."

Nobody has ever done this, period, but never mind. The point was they were proud. Aung San Suu Kyi told the gathering of her love of literature and lighter reading, including Harry Potter and detective stories. Someone asked her whether the current situation in Myanmar should be told as a detective story or a poem. "Oh, a poem," she said emphatically. "I hope that Myanmar will be the kind of country worth writing poems about."

Well, there are all sorts of poems. As a kid I heard the one about Algy, who gets eaten by a bear.

Subsequent events in Myanmar would certainly make for a tragic ballad. Aung San Suu Kyi herself was widely criticized for failing to stand up for Myanmar's persecuted Rohingya population. And then things got much worse. On February 1, 2021, the military staged a coup and returned her to detention along with other civilian officials. As of early 2023, the Assistance Association for Political Prisoners estimated that close to three thousand protesters and activists had been killed and many thousands more imprisoned. The United Nations Office for the Coordination of Humanitarian Affairs has estimated that at least one million Myanmar residents have been internally displaced, and seventy thousand refugees (mostly Rohingya) have fled the country. Not all travel is tourism.

The people I met in Myanmar were thrilled to welcome the world. The arrival of foreigners meant something to them—it signalled a new day. That dawning sense of joy and possibility proved to be a mirage. The authoritarian curtain has come down again.

Whether or not tourism ultimately helps or harms a location, there is no doubt that the conditions allowing for tourism are precious. They are worth fighting for.

CHAPTER THIRTY-THREE

Final Reservation

The day has arrived. It is August 25. Eight years have passed since Kyoko and I toured Japan together. At two p.m., if Kyoko's design is realized, we will reunite at Caffè Artigiano at the corner of Pender and Thurlow in Vancouver. It is clear, however, that the plan will not, cannot work out exactly as prescribed. There has been a hitch. As the clock ticks toward zero hour at the designated meeting spot, I am over two thousand kilometres away.

It's been a bad year for my family. My mother died the previous March. In July my father, showing increasing signs of dementia, landed in hospital with a recurrence of the heart trouble that has dogged him for years. A family conference concluded I was the sibling best situated to spring Dad from hospital and shepherd him for a while. And so in late August I am in Manitoba—specifically, in Clear Lake, the scene of so many happy family vacations and reunions. Dad and I are sitting on the beach in lawn chairs, gazing out over choppy waves on the lake. It's a blustery day.

Since the days when Clear Lake was virtually the sum total of my travel experience I have been around the world. The world has proven to be quite a place. Yet perhaps inevitably, as I have grown older this beloved location has called to me with greater insistence. It has not been diminished by comparison with more exotic destinations. If anything it has grown in my eyes, appreciated for the quiet little miracle it is. How many places on our once-lonely planet are so beautiful yet so peaceful and free of mobs? There's a lot to be said for being three hundred kilometres from the nearest major airport. Even better if that airport is Winnipeg International, located approximately 35,000 feet below most international air traffic. Clear Lake, Manitoba, is not on Agoda. *Condé Nast Traveler* subscribers couldn't find it with Google Maps and a complete DVD set of *Little House on the Prairie*. On this cool summer afternoon, Dad and I don't have much company.

Dad's eyesight is poor and his mind elsewhere. So he neither sees nor notices that I am keeping one eye on my phone. Commitments may have called me away but I have made arrangements. I've enlisted my Vancouver friend Chris to stand in for me at Caffè Artigiano. Armed with a photo of Kyoko, he is perched at a table beside the door, waiting to send photos and reports. Far away, I sit with Dad gazing at a cold lake in the heart of fly-over country.

Normally the most upbeat of humans, Dad is blue today. He is grieving. This familiar place, so powerful for our family, has become for him a cruel reminder. Almost everything we knew is still here—the townscape is largely unchanged, give or take the odd grocery store or playground. Our cottage, now owned by family friends, still stands, clad in bright yellow on Marigold Street. Yet what gave it all meaning for my father is gone, and now the familiar sights merely recall his loss more sharply. "I wish Joan were here," he says repeatedly.

I do too. Yet although I would never tell him so, I feel differently about this place than my father. On return visits I have managed to forge a new relationship with our old turf, one that is both rooted in family history and open to discovery. As a kid I rode my bicycle to the Trading Post to buy pop and a chocolate bar (all for a quarter, damn it). Now I ride into the countryside, camera in satchel, seeking to capture the vision of prairie beauty that had quietly taken root in my young mind so long ago.

Here there are no questions about belonging, no effort required to forge bonds with a distant place. I still have old friends, connections that offer a bridge from past to present. For me, Clear Lake is both a landscape of memory and a vital destination. Every square metre is imbued with personal meaning, and yet I often encounter places I feel like I am seeing for the first time. Sometimes I am.

That sort of renewal is beyond Dad now. His eyes, his mind beginning to fail, his heart afflicted both physically and metaphorically, Dad lacks either the capacity or the motivation to see the familiar anew. What vision he has left is directed backward. He made a life with my mother and now that life is past. What surrounds him here today is mostly pain.

My phone pings with a message from Chris. "Nothing so far," he writes.

When I consider the experience of travel I often think back to the 1981 movie *My Dinner with Andre*, starring Wallace Shawn and André Gregory as fictionalized versions of themselves. On a list of the all-time great action flicks, it lands somewhere outside the top four hundred thousand. But it is a classic, perhaps one of a kind—a film that consists almost entirely of two men having dinner and talking. After listening to Gregory's wild tales of globe-trotting, his experiences of bizarre rituals and searing personal revelations, Shawn pushes back with a defence of the everyday. "Why do we need to travel to Mount Everest in order to perceive one moment of reality?" Shawn asks. "Is Mount Everest more real than New York? I think if you could become fully aware of what existed in a cigar store next to this restaurant, I think it would just blow your brains out."

The universe in a drop of water—I have experienced that revelation chiefly through photography. I have become lost in the unfolding drama of a daisy, a bee and a lurking spider, a drama that might play out almost anywhere from Tibet to Tuscany to Saskatchewan. Perhaps, as Shawn suggests, perfect awareness of a place and a moment is what matters most, regardless of where you may be. But that is a tall order for ordinary humans who have not achieved enlightenment under the bodhi tree. And novelty is a potent drug. Even Manitoba offers it to me now. It is no longer home—my home is a two- or three-day drive to the west. Getting to Manitoba now means a voyage. Perhaps my old terrain has acquired the allure of the novel, even a touch of the exotic. It benefits from the selective view that comes with tourism. It's not like I come back in January when the daisies and bees and spiders are long dead and your choice of outdoor clothing can be a matter of life or death. Nowadays I get to choose my season. Where Manitoba is concerned, that makes it much easier to nurture fond feelings.

That train of thought brings me back to Kyoko. In the years since our last meeting I have spent a fair amount of time wondering what might have been. My friend Martin never fails to remind me of how I behaved at the time, my panicky thrashing about, my desperation to escape. And there is no doubt that my life would have been different with Kyoko in it. The life I have lived is the life I have chosen, and a significant part of that choice was to be alone. It's telling that I have had no serious romantic partners since— it would seem my memorable time with Kyoko helped me figure out some things. People are often eager to tell you what you miss by being alone. What you might gain, I don't think they realize.

Single life certainly holds no appeal for my father. It makes a difference whether your independence is the result of your own choices or was thrust upon you. For at least sixty-five years, fifty-eight of them as man and wife, my father desired above all the company of my mother. My parents cherished their own travels, particularly after they had both retired. They toured the continent in a used Mercedes sedan, visiting their children and making time for their favourite spots, like a beachfront cabin in Lincoln City, Oregon. I know love can work, and I know it can go on the road. I saw it.

It is well past four local time, two p.m. Vancouver time. My phone buzzes. "No sign of her," Chris texts. "Doesn't look good. How long do you want me to stay?"

I look over at Dad, staring glum and unseeing out over the lake. Father and son together, waiting for people who will never return.

It's chilly and Dad is tired. I help him to his feet, fold up the lawn chairs and the blanket, and take his arm.

Time to go.

Acknowledgements

My intention was to have ChatGPT write this entire book while I stayed on the couch. But it turns out even a chatbot will balk at the prospect of a seven-hour budget flight, of being injected into a middle seat without so much as complimentary water or pretzels. So I had to write it after all. Not by myself, though—I had plenty of help.

This book would not exist without David Beers. He was there at its genesis, steered me toward the proper approach, then went to bat for me to make it a published reality. Dave essentially worked as an unpaid agent and sometime editor as well. On occasion we yelled at each other, which does happen in healthy relationships. I can't adequately express my gratitude for all his help and support.

I assume Derek Fairbridge did not do his editing work pro bono but I am thoroughly grateful for that, too. A sympathetic and perceptive editor is a gift every writer should pray for, and my prayers were answered. Thanks as well to keen-eyed copy editor Emma Skagen, who went above and beyond with wise advice and corrections that saved me from some serious embarrassment.

A big thank you to everyone at Douglas & McIntyre, including Anna Comfort O'Keeffe and Caroline Skelton, for their help, advice and support.

There were many interview subjects good enough to talk to me on the record—my apologies if I forget anyone: Giulio Mattioli at the TU Dortmund University was a tremendous resource for me—wise, thoughtful, informative and patient when I kept taking advantage of his good nature in order to ask more questions. Seth Wynes of Concordia not only granted me a great interview; he was the one who suggested I contact Giulio. Paul Chiambaretto was another great aviation resource. Dr. William Rees, as you will have noticed, is a man who pulls no punches. His input was much appreciated.

I am so glad to have stumbled across Susan Trollinger's book *Selling the Amish: The Tourism of Nostalgia* at the Vancouver Public Library. Susan educated me on both Amish tourism and the Creation Museum. (On that note, I would also like to thank the VPL and the North Vancouver District Public Library. They are essential public resources and deserving of all our support.)

Dr. Hazel Andrews was gracious in offering her time and wisdom, as was Dr. Ulrike Gretzel. Both of them provided me with more insight than I could ever have expected. Claire Newell of Travel Best Bets was very helpful, as was Karen Stein, author of *Getting Away from It All: Vacations and Identity*.

Thanks to Elizabeth Becker, author of *Overbooked: The Exploding Business of Travel and Tourism*. I highly recommend reading it.

I owe both thanks and an apology to Jack Reid, author of *Roadside Americans: The Rise and Fall of Hitchhiking in a Changing Nation*, and Jonathan Purkis, author of *Driving with Strangers: What Hitchhiking Tells Us about Humanity*. They both granted me great interviews for a chapter I ended up cutting, through no fault of theirs. Next book, I hope.

In writing about the *Diamond Princess* I drew extensively from the excellent documentary *The COVID Cruise*, directed by Mike Downie and available online at CBC Gem.

My old radio friend John Beaudin dug up the ancient tape of my conversation with Al Stewart, cleaned it up, digitized it and sent it to me. Thanks, John.

Chris Ferguson was my sentry at Caffè Artigiano on that fateful day in August. Thanks, Chris. He also mastered the Tigers and Goats game I brought back from Kathmandu. Chris could even win playing as the goats.

Tamotsu Nagata was very helpful with translations. He and his wife Yumi Araya also fed me lavishly when I visited Tokyo. This is the inadequate thanks they get.

Waka Takamido was kind enough to meet me in Miyama. I couldn't find her office and a local had to call and explain that some clueless Canadian was wandering around the village asking for her.

Peter MacIntosh was good enough to share his knowledge and experience with me in Kyoto.

Alex Temblador not only gave me an informative interview, she introduced me to the Otter transcription service, which I wish I had known about earlier. Shalene Dudley also gave me her fresh perspective on the industry—thank you.

Thanks to Claudia Milia at Prince of Whales, and the biologists and crew of the *Salish Sea Dream*.

Charmian Nimmo has only one line in this book but she nails it. Her ceramic work, both pottery and sculpture, is amazing and can be found at Kingsmill Pottery on Granville Island in Vancouver.

Sue Ridout, my old TV boss, threw a party one day, and it was while talking to people at that event I resolved to try—again—to make this book happen. Maybe that wasn't her intention but anyway, she was nice enough to invite me. Thanks, Sue.

Zak Vescera and his head-to-toe airline wardrobe were a bonus addition to this book. I think he has since changed into fresh togs.

Thanks to Dr. Edward Koh, Per Unheim, Hlynur Guðjónsson, Filip Schmidt, Tara Winkler, Greg Oates, James Higham, Egill Bjarnason, Valerie Weaver-Zercher, Andrew Dumbrille, Pablo Tejedo Sanz, Jeroen Oskam, Paul Nursey, the staff at Hidden Japan, Andrew Clark and Dan Fraser at Smiling Albino. And of course, Socrates and Seneca. You both got a raw deal.

Thank you to my brother John Burgess, who lets me sleep on his dining room floor, feeds me boiled cabbage and offers advice, some of it requested.

Meeting people is among the greatest joys of travel. Some of those people are in this book, many more are not, but I am grateful to almost all of them. Even that customs guy at Charles de Gaulle Airport.

Many of the names in this book have been changed to protect privacy. But if you book a room at Hotel Orlanda in Rome you will find that Marco, Paolo and Teresa are indeed Marco, Paolo and Teresa. Unless you are travelling alone, you won't want to book my favourite room, number 505. For one thing, the bed will be too small for two people. But most importantly, it's my room. Keep out.

About the Author

STEVE BURGESS is a writer and broadcaster whose honours include two Canadian National Magazine awards. Burgess is a contributing editor of The Tyee and an award-winning documentary director. He is the author of *Who Killed Mom?* (Greystone, 2011) and his stories have been featured in publications including *Reader's Digest, Maclean's* and *The Globe and Mail*. He lives in Vancouver, BC.